More...

THE TAO OF NEGOTIATION

"*The Tao of Negotiation* is a wonderful book. I highly recommend it to anyone who would understand the nature of conflict and the techniques for making all of life's relationships work better."
—JAMES A. AUTRY, FORMER SENIOR VICE PRESIDENT OF THE MEREDITH CORPORATION, AND AUTHOR OF *Love and Profit: The Art of Caring Leadership*

"*The Tao of Negotiation* is a landmark book! It cuts to the very core of the human predicament where our strong sense of rightness and raw emotions often conflict. The authors' vast experience in mediating the human plight, which incorporates their impeccable wisdom in both psychology and the law, is not only timely but compelling for any type of human relating. This book is a must for all people who consider themselves in a relationship of any kind. I felt a shift in consciousness concerning my attitude toward conflict from just one quick reading."
—JACQUELYN SMALL, FOUNDING DIRECTOR OF EUPSYCHIA, INC., AUTHOR OF *Becoming Naturally Therapeutic*, *Awakening in Time*, AND *Transformers: The Artists of Self-Creation*

"*The Tao of Negotiation* is a basic relationship manual for the breakfast table as well as the United Nations Roundtable. It contains very useful operating instructions for living in a conflicted world. Joel Edelman and Mary Beth Crain have skillfully measured

the distance between the heart and the mind and built an infrastructure to traverse momentary gulfs. When minds meet there is one heart; the end of warring is the beginning, middle, and ultimate peace."
—STEPHEN LEVINE, AUTHOR OF *Who Dies?*

"Anyone who lives and works in the world of business knows two things: It is by definition full of conflict. And the options for resolving conflict are few. *The Tao of Negotiation* is the first resource anyone should turn to when faced with conflict, in their business, marriage, or their lives."
—LARRY WILSON, FOUNDER AND CEO OF THE PECOS RIVER LEARNING CENTER, AND COAUTHOR OF *The One Minute $ales Person*

"*The Tao of Negotiation* is an invaluable tool to assist us in the most critical endeavor of our time: maturing our relationships to reflect our higher wisdom."
—BARBARA MARX-HUBBARD, FOUNDATION FOR CO-CREATION

THE TAO OF
NEGOTIATION

*How You Can Prevent, Resolve
and Transcend Conflict
in Work and Everyday Life*

JOEL EDELMAN

and

MARY BETH CRAIN

HarperBusiness
A Division of HarperCollinsPublishers

A hardcover edition of this book was published in 1993 by Harper-Business, a division of HarperCollins Publishers.

THE TAO OF NEGOTIATION. Copyright © 1993 by Joel Edelman and Mary Beth Crain. All rights reserved. Printed in the United States of America. No part of this book may be used or reproduced in any manner whatsoever without written permission except in the case of brief quotations embodied in critical articles and reviews. For information address HarperCollins Publishers, Inc., 10 East 53rd Street, New York, NY 10022.

HarperCollins books may be purchased for educational, business, or sales promotional use. For information please write: Special Markets Department, HarperCollins Publishers, Inc., 10 East 53rd Street, New York, NY 10022.

First paperback edition published 1994.

Designed by Irving Perkins Associates, Inc.

The Library of Congress has catalogued the hardcover edition as follows:

Edelman, Joel.
    The Tao of negotiation : how you can prevent, resolve and
transcend conflict in work and everyday life / Joel Edelman, Mary
Beth Crain. — 1st ed.
        p.   cm.
    Includes index.
    ISBN 0-88730-643-8
    1. Negotiation. 2. Conflict management. 3. Interpersonal
conflict. 4. Lao-tzu. Tao te ching. I. Title.
    BF637.N4E29   1993
    158´.5—dc20   92-56236

ISBN 0-88730-702-7 (pbk.)

94 95 96 97 98 PS/RRD 10 9 8 7 6 5 4 3 2 1

To our loving spouses, Jeannine Farr-Edelman and Adam Shields, who taught us about preventing conflict by giving us no unsolicited book advice, who taught us about encouragement by their neutrality and who taught us about patience by not having read the book, yet.

Peace is not simply the absence of war. It is not a passive state of being. We must wage peace, as vigilantly as we wage war.
THE XIV DALAI LAMA

Every fight is one between different angles of vision, illuminating the same truth.
MAHATMA GANDHI

Peace is easily maintained;
Trouble is easily overcome before it starts.
The brittle is easily shattered;
The small is easily scattered.

Deal with it before it happens.
Set things in order before there is confusion
LAO TSU, *TAO TE CHING*

Contents

Preface

In dealing with others, be gentle and kind.
In speech, be true.
In business, be competent.
In action, watch the timing.

No fight: No blame.

The *Tao Te Ching**

In order to fully understand the basic underlying idea of *The Tao of Negotiation*, we need to ask four questions. First, what is "Tao"? Second, how does it apply to "negotiation"? Third, why did we write this book? And fourth, why are you reading it?

In its simplest translation, "Tao" (pronounced "Dow") means "way" or "path." The *Tao Te Ching*, written by the Chinese sage Lao Tsu in the sixth century B.C., is, on one level, a book about how best to conduct one's life in accordance with the laws of nature and the universe, so as to experience both inner and outer peace. Those who follow the Tao find their feet

* Translation by Gia-Fu Feng and Jane English, Vintage Books, 1972.

toughened on the sharp stones along the road less traveled. The path of the Tao leads away from the sensations of desire and expectation that make up the world of the ego—that is, suffering—and takes us into a new dimension of detached awareness—that is, joy.

Through the Tao, one experiences the true strength born of humility and grace. In the process, we as individuals take upon ourselves the full responsibility for discovering and engineering our own salvation.

How does the Tao apply to negotiation?

Typically, negotiation is thought of as the process of discussion engaged in by two or more parties, each of which wants to achieve a desired aim. Negotiation can be a selfish experience in which each party is concerned only with their own needs. Or, it can be a mutually beneficial experience, in which everyone's needs are taken into equal consideration by each participant.

But traditionally, negotiation has been conceived of as a process of bargaining or conflict-resolution that *requires the participation of both sides.*

The Tao of Negotiation takes a new approach to this concept of negotiation. Because the Tao is concerned with "personal cause and effect"—the individual's perception of and responsibility for his or her own actions and their effect on the self and others—it believes that the individual plays the key role in creating the external events in his/her life. Not *shaping* those events, but *creating* them. Therefore, the basic premise of *The Tao of Negotiation* is that while a conflict may involve two or more people, *it often only takes one person to resolve that conflict, or to prevent it from occurring altogether.*

Attitude and intention are, to the Tao, the most powerful tools of human existence. How we perceive a situation—how we *choose* to perceive it—will often determine its outcome, says the Tao.

> He who is attached to things will suffer much.
> He who hoards will suffer heavy loss.
> A violent man will suffer a violent death.
> But a contented man is never disappointed.

When we take the approach of the Tao to negotiation, we deal first with ourselves. Instead of concentrating on the other person in a defensive or offensive manner, we stop, grow calm, look inward. Instead of blaming someone else, or expecting a battle, we study the situation, exploring our own intentions and actions. How are we really feeling? What do we really believe? How might we have contributed to the problem? Do we want war—or peace?

> Knowing others is wisdom.
> Knowing the self is enlightenment.
> Mastering others requires force.
> Mastering the self needs strength.

Once we are clear about our own needs, wants, beliefs and responsibilities, we can proceed to the situation or problem itself. Do we want a conflict? Often, that's the case. We may feel so angry at someone else, and so justified in our anger, that we may take an overwhelming satisfaction in locking horns with the other person, "standing up to" them and "beating" them. If this is our attitude, then a conflict will surely be the result, for we expect conflict and tailor our actions accordingly.

If, on the other hand, we want to end existing hostilities, prevent them from escalating or prevent them altogether, we have the power to create that scenario. By having *the intention and willingness to negotiate from a position of peace, we can unlock the truth.* By being open and honest ourselves, we can create an environment in which the other person feels safe enough to become equally vulnerable. By being willing to understand and accept the validity of the other person's point of view, regardless of whether or not we agree with it, we can escalate understanding and acceptance—and eventually agreement—on both sides.

The Tao of Negotiation is not a book about "compromise"; it is a book about awareness. A person who negotiates from the Tao negotiates in the spirit of *watchful humility.* He/she does not fear conflict, or try to appease it. He/she accepts it with neutrality, as another form of energy that can either be used or diffused. Conflict in and of itself is not a negative experience—it can be as illuminating as it is uncomfortable. It is *how we choose to respond to conflict* that determines whether its effect will be positive or negative.

We wrote *The Tao of Negotiation* because we believe that learning how to *prevent* conflict is just as important as learning how to resolve it.

When we become involved in a conflict situation, we often automatically assume a conflict where none yet exists. We become embroiled in emotions that may have nothing to do with reality. We become angry and afraid. What if the other person is feeling like this? What if he/she does that? Fear and anger lead to expectation of the worst. Our emotions escalate, and pretty soon we've created a scenario that hasn't happened yet, but that very well might because we will respond to the other person as if it has.

The Tao of Negotiation is intended to show you how you—and you alone—can prevent conflicts from occurring in your life, and how, in the process, you can make your relationships more energizing, enlightening and fulfilling. When we choose the Tao, we choose harmony. The more we understand the Tao, the more harmonious our attitude toward life becomes. We learn to stop, look and listen before we act, even before we think. We become more objective, less fearful. Instead of believing that we know all the answers, we embrace curiosity. We move from the delusion created by fear to the awareness born of inquisitiveness.

The Tao of Negotiation is a practical approach to conflict enlightenment. By reading it, you can learn how to know yourself, and how to know—and deal effectively and compassionately with—others.

And *The Tao of Negotiation* is a book for warriors: warriors of peace.

The ancient masters were subtle, mysterious, profound, responsive.
Watchful, like men crossing a winter stream,
Alert, like men of danger
Courteous, like visiting guests.
Yielding, like ice about to melt.

Peace is as active a state of being, after all, as war. When we negotiate from the perspective of the Tao, we study the terrain, plan our strategies. We are not passive; we are aware, at all times, of the stirrings in the bushes, the footsteps of the intruders and the proper way in which to meet them and disarm them. We are in inner control; outer events respond accordingly.

The Tao of Negotiation is, like the Tao itself, a guide to taking control of one's life by first taking responsibility for it. Because as transcendent and metaphysical as the Tao may seem, it is equally tangible and down-to-earth. The beauty of Taoism lies in its ability to practically apply itself to the difficulties and ponderings that are part of the eternal human condition. Culture and time mean nothing to the Tao; it is, as Lao Tsu explains, "unborn—so ever living," a timeless, infinite, benevolent constant to which all of us can turn for insight, comfort and ultimate liberation.

Why are you reading this book?

Only you, of course, know the answer to that. You may currently be experiencing conflicts with family, friends, lovers, coworkers, subordinates, superiors. You may be interested in learning how to "read" another person for business and negotiating purposes. You may want to know more about the types of relationships to pursue in your life and those to avoid. You may be looking for a more spiritual way to deal with others. Or a more practical way.

Whatever your reasons, you've picked this book up. And we hope you enjoy it and profit by it. The principles of *The Tao of Negotiation* are easy to understand—befriend them, and conflict will, we hope, be, if not a stranger to you, then at least a distant relative who rarely comes to visit.

MARY BETH CRAIN
Santa Paula, California

Acknowledgments

I began making random notes about the acknowledgments from the moment that I had the first inspiration for the book during a three-week silent meditation retreat in 1986.

I begin with thanks to my parents, Doris and Sam Edelman, whose influence and conditioning came to mind regularly as I confronted myself with the conflict response patterns I observed, received and created at home. As the middle child between my two loving sisters, Paula and Lauren, I had an early dose of "being in the middle"—a crucible for learning about negotiations. My adult son, Adam, has been available through the seven-year writing process as a sometime writing coach, full-time cheering section and as a pride and joy.

I have been blessed by large numbers of close and supportive friends who encouraged me when I most needed it. Jim Autry, Bob Chartoff, Hyla Cass, Michael Goldberg, Bonnie Newman, Loren Roche, Stan Levy, Rickie Moore, Henry Marshall, David Phillips, Isolina Ricci, Nesa Ronn, Raymond Shonholtz, Ruth Strassberg, David Surrenda, John Vasconcellos and Larry Wilson have been most available to me. Many of these friends also read and provided extremely valuable feedback on early drafts of the manuscript.

In the past twenty-two years of practice I have had thousands of mediation clients and hundreds of legal and counseling clients. The majority of case studies and anecdotes in the book are based on these situations (with names and other identities changed, of course). I thank them all for trusting me and allowing me to tune into and to work together with them on their unfolding life dramas.

What is most special to me about this book is its balance between practicality and spirit. I would like to thank the many teachers, especially the spiritual teachers, who have graced me with their presence and their wisdom. Among the many teachers, His Holiness The XIV Dalai Lama stands out as a person who embodies the finest in human spirit and worldly behavior. It has been my honor to play a small part in his lifelong campaign of waging peace when I was Conference Coordinator for the three-day Transformation of Consciousness Dialogues in 1989 in Newport Beach, California. Just a few hours after these dialogues were completed it was announced that he had been awarded the Nobel Peace Prize for 1989.

Before *The Tao of Negotiation* took on its present intention, structure, style and title, I worked closely with a number of people. Connie Zweig, long-time friend and collaborator, and Jeremy Tarcher were very helpful, knowledgeable and supportive. Art Franklin, insightful teacher, friend and all-around wise man was ever-present at crucial times. Maureen Crist, writing coach and close friend, was always available for honest dialogue and great humor. Marilyn Ferguson, another "sister," was there at all stages with regular advice, feedback and heartful energy.

When Daniel Kaufman introduced me to Mary Beth

Crain the book began to take on its present focus and depth. My friend Stephen Levine suggested that I send a completed manuscript to literary agent Loretta Barrett, who had been Stephen's editor. We could not have asked for a more caring and professional agent.

The enthusiasm, warmth and support of Susan Muldow, Editor-in-Chief of HarperCollins, captured us. Our editor, Virginia Smith, Executive Editor of HarperBusiness, has been discreet, knowledgeable and extremely helpful. Our dealing with HarperBusiness Publicity Director Lisa Berkowitz has been wonderful and we wish her great success in these efforts.

My long-time assistant and friend Ruth Petal has been with me through every step of this process—cheering, typing, advising, alerting, reminding and generally doing anything and everything that good assistants are supposed to do.

Although I began working on this book three years before I met my future wife, Jeannine Farr-Edelman, I became much clearer and more grounded thereafter. Shortly after we married, the manuscript was finally ready for presentation. I attribute the good fortune of publication by HarperCollins to the success of my loving relationship with Jeannine.

Finally, I could not have wished to have a better cowriter than Mary Beth Crain to help communicate my sometimes unconventional ways of seeing how we humans blunder our way into conflict and how we can mobilize our best selves to prevent and respond to such conflict.

JOEL EDELMAN
Malibu, California

. . .

This is definitely the best part of the process: Sitting down to thank all those cheerleaders in the game of my life who helped to make this book possible with their enthusiasm, support and undying optimism.

To my dear friends: Sister Janet Harris, who believed in the project from Day One, and who has successfully used the principles of the book in her work with staff and inmates in Los Angeles and San Bernardino correctional institutions; Deborah Tracy, for her constant love and encouragement; Terry Taylor, for her magnificently irreverent sense of humor; Dan Kiernan and Steven Vance, for always seeming to be there; Ron and Maria Reifler, for their belief and pride in my talents and their wonderful work in self-esteem; Deb Bowers, for her metaphysical perspective; Grusha Paterson/ Mills, for being my "adopted" mom and one of the most inspirational role models anybody could have; Marilyn Ferguson, friend, fellow writer and incorrigible Mysterian, for her insightful comments and the talks 'til dawn and beyond; Daniel Kaufman, for aligning Joel's and my orbits.

To our agent, Loretta Barrett, for her wonderful energy and enthusiasm and extraordinary ability to make things happen.

To our editor, Virginia Smith, for her openness, sensitivity and respect for and commitment to our work.

To my family: my mother, Hazel Gersten, for always being proud of her daughter's accomplishments, no matter how strange they may have seemed; my twin brother, David Gersten, for forty-two years of special closeness; my cousin, Claire Schwarz Bucalos, for always being "tuned in"; my ex-husband, Bob Crain, for all the years of support and unconditional love.

To Joel, for four years of patience, resilience and

vision and for being the best collaborator a writer could have.

To my incredible husband, Adam Shields, for his love, support, artistic soul, thoroughly mad take on life and tendency to brag about me to everyone within earshot.

And to my father-in-law, "Boss" Shields, for teaching me about life, death and the importance of believing in things unseen.

MARY BETH CRAIN

THE TAO OF
NEGOTIATION

Introduction

Doesn't it take just one side to start a conflict? Isn't that usually how it happens? And doesn't it take two sides to end it? How can you possibly have peace unless both sides are really, willing and able to agree to it?

There seems to be a worldwide human assumption that conflict happens because of the actions of one side. I find this, however, to be the naive approach to a complex topic. Conflicts always happen because of real—and what are perceived as legitimate—grievances on both sides.

Generally, of course, one side is going to "start" the conflict. There has never, to my knowledge, been a formal agreement stating that at 3 P.M. on April 26, the guns on both sides are going to simultaneously go blazing. But the reality is that the way people and organizations and countries often approach difficult, delicate and conflict-laden situations is through the unspoken, unconscious conspiracy of signing each other's conflict certificates—by assuming, in advance, that there will be a conflict in the first place.

If this is true, the reverse must also be true: That if one person or one side refuses to enter into that

1

"agreement," to be a party to that conspiracy, then conflict will be, at the very least, delayed.

I believe that through the willingness of one side to peacefully negotiate, and, more importantly, through its firm *unwillingness* to move into an attack mode, there's a high probability of conflict being completely prevented. Not by rolling over and playing dead or crying "uncle," but by understanding enough about the nature of conflict to know our responsibility, the part we play in it and the power we have to influence the other side in a healthy way, so that it doesn't perceive conflict as inevitable.

For nearly thirty years, I have been involved in various aspects of the law. I have been both a defense attorney and the Deputy City Attorney in Los Angeles. I have been an Adjunct Professor of Law at Loyola Marymount University and the University of Southern California. I was a Directing Attorney for the Western Center on Law and Poverty, and the Executive Director of the Neighborhood Justice Center of Los Angeles, where I organized some of the first gang mediations in the city, helping warring gangs to resolve their conflicts, and giving the police and community tools with which to better understand and communicate with gangs.

In short, I have been an active participant in our legal system, and I have seen the wounds inflicted on the battlefields of litigation and the criminal justice system turn to scars that often never completely heal.

I knew that there must be a better place than the courtroom or the jails for people to come together, and a better way than a lawsuit or a prison term for them to resolve their difficulties. I found the answer in mediation, a process whereby two or more parties agree to explore a conflict through the services of a third person—the mediator—who helps them to better understand both their own and the other's position and, hopefully, come to a peaceful resolution that satisfies everyone.

As a mediator, I have found a great deal of joy in helping people to amicably—or at least non-adversarially—resolve conflicts that, if allowed to escalate into litigation, might pose a significant threat to their long-term emotional well-being. I have also found great satisfaction in utilizing the principles of mediation on community and global levels. As everything from a gang mediator to a facilitator of communications for delegations to the Soviet Union, China and Costa Rica, I have discovered that regardless of differences in race, religion or culture, people everywhere share the same basic need to be understood and valued—a need that, when unmet, is at the bottom of virtually every conflict.

And, during my sixteen years of experience as a professional mediator, I also discovered something else. *The Tao of Negotiation* springs from the premise that in a dispute, or potential dispute, both parties do *not* initially have to be committed to working out the problem. If only *one* of the parties is willing to head off a conflict at the pass or to amicably resolve an existing conflict, there is a high probability that, given the necessary tools to work with, their efforts can succeed.

Thus, while *The Tao of Negotiation* is concerned with *preventing* and *resolving* conflict, its primary focus is on *responding to* conflict. For *how we respond* to a conflict or potential conflict can determine whether it is prevented, resolved or allowed to escalate into an all-out dispute.

Although I work as a third-party mediator, I have also spent a significant part of my practice as a back-stage adviser/coach to one side of a dispute. My whispering in the ear of one person has often been as effective as counseling in the presence of both parties. Why? Because when one side is willing to listen rather than fight, the other side will usually *respond to that willingness* in the same spirit, entering into a process toward a final resolution that feels good to everyone involved.

In other words, while a difficult or problematic situation may involve two or more parties, *one* person's decision to *respond* rather than *react* to that situation— to come from a thoughtful, inquiring, listening space rather than an automatic "knee-jerk" frame of mind— can set the stage for dialogue and openness. So in many ways, *The Tao of Negotiation* is a guide to "self-mediation," whereby you alone can learn how to resolve—and even prevent—your own conflicts. That is *my* kind of negotiation.

MEDIATION, MEDITATION AND CONFLICT

The Tao of Negotiation takes both a "mediative" and a "meditative" approach to conflict.

Basically, the work that I do as a mediator is an approach for people who don't want to kill each other; for people who don't want to get caught up in the legal adversary system of spending all their time, emotion and energy in a court battle; and for people who intend to find a way to go their own way with the least amount of pain possible. In other words, I help people to talk to each other, and to understand what they and those they're in conflict with really want. I don't represent one person *against* another; I simply provide a service to help everyone to make some decisions together.

Mediation and meditation are the cornerstones of the philosophy I have developed in dealing with conflict. That's because both activities involve the willingness to take personal responsibility for the conflicts, both inner and outer, in one's life, and the intention to approach and resolve those conflicts in a nonaggressive, integrative and positive manner.

In *meditation*, we essentially make an agreement with ourselves to explore the conflicting sides of ourselves, and to make peace with the many different personalities that coexist, sometimes peaceably and sometimes not, within us.

It's really no coincidence that "mediation" and "meditation" are so close in spelling, because they are so close in substance. And it's also no coincidence that these two endeavors have been traditionally treated with suspicion by Western society, which views conflict as a battle in which one side can't win until the other loses, and which values blaming the other party above taking personal responsibility for one's own contribution to the existing problem.

What it all boils down to, essentially, is the willingness to confront pain, and in so doing to learn from that pain and eventually transcend it.

In many kinds of quiet meditation, for instance, you have to deal with all kinds of pain—physical, psychological and spiritual. If you sit for any length of time, your legs go numb or your back feels as though it's going to break. When you try to empty your mind, terrible thoughts pop up like irrepressible demons. You want to kill your boss; you want your kids to disappear. You're horrified to realize that you might not be as nice a person as you thought you were.

You want to run away from the pain. But you can't, because the intention of the meditation is self-observation. When your shoulder aches, you are taught to simply look at what's happening without judging it. "Okay. My shoulder aches." When an awful thought pops up, you merely make an internal note of it. And eventually, the pain dissipates and thoughts fade and you find yourself at peace as you step out of the prison of the mind into the free world of self-realization.

Similarly, mediation involves a willingness to experience the pain of self-examination in an effort to reach peace. It's a little like doing a "conflict root canal." Instead of pointing the finger at the other person, both parties try to get to the root of the problem, to admit its true nature and the part they've each played in allowing it to abscess. When they can individually take responsibility for their own actions and intentions, healing takes place and peace is possible.

In Western society, however, we're taught to avoid discomfort of any kind. If we feel the slightest twinge, we grab an aspirin, lie down, call the doctor. This idea of being with the pain, accepting it and not trying to deaden it, is a radical notion, especially for those of us who have grown up with the idea that if something hurts, then it's wrong. Thus, when you suggest meditation to a confirmed Western ideologist, you're generally met with skepticism because nobody likes to have his or her life flipped over onto its head.

In a similar way, the whole idea of a mediative attitude is regarded with alarm in our culture. Why? Because mediation turns our established aggressive way of thinking upside down and inside out.

THE CONFLICT "HIGH"

How has the media and society taught us to deal with disputes? If you're angry, show it and get even! If you're upset with somebody, hit them!

How are we counseled to handle our disagreements by the guardian of mass unconsciousness, television? Well, if you're really annoyed with someone, you pick up a gun and shoot them. If you want to be nice about it, you beat them up a bit, physically and emotionally. If you want to be truly civilized, you berate them and make them look like fools. And if you want to be *super* nice, you "just" sue them.

Conflict, you see, is a kind of drug. It's exciting, it gives us a sense of false empowerment, it's highlighted by the media, and we've gotten so used to it that while we hate it on the one hand, we're almost addicted to the idea of its presence in our lives.

Aggressive behavior often provides us with a "high" that we are loathe to give up. It's exhilarating for many people well trained in the school of competitive thought to "beat" someone else, either on a football field or in a courtroom.

That's why, in the world of hardball legal strategies, mediation is often considered by many people to be too "soft" an approach to disputes. Through some strange permutation in mass reasoning, it has somehow become "unmanly," and "unwomanly" as well, to admit that the other person might have just as much right to his or her opinions and feelings as you have.

So, when I say to people, "Now, the real way to deal with conflict is, first of all, to prevent it," it's as though I'm taking their candy away. I'm taking the excitement of conflict out of their lives. I'm also supposedly taking away their right to act on their feelings and beliefs, whatever they may be. When you propose the radical notion of sitting down and talking with somebody and trying to come up with a common solution, people act as though you'd just suggested that they give up their birthright!

It's true that conflict is an inevitable part of life. But it is not true that the only way to deal with conflict is to provoke more of it, by the angry insistence upon our God-given right to become the enemy of everybody.

The only *real* way to win a dispute is to make sure that both parties come to an understanding in which as many mutual needs as possible are met. A victory based on revenge, force or the emotional/legal battering of the opposition into submission is not, in my terms, a victory; it's a rape.

The "winner" may have gotten what he/she *thinks* he/she wanted, in the way of money or control or the satisfaction of having been proven "right." But the essential conflict has not been resolved and will continue to pollute the lives of the participants, possibly forever.

Unfortunately, our litigious society has promoted the insidious notion of "attack and defend" to the heights of absurdity. Based on the three traditional methods in the United States for dealing with disputes—litigation, arbitration or adversarial negotiation—we promote one basic underlying tenet: In difficult situations, the other person is an adversary.

Thus, the two sides must inevitably face off in some

kind of hostile encounter, or at least threaten such an encounter. Because of this deeply ingrained and culturally approved attitude, most of us have been conditioned to view the other person as the "enemy." In every exchange we search constantly for "right" and "wrong." Finger-pointing becomes the accepted mode of conduct; taking responsibility for one's own actions and looking inside for honest answers is righteously and consciously avoided.

TURNING CONFLICT INSIDE OUT

It may surprise many people to learn that the external conflicts we experience are almost always the mirror of our own internal conflicts—the inner problems that we haven't resolved or even acknowledged.

Most of us become embroiled in conflict because we aren't clear as to who we are or what we want. We resent others for taking advantage of us when, in truth, we allowed ourselves to be taken advantage of. We are faced with conflicting choices in a career move and do not know where to turn. We desperately want to tell our husband, wife, lover our deepest feelings but are terrified of his or her response. And so we remain silent, frustrated and unhappy.

These conditions are usually a result of our reliance upon our "rational" thought processes, and our unwillingness to give ourselves enough time and space to reflect silently and patiently in order to discover what's percolating inside ourselves. We tend to make quick decisions based on mental phenomena or societally encouraged actions.

But the more significant a decision is in terms of our life purpose or direction—be it a relationship that we want to get into or out of, a job transfer or a career move—the more we need to take an hour, a day, a week, a month, even a year off with no particular goal other than to listen to our inner voice without any preconditions.

The rational mind simply cannot get down to the level of intuition at which major decisions need to be made. It can work with intuition, but it can't force it up. And listening to your intuition—to the nonverbal, non-rational messages you receive—is the first step on the way to knowing yourself and understanding someone else. Which is, in turn, the most essential ingredient in the successful prevention and resolution of conflict.

GOOD MEDICINE

There is a third word that is very close to the words "meditation" and "mediation," and that carries with it similarly volatile connotations. That word is "medicine," and it's a word that has just as important a place in my practice as the other two.

I like to think of myself not so much as a lawyer, marriage and family counselor or even a mediator, but more as a healer—a "dispute doctor," with the preventive approach to the disease taking precedence over the curative.

We've often heard the maxim, "an ounce of prevention is worth a pound of cure." This holds true in terms of psychological as well as physical health. If you do all the things that you can to prevent a dispute from occurring, you're way ahead of the game.

Just as you are less likely to become ill if you eat well, exercise and reduce stress in your life, so you will increase the chances of maintaining a state of harmony and balance in your life through the "medicine" of a mediative approach to life, which heals relationships, and meditation, which heals the soul. But the deeper you get into a dispute, the harder it is to deal with the situation. And when it gets to the extreme point where both sides engage lawyers to fight for them, it's exactly like having the body so out of kilter that surgery may be the only avenue left.

The holistic approach to medicine is still regarded with suspicion by a pill-popping society that doesn't like to take responsibility for its own health. And so, preventive medicine is considered as heretical to the established Western medical profession, as mediation is to the legal profession, and meditation is to the concept of "rational" Western thought.

I suppose, then, that I'm asking all of you who read this book to commit heresy.

In these pages you will be asked not to avoid or fear the pain of conflict, but to stay with that pain—to watch it, accept it, embrace it. And you will be asked to commit to the intention, in any conflict, of resolving that conflict in a manner that assures that the other party will be respected and understood.

You'll find ways of communicating that will help to solve the mystery of another person's perspective and dissolve dissent before the dispute stage is ever reached. You will be asked to look at yourself honestly, to catalogue the virtues and the flaws that helped bring a dispute into existence and to accept responsibility in every conflict you encounter, either as a participant or as a balancing force.

You'll find techniques of centering yourself, of inviting periods of silence into your life in which your physical body will not be "accomplishing" anything but your mental and spiritual selves will be reforming your consciousness in such a way that you will achieve far more than you ever have.

In short, *The Tao of Negotiation* will show you how you can act from the highest and best part of yourself in trying to make your life as conflict-free as possible.

This does not mean that you won't ever have conflicts to face, for you inevitably will. Nor am I promising you that they'll always be resolved; there are always circumstances beyond our control, not the least of which are the responses of other people.

Rather, this is a book about how you can do your best, as long as you focus not on the dispute, not on the other person, but on yourself—what you're doing and not doing, how you're doing it, and what your needs really are. These are the true bases of negotiation. If you keep this focus, I *can* guarantee that the conflicts in your life will have a much higher probability of either being resolved or prevented altogether.

With the suggestions in this book—which involve everything from approaching conflict as a "research" project to learning how to change our own responses to conflict—we can maximize our chances for either preventing disputes altogether, or resolving them in such a way that both we and our apparent "antagonist" both emerge "victorious."

And, as we begin to understand and make use of the principles and techniques in the following pages, we stand a good chance of improving our relationships and our negotiations with friends, lovers, husbands, wives, children, parents, employers, employees, business partners, the store clerk, the creditor, the phone company, the IRS—in short, all the other human beings who will fill, at some point or another, the giant dance card of our lives.

Above all, this book does not come from an abstract, theoretical place. It is about *effective negotiation*: thought patterns, intentions, actions, procedures and techniques that *work*.

In the past sixteen years, I have helped more than a thousand clients to deal with divorce, partnership disputes, employee/employer clashes and most of the other conflict dilemmas to which human beings are prone.

Many times the people involved in these situations are so primed for battle that I feel like diving under the nearest table to escape the hostilities. But I'm pleased to say that my clients usually leave my office calmer, happier and more attuned to what it was they had really been seeking in the first place: understanding and acceptance.

These basic human needs are, after all, at the heart of every conflict. We all want to be loved; we all want to be appreciated, respected, acknowledged. When we feel that these needs are not being met, we become angry and hurt. And if we allow these emotions to dominate us, we have prepared the ground for a dispute.

Based on my own experiences as both a "professional" and as a man who has been through his own share of conflicts—some of which he handled as badly as anyone—*The Tao of Negotiation* is also the story of my own journey toward trying to become a compassionate, responsible human being. It is the story of personal growth, both my own and that of the many clients and friends who have taught me all about conflict: what it is, how we invite it into our lives, how most of us handle it, how most of us can handle it better.

I have been helped enormously by my coauthor, Mary Beth Crain, who has performed the ultimate Tao act of setting her own ego aside to take on the task of supporting and enhancing my own work on this book. As you can see, this book is written in the "I" of Joel Edelman because it expresses my voice, observations, ideas, life experiences, cases, suggestions and my ultimate responsibility for the material. But it has been a true collaboration in every sense of the word. And while any collaboration such as ours contains the seeds of a potential conflict, Mary Beth's uncanny ability to make the writing echo my way of thinking and my voice has helped us to stay true to our purpose and to work together in genuine partnership.

Finally, *The Tao of Negotiation* is the story of learning how to embrace our conflicts, to observe rather than condemn them, in order to learn the many invaluable lessons they have to teach us. It's how we choose to *respond* to the conflicts in our lives, after all, that determines whether or not they will become exercises in what the great Hindu master Paramahansa Yogananda so aptly termed "the soul's bad habit of translating sensation into pain"—or invaluable opportunities for self-awareness and growth.

JOEL EDELMAN
Malibu, California

1

The Nature of Conflict

Conflicts come in all sorts of shapes, sizes and guises, and as a lawyer and mediator, I have undoubtedly encountered most of them. Yet it's in my work as a judge at Small Claims Court that I often get the dubious privilege of seeing conflict at its most severe and most fascinating.

One of the more energetic disputes I judged occurred not long ago. It was a real media case, involving the daughter of the head of a major record company, the defendant, and her erstwhile agent, the plaintiff.

The case itself was not particularly earthshaking. The defendant, who was an aspiring actress, had engaged the plaintiff to act as her agent. The plaintiff, she claimed, had made grand promises of signing her to a movie deal. The agreement was an informal one, with no detailed contract as to expectations and fees for services.

The plaintiff was under the impression that she would not only get a percentage of the deal, but would be paid for any time and effort she put into it, regardless of whether or not her efforts led to a job for the

15

defendant. So, she made several trips to New York, a lot of phone calls, and put forth, she claimed, considerable effort on her client's behalf.

However, after three months and no deals, the defendant decided that the plaintiff wasn't doing her job and pulled out of the agreement without paying a nickel for any services, real or imagined. The plaintiff subsequently sued successfully for $2,500 worth of travel and related expenses, and the case made its way to my small claims appeals. (Attorneys are allowed to represent clients at small claims appeals; in effect, it is a new trial.)

When the two parties stood before me, they were armed for battle. The record mogul's daughter arrived with a full entourage that included her lawyer, a stable of pompous "expert" witnesses and a pushy mother who ordered everyone around like a circus ringmaster. The plaintiff, a young woman new in her profession, was also auspiciously padded and showed up with her own attorney and witnesses.

All the participants treated the affair as if it were a huge federal case. Every time the defendant opened her mouth, her mother would interject, with statements like, "See? If you'd listened to me, none of this would have happened!" One of the "expert witnesses," whom the mother had engaged, was a top Hollywood agent who had a list of credentials as long as my arm and wanted to make sure I knew every one of the 37,000 things he'd done, and that he knew the agent's code of ethics up, down and inside out. It was a real zoo; everybody was talking at once, and I felt more like Arnold Schwarzenegger in *Kindergarten Cop* than a judge, as I valiantly tried to maintain order in the court.

Meanwhile, the plaintiff came loaded down with

documents showing all of her expenses, as well as written evidence that the defendant had kept encouraging her to proceed in her efforts. However, since there were no signed agreements, the defendant maintained that the plaintiff should be paid nothing at all, that she had worked totally on contingency, and that she had pulled out when she found out the plaintiff was acting "unethically."

Now, one of the ways I differ from many of my colleagues on the small claims bench is that I'm always trying to find out what's really at the bottom of any conflict. So, after I hear all the evidence, I always ask both the plaintiff and the defendant two unexpected questions. The first is, "If this situation were ever to arise again, what would you do differently, if anything, from what you actually did?" And the second is, "What have you learned from everything that's happened, including this trial?" If there has been any question in my mind as to what the decision ought to be in the case, I will make a judgment according to how the two parties answer these questions.

As you might imagine, both the record mogul's daughter and the agent were taken aback. The agent finally decided that she would never enter into any work in the future without having a clear and detailed written agreement. The daughter was so flabbergasted by the "pop quiz," and so used to having answers put in her mouth by her mother, that she stood there in bewildered silence.

I didn't believe the plaintiff, because I knew that the record mogul's daughter was such a big plum for a struggling new agent to get that she would have been willing to sacrifice anything to land the account. As for the defendant, she acted so guilty and ashamed of herself that I guessed that the real issue was not the money or the quality of the agent's work. Rather, at some point the agent probably got too bossy and reminded the defendant of her mother, setting off an explosion and causing her to rebel against this unwitting symbol of obnoxious parental authority. But at the same time, she was so embarrassed by her inability to make a go of her career that she felt she had to cover up her failure in the ultracritical eyes of her family. So she allowed mother to run the show and make the agent the scapegoat.

I ended up giving judgment for the plaintiff in the amount of what she was able to show were her on-the-record out-of-pocket expenses. But I awarded her nothing for the hours she spent; I decided that her time was her lesson. My decision, however, isn't really important. What is far more crucial to this book is what this particular incident of locked horns illustrates about the nature of conflict.

WHAT IS A CONFLICT?

The simple definition of conflict, and the one most of us would easily subscribe to, is a situation in which two people cannot agree on the actions that one person takes or that he or she doesn't want the other to take.

If Harry wants to go to Bermuda, and Mary wants to go to the Catskills, they are having a disagreement. If Harry agrees to go to the Catskills, or Mary agrees to go to Bermuda, or if both settle on Las Vegas, there is no conflict—only a disagreement that's been resolved. But if neither of them will budge in their desires, a conflict will be the result.

Unilateral and Bilateral Conflicts

Conflicts can either be *unilateral* or *bilateral*. A unilateral conflict involves a situation in which only one side has a complaint. For instance, if a tenant withholds rent for no legitimate reason, the landlord can be said to be engaged in a unilateral conflict. In a bilateral conflict, on the other hand, each person wants something from the other. If the tenant isn't paying rent because there's no heat, or the roof is leaking or he broke his leg on the cracked stoop, he and his landlord have a bilateral conflict on their hands. The tenant wants repairs done; the landlord wants his or her money. If neither agrees to the other's demands, there's conflict on both sides.

This is the most basic definition of conflict. But it isn't as straightforward as it seems, because often unilateral conflicts are bilateral conflicts in disguise. While one party may seem to have no complaint, no reason for aggressive behavior, he may not be aware that on an unconscious level he actually is angry with the other person.

Let's take our landlord/tenant dispute. The tenant hasn't paid. It isn't because he doesn't have the money or that the landlord is negligent. It's a passive-aggressive act that has no outward rationale; the tenant can't even explain his own actions. He just keeps "forgetting" to put the check in the mail.

But in reality, what's going on is that several months ago the landlord passed by the tenant in the supermarket without saying hello. The tenant thought it was strange at the time; it even irritated him a little. As time passed, he buried the memory of the insult, real or imagined. But the incident took an unconscious turn, in the form of late payment on the rent.

In a way, then, there is really no such thing as a unilateral conflict, because every conflict has its underlying causes, conscious or unconscious. Where conflict is concerned, there's no such thing as an immaculate conception; somewhere, somehow, the seed or seeds are always sown, no matter how deeply in the earth they're buried.

Personal Versus Structural Disputes

There's an important distinction to make between those types of conflicts that can be termed "personal," and those that are of a "structural" variety.

These two types of conflicts are, by nature, quite different. A *personal* dispute involves specific individuals, and specific feelings toward those individuals. A *structural* dispute is more of a "generic" conflict, that is endemic to the circumstances or the group of people involved. Of course, any *structural* dispute must also be *personal*; otherwise it could not generate the energy necessary to create a dispute.

By way of illustration I like to use the following scenario.

Betty and Max are going at each other with both barrels loaded. "He's so uncommunicative!" screams Betty. "He's like a statue! He never talks about his feelings, and when I try to talk about mine, he just grunts and goes on reading the paper!"

"Ah, she's the one with the problem!" growls Max. "She's always on the emotional edge. You look at her cross-eyed and she bursts into tears! She's always wanting to 'talk'—which means beating an issue into the ground. She never lets up. And she's nosy. 'Why, why, why?' That's all she wants to know!"

At this point I'll stop the proceedings.

"Betty. Max. Did you know that what you're in the middle of right now is not just a *personal* argument?"

This stuns them. "What do you mean, it isn't just 'personal'?" says Betty. "I'll say it's personal! He drives me crazy!"

"Wait a minute," I'll reply. "What you're involved in is a classic dilemma between the sexes. Yes, of course it has to do with you, Betty, and with you, Max. But if it weren't Max here—if it were Clem or Sam—you'd probably be raising the same complaints, Betty. And Max, if it weren't Betty, if it were Edna or Dorothy, you'd be climbing just as high along the wall. Why? Because this is very much a 'male-female' issue, where the majority of women will be saying one thing and the majority of men will be saying another."

This is what I call a *structural dispute*—a problem arising as much out of the *situation* as out of the particular individuals involved. A statistical truth: Max is speaking like most men; Betty is speaking like most women. And once they discover that this is the case, they are likely to feel relieved and to go on to something else.

Structural disputes are *not* personal. In international business negotiations, for example, disputes or misperceptions can arise out of what are essentially cultural differences that have nothing personal to do with the parties involved. If you don't understand the established negotiating practices of the country with which you're dealing, you may feel that its representatives are being insensitive, deceitful, insulting—and they may feel the same about you. Anyone encountering a structural dispute has to realize that that's what it is: a situation whose elements have been in large part predetermined. If you expect the other person to change their nature, conditioning or reactions, you're in Disneyland, not the real world.

SOME COMMON SOURCES OF CONFLICT

How do conflicts begin? The same way the universe began: Nobody really knows.

"You called my mother a liar!"

"I did not! She called *me* a liar!"

"You never tell me you love me!"

"I just told you Sunday!"

"He agreed to go fifty-fifty on this deal!"

"I never said any such thing!"

More often than not, who "starts" a conflict is open to debate. The exact moment at which a conflict begins is usually equally vague. But remember: Every conflict has its underlying causes, whether conscious or unconscious.

Conflicts can always be traced to a source, the most common of which are: (1) misunderstanding and miscommunication; (2) dishonesty; (3) negligence; (4) intention; (5) exclusive investment in one's opinions and belief system; (6) failure to establish boundaries; (7) mishandling of conflict; (8) fear; and (9) hidden agendas.

1. *Misunderstanding.* A misunderstanding occurs when the entire feeling and intention of a course of conduct is translated by the receiving party in a manner contrary to that in which it was intended.

Because he hates the theater, Ralph has an agreement with his wife, Stella, that she gets season tickets with a girlfriend and he picks them up after the show. But one evening, Stella's girlfriend cancels out. Ralph drops her off at the theater, where she unexpectedly meets an old coworker, Jim, following the performance. When Ralph pulls up, he sees Stella talking and laughing with Jim. Enraged, he accuses her of two-timing him and her girlfriend of being in on the conspiracy. Because Stella did have an affair at one time long ago, she can't convince Ralph of her innocence now. He spends the weekend at his buddy's house, and, due to anger and fear, a simple misunderstanding has become a conflict.

2. *Dishonesty.* Dishonesty is a certain source of eventual conflict. When people don't tell the truth to each other, there's a 100 percent guarantee that sooner or later a conflict will be the result. And it doesn't take a full-fledged, bold-faced lie to cause conflict; partial dishonesty, where conflicts arise not because of lies but because of half-truths, things left unsaid, are just as incendiary—or just as debilitating to a relationship.

Craig, a man in his sixties, had never been able to truly communicate with his father because his father never revealed what he was thinking or feeling. As a result, Craig felt as though he and his father were somehow always at odds. "I never seemed to be able to please him," he recalls, with more sadness than bitterness. "Nothing I did, or wanted to do with my life, was good enough for him. Yet he never once said this in words. He never gave me any indication of what he would have liked me to be. He was merely cold and distant, showing no interest in my interests, communicating his displeasure to me nonverbally.

"Because my father was so distant, I found it impossible to ask him what he was really thinking. The thought of trying to really talk to him was virtually paralyzing. It wasn't until he was dying that I was finally able to say, 'What would you have liked me to be?' And he replied, 'A doctor.'

" 'A doctor?' I was stunned. 'But you never said a word about my becoming a doctor.'

" 'I know,' he replied. 'I didn't want to influence you in any way. I wanted you to make up your own mind about your life.' "

This is a particularly poignant example of how the inability to be honest—to communicate from the heart—destroyed what could have been a warm, loving and caring relationship, and created in its place a state of chronic unexpressed conflict. (In the next chapter, we discuss dishonesty in more detail: Why many of us are afraid to be open, and how communication is vastly improved when we are willing to risk revealing our true feelings.)

3. *Negligence*. Many conflicts are due to simple negligence. The words we use, the promises we forget to keep, the responsibilities we shirk are all potential sources of conflict. Your son refuses to mow the lawn, no matter how often you've told him to do it. You promise to keep a friend's confidence secret and inadvertently spill the beans to a mutual acquaintance, who calls your friend and creates a rift between you. Your employee is late on a crucial project, putting the department in jeopardy. What we don't do can be just as conflict-provoking as what we do.

4. *Intention*. Our intentions are perhaps the most powerful sources of both conflict resolution and con-

flict provocation. When we have the intention to understand another, and to act in a manner that's mutually beneficial, conflict can almost always be prevented. If, however, we have the intention of doing harm, either physical or emotional, to someone, we are sure to create and maintain a state of conflict. It doesn't matter how justified we think we may be in our actions. A wife may feel it's her right to "take her husband to the cleaner's" after finding out about his affair. Bill might be convinced that Larry "deserved" that punch in the jaw after making an insulting comment about his failed business venture. Whatever the reasons, when our intentions are less than honorable, understanding and forgiving, we will inevitably find ourselves in a state of war rather than peace, conflict rather than harmony.

5. *Exclusive investment in one's opinions and belief system.* Another common source of conflict concerns "conflicting" beliefs. As we are tied to our egos and our identities in the world, so we are often tied to the philosophical, political or moral approaches to life that go along with them. When two people have opposing belief systems, and each of them is firmly convinced that they are in the "right," conflict can't be far away—regardless of whether this investment in an opinion, bias or belief is stubborn or sincere.

6. *Failure to establish boundaries.* When we don't set limits and make our personal boundaries clear, others can and probably will overstep them. This failure to clearly define what we need and want, and what we don't need and don't want from others is an invitation to conflict. By allowing another to "take advantage of us," chances are good that we will eventually

become resentful of them. And resentment leads to conflict.

Let's say that Ethel, a recent widow, calls her friend Evelyn every night and talks for at least an hour. Evelyn eventually grows tired of Ethel's phone calls. But she doesn't want to "hurt her feelings" because "poor Ethel is so lonely." So Evelyn deals—or doesn't deal— with the problem by buying an answering machine and screening her calls.

Ethel begins to suspect that Evelyn is avoiding her, and rightly so. Now her feelings *are* hurt. And when they meet at a church luncheon several weeks later, Ethel is very cool to Evelyn, who in turn takes offense at being "snubbed." Word quickly gets around that Ethel and Evelyn are "on the outs."

Had Evelyn been able to confront Ethel calmly and sympathetically *at the outset* about the too-frequent phone calls, this unhappy denouement could have been avoided. It would have been very easy for her to say, "You know, Ethel, I really value our friendship and I want to be here for you, especially at this difficult time. But sometimes I'm just too tired for long stretches on the phone every night. What do you say we limit our calls to a couple of times a week? If you really need me, you know I'm here. But I feel that I can be more genuinely present to you when I'm not worn out."

The basics of responding to and preventing conflict are essentially the same in any situation, whether it involves business partners, lovers, parents and children, organizations or countries. We need to be clear with *ourselves* first, as to what our intentions, needs and limits are. And then we need to be able to communicate this information calmly, clearly and concisely to the other party. When we define our boundaries at the moment they're threatened, we communicate respect for ourselves, and we give the other person a chance to respect us as well.

7. *Mishandling of conflict.* Perhaps the greatest source of conflict, one that is greater than all the others combined, is an unwillingness to deal directly with conflict. Because most people have no idea how to approach conflict situations, they mishandle them. Most conflicts are difficult situations that started out as molehills and were made into mountains by lack of awareness of what conflict is—and what it isn't. When we feel tension or conflict with another person, we often react emotionally, out of anger or fear. We may become defensive. We may attack the other. We may placate him or her. We may go into denial. Or we may withdraw completely. Because many of us often make a premature assumption that a conflict exists before it actually does, or because we are threatened by confrontation and/or uncomfortable feelings, we are apt to create or inflame conflict rather than prevent or resolve it.

8. *Fear.* Fear is at the root of the majority of conflict situations.

Fear can be considered the primary motivating force behind dishonesty, exclusive investment in one's own belief system, failure to establish boundaries and other defensive actions that create barriers to open communication. Usually, when we are involved in a conflict or potential conflict, we are feeling, on some level, threatened. We may have deemed it *unsafe* to be honest or vulnerable, fearing another person's anger, rejection or retribution. Or, we may be afraid of losing something that is very important to us. A wife or husband may remain in an unhappy or abusive marriage because they are afraid of losing what they perceive as security or love. We might stay in an unfulfilling job for essentially the same reason: We're afraid that we won't be able to find anything better, that present security is better at any cost than none at all.

We become invested in our own belief systems out of fear. More often than not, people who are very rigid in their opinions are those with the most fragile senses of self. Because they are afraid of being seen as "wrong" or "imperfect," they view a challenge to their belief system as a personal attack, a threat to their very identity.

Fear is also behind the failure to establish boundaries. When we allow others to take advantage of us, it's generally because we are afraid of confrontation or rejection. We shy away from expressing our real feelings and needs because we don't want others to be angry with us, or to turn away from us altogether.

In the next chapter, we explore some of the different dimensions of fear—how they pose obstacles to honesty, and how to overcome them.

9. *Hidden agendas.* A hidden agenda involves a situation in which one party has an undisclosed intention or motivation.

Hidden agendas come in two categories: conscious and unconscious. An example of a conscious hidden agenda is an organization making an extremely generous bid to buy a company, not because of the market, but because that organization can get a foothold in the door to other activities later on. Another example of a conscious hidden agenda would be the classic situation in which a junior executive "brown-noses" his superiors in hopes of a promotion.

An unconscious hidden agenda, on the other hand, is far less obvious. That's because it's hidden not only from the other person, but from the person who has it.

Unconscious hidden agendas are invariably the cause of a large class of disputes known as "personality" disputes, in which people find themselves acting out without really meaning to. They do and say things that cause conflict without understanding why they engage in that behavior.

Personality disputes are probably the most common kind of conflict situations that we encounter on a daily basis. In chapter 4, we'll take a look at this type of dispute, analyzing a typical unconscious hidden agenda that most of us have undoubtedly encountered at some point in our lives.

WHERE DISAGREEMENT ENDS AND CONFLICT BEGINS

The case of the record mogul's daughter was a perfect example of a disagreement that could easily have been resolved through a mediative approach. The actual value of the services of everyone present, from the multimillionaire Hollywood agent and the lawyers on down, was so extraordinarily high that if the parties involved had been willing to sit down and talk about the whole thing in a neutral, reasonable setting, it probably could have been resolved in two or three hours, saving both parties thousands of dollars.

Instead, however, the affair escalated into a full-blown conflict. Why?

Very simply because the elements that are necessary to *prevent* a conflict were missing, and those that cause conflict went unacknowledged and unchecked.

The basic elements necessary to prevent conflict involve (1) awareness; (2) honesty; (3) the intention to resolve the disagreement in as peaceful and mutually beneficial a way as possible; and (4) the willingness to divest oneself of the attachment to being "right."

The basic elements that in this instance caused conflict were (1) fear; (2) hidden agendas; (3) miscommunication; and (4) the need to be vindicated.

In the example we're using, the parties involved were guilty on all counts. The defendant was *afraid* of being labeled a failure by her family; the plaintiff was afraid of the effect the loss of her client would have on her career. Operating with the *hidden agenda* of wanting to land a big client to boost her fledgling business, the plaintiff agreed to enter into a "friendly" working relationship with the defendant, in which formal contracts were dispensed with. The defendant also had a hidden agenda—she wanted to make a name for herself and create her own identity in order to get out from under the oppressive wing of her domineering mother.

As far as *miscommunication* goes, neither party took the preliminary precaution of outlining, clearly and concisely, all of her expectations before entering into a working relationship. And in order to *"save face,"* both became attached to "winning" the war rather than preventing it. Thus, each immediately took an adversarial approach against the other, and what started out as a disagreement ended up as a dispute.

THE FOUR TYPES OF "CONFLICT PERSONALITIES"

When it comes to dealing with a conflict, most people can be classified as one of four types: (1) the attacker-defender; (2) the accommodator; (3) the avoider; and (4) the stalemater.*

Attacker-Defenders

The attacker-defender views the other person as the "enemy." He/she focuses on why the other is wrong, and what he/she wants out of the situation.

This is essentially a warlike mentality. This type of mindset—which is actually a "gutset"—is antithetical to the successful negotiation and prevention of conflict, in terms of coming up with a peaceful resolution that takes into account, as much as possible, the needs and objectives of each party.

"That SOB!" the attacker-defender bellows. "He/she had no right to do this to me, and this is what I want and this is what I'm going to get!"

As long as we approach conflict situations from this belligerent perspective, we can never really "win." We may momentarily get what we think we want, such as revenge, or money, or destroying the other person. But since we will probably not have achieved a truthful, sincere end to the enmity, the internal conflict is likely

---

* I would be happy to credit the psychologists who originated these terms, but unfortunately I came across the material some years ago, and cannot remember the source. If you happen to be reading this, please come forward and receive your due!

to continue long after the immediate material aspects of the problem have been taken care of.

Accommodators

Accommodators seem, at first glance, to be the polar opposites of attacker-defenders. Instead of using the slightest provocation as an excuse to go to war, the accommodator will do anything to "keep the peace."

The perfect historical example of the Great Accommodator was the British Prime Minister Neville Chamberlain, who agreed to cede Czechoslovakia to Adolf Hitler in the mistaken belief that this action would mollify the aggressor. Chamberlain's famous last words on leaving the Munich Conference were "I believe we have secured peace in our time." Instead, as we know, Chamberlain's "generosity" gave Hitler the green light to begin World War II.

Accommodators do not generally act from a position of strength. Their motivation is fear and a basic belief that they have no power. When facing opposition, they throw up their hands and tell themselves, "I can't get what I want anyway, so I might as well give in." Or, "I hate to fight—fighting never solved anything. It's better to turn the other cheek."

In their own way, then, accommodators are just as insecure as attacker-defenders. And they are just as adept at not taking responsibility for the problem they're facing—even though it may seem like they are. Very often accommodators will appear to take full responsibility for a conflict situation. But down deep, they're usually as angry as attacker-defenders, and as convinced, albeit silently, of their own rightness. The difference is that they're passively rather than actively hostile.

Avoiders

Avoiders are an extreme variation of accommodators:
They do not even want to acknowledge that a conflict
exists. Like the attacker-defender and the accommodator, the avoider eschews responsibility for the problem,
but in a different way. He/she simply denies that there
is a problem.

As anyone who has been involved with classic
avoiders, like many alcoholics or other substance
abusers, can tell you, this type of "conflict personality"
is extremely difficult to deal with. These individuals
typically have a need for denial that runs so deep that
they will do almost anything to resist confronting their
dependence or codependence. Communication and
honesty are foreign behavior patterns to them. They
are paralyzed by fear. Like accommodators, avoiders
have an extremely low concept of their self-worth,
which in turn leads to a "victim" mentality of hopeless-
ness and despair. But the avoider's way of dealing with
his/her feelings of powerlessness is to pretend that
everything's just fine and "let's maintain the status
quo."

Stalematers

There's a wonderful novel about turn-of-the-century
Charleston called *Pride's Way*. The central characters
are two sisters, Miss Julie and Miss Tessie, who haven't
spoken to each other since the Civil War.

What was the source of their disagreement? Actually,
neither of them really remembered it anymore. Or if
they did remember it, it had long since ceased to have
any relevance in their lives. But the sisters still continued

to stubbornly maintain their positions of mute intractability—even when they unexpectedly ran into each other at mass after having privately resolved to bury the hatchet.

Miss Tessie and Miss Julie are good examples of stalematers, people who are more concerned with maintaining the sanctity of their positions than in taking any action whatsoever to end a conflict. Stalematers feel no impulse either to attack the other person or to win them over. Rather, their payoff is to feel "validated" by remaining entrenched in their views.

Like attacker-defenders, stalematers suffer from an overwhelming need to be right—one of the greatest causes of human suffering. Its corollary, of course, is the need to prove others wrong—always a deterrent to genuine, honest conflict solving.

A good example of the extremes to which the stalemater will go is the reaction of the Iraqi government to the withdrawal of their forces from Kuwait. Despite their overwhelming losses, and the overwhelming victory of the Coalition Forces, Iraq continued to broadcast that it had won the Gulf War. And even those pro-Saddam groups who were forced to admit that the war had been technically lost claimed a "moral" victory—the victory of an Arab nation standing up to U.S. imperialism in a "holy" cause.

These four conflict personality types usually tend to overlap to some degree in all of us. The attacker-defender mentality generally contains aspects of the avoider and the stalemater—the Iraqis attacked Kuwait, denied that they had done anything wrong and remained firmly entrenched in their belief that they were "right." The accommodator can also be an avoider—attitudes like "It's all my fault" or "You're

100 percent right" or "You're wrong but I'll give in because I don't want a fight" are actually a means of masking the real problem and the accommodator's actual contribution to it.

But regardless of the personality type involved, the end result of all these positions is the same: a "win-lose" approach to conflict solving, which is really a "lose-lose" situation for everybody concerned.

Just as there are many different sources of and responses to conflict, there are many different levels of conflict. I like to approach these levels with something called a "Conflict Continuum."

THE CONFLICT CONTINUUM

At each end of the continuum is an extreme: *peace* and *war*. A state of peace is a state of compassion. A state of war is a state of the ultimate conflict, the most negative extreme, where there is physical hostility leading to death. Wars can take place between countries, tribes, drug kings, gangs, corporations, partners and individuals. Whatever the circumstances, they will all have the common denominator of a complete breakdown in

The Conflict Continuum

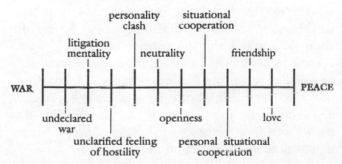

communication and a refusal to see the "other" as a human being who has the right to life.

One step down from war we have *undeclared war*, which is really a war by other means. For example, in the period just preceding World War II and the Japanese attack on Pearl Harbor, we were doing things like boycotting the Japanese, making sure they weren't able to get raw materials, denying them access to financial markets and committing otherwise "provocative" acts. While we hadn't made a formal declaration of war, we were actually in an informal state of war.

This level of conflict applies to personal relationships as well. If we are engaged in open hostility with someone else, where provocative statements and actions abound and there is the intention to hurt or overpower another, we can be said to be engaged in an undeclared war with that person. In this type of relationship, disagreement or opposing worldviews have escalated into full conflict, with each side squared off against the other. Many unhappy marriages, for instance, are in a state of undeclared war, with both spouses constantly "sniping" at each other. Also, many ongoing on-the-job conflicts are endless sources of tension and frustration for hostile coworkers.

Next to "undeclared war" on the continuum comes what I call the *litigation mentality*. This is where you're really at war, but you're being "civilized" about it. You're using the judicial/economic system, playing by all the legal rules. But you are nonetheless engaged in a form of open hostility. In litigation, someone is usually "out to get" someone else. They're simply doing it in a "nice" way. But the parties involved become adversaries, one of whom must win and one of whom must lose.

The next step on the continuum is an *unclarified feeling of hostility*. Here the people involved may sense that a conflict is in the air, but nobody can quite define it.

When Jane, a divorcee with two children, went to visit her fiancé Rory's family, they were all very polite and hospitable. But, although she couldn't put her finger on anything in particular, Jane sensed that something wasn't right, that she wasn't being totally accepted.

When she mentioned her concern to Rory, he laughed it off and told her she was being "too sensitive." "My family loves you!" he insisted.

A month later, however, Rory received a nasty letter from his aunt, berating him for his choice of a wife and announcing that she spoke not only for herself, but for a number of people in the family. Jane's intuition had been correct; there was hostility toward her. It just hadn't been acknowledged or defined until Rory received the letter.

Moving down from unclarified hostility, we have a *personality clash*. This is a situation where it can be said, "Okay. Culturally, astrologically or whatever, these two people just can't get along with each other." Whether they're relatives, friends or business associates, they simply clash. One person's one way, the other person's the other way, and when they get together it's one big explosion caused by bad chemistry. This sort of interaction doesn't even have to involve actions or words; just the physical presence of one will set the other off.

At the middle of the continuum we have *neutrality*. Here interactions are neither positive nor negative. There's no friendship or love; neither is there hostility.

The parties involved interrelate amicably, but they are emotionally removed from each other.

Beyond "neutrality" is a state of *openness*, where, although there may not be extensive dealings between two people, there is an unspoken comfortableness and invitation to friendship or cooperation.

After "openness" comes *situational cooperation*, in which people are engaged in an activity or as co-workers, and "personal situational cooperation," where the parties who are involved in business or work dealings are also friends.

As we continue along the continuum, relationships deepen, to *friendship* and finally, *love*.

The Conflict Continuum: Where Do You Fit In?

Stop here for a moment to take a look at the various relationships in your life. Where do they fit on the Conflict Continuum?

Do you feel as though you're at war with someone when it's really only a personality clash? Are you and a coworker in a state of "unclarified hostility" that's got you both confused? Who are the people you feel closest to, most open with? With whom do you peacefully coexist?

You may find that some of your relationships can't be relegated to one point or another on the continuum. Perhaps you fluctuate between "neutrality" and "openness" with one person, or "personality clash" and "undeclared war" with another.

The Conflict Continuum can be a useful gauge in assessing how and why we interact with others in a certain way, and what stage we're at in terms of the levels of conflict we're experiencing in our lives. Perhaps we didn't realize, if we're engaged in litigation, that we are actually at war with someone else. We may discover that we'd like to get better acquainted with the "friendly stranger" at work whom we've put in the "openness" category. Or, if a high percentage of our relationships fall closer to the "war" or "peace" end of the spectrum, we may gain greater insight into the kinds of relationships we tend to create, and why.

Above all, the Conflict Continuum is a reminder that the world of conflict is neither black nor white, that many subtle gradations exist within it, and that we have the power and capacity to choose and to alter our relationships in order to minimize the conflict and maximize the harmony in our lives.

2

A Dispute Isn't a Dispute
Until It's a Dispute

A friend of mine is fond of relating the following story, her version of a "Zen" moment of enlightenment. She had just begun an intense, love-at-first-sight relationship, only to have her lover go off to Europe three weeks later. For seven tortured weeks she was plagued with doubts. What if he decided he didn't love her after all? What if he met someone else during his trip? What if he didn't call her as soon as he returned?

Full of all these what-ifs, my friend's brain was about to short-circuit, until a wise friend of hers put things in perspective.

"Why worry? Whatever he does, he does. Remember: *You don't know until you know.*"

You don't know until you know. My friend stood there, awestruck by the brilliant simplicity of this observation. There was really nothing she could do about the situation, after all. And worrying about something before it actually happened suddenly came into focus as the waste of time and energy that it is. In an instant, it seemed, she was free of the problem, able to settle back and take each day at a time until her lover returned, at which point things progressed just as beautifully as she could have hoped and her fears turned out to be groundless after all.

So, the moral of this story is, "You don't know until you know." Which leads me to the moral of this chapter: A dispute isn't a dispute until it's a dispute.

Now, the human imagination is, admittedly, a wondrous thing. It has created great works of art, soared to the most magnificent heights of invention, pulled us through times of adversity by opening windows onto dreams, allowing us to glimpse the virtually limitless alternatives at our disposal for creating new life scenarios.

Yet our imaginations can just as easily run away with us. And they usually set a record for the 100-yard mind dash by worrying about something in advance and *creating conflict before any actually exists.*

It's probably safe to estimate that 90 percent of the things we worry about are simply fears that have not yet materialized and that may never do so. Thus, I constantly remind clients—as well as myself—of rule number one in resolving any disagreement: A dispute isn't a dispute until it's a dispute.

The ground may be fertilized with the *seeds* of a dispute. If it's been over a week and the project you've submitted to a client hasn't been approved, you might be gearing up for a clash of wills or a battle for payment. Your friend Harry might not have responded to your phone message about the $100 you loaned him, leading you to surmise that he's an SOB who has no intention of repaying you a single dime. You might be ten days late on your rent and hiding out from your landlord. Or, you might be courting a foreign company and may have said or done something that, when they didn't respond immediately, led you to fear that you'd offended them.

But your client hasn't rejected your project *yet*; Harry hasn't said he won't pay you back; your landlord hasn't presented you with an eviction notice; the foreign company hasn't accused you of committing a heinous insult. If and when these possibilities become reality, then a dispute *could* be the result. But unless the "worst" happens, anything is possible. Before anything happens is a perfect time to nip a potential dispute in the bud.

The "Miracle" of Open Communication

One evening Sally, an executive in a computer software corporation, called me in the throes of deadline panic. She had a report due, but, troubled with other deadlines and personal crisis, she had put the assignment on the back burner because her boss had gone out of town unexpectedly and wasn't due back until the following week.

But that evening, out of the blue, her boss called her to ask if the report was finished. Caught off guard and fearing his wrath (he was the kind of person we politely term "difficult"), Sally reacted by not telling him the truth.

"Oh, yes, it's finished, Mr. Babcock. I just have to print it out."

"Great," said Mr. Babcock. "Fax it to me tomorrow morning. I want to read it before I get back."

When Sally called me, she was really panicked and afraid that she was going to be fired.

"Hold on a minute," I replied. "Is Mr. Babcock angry with you?"

"No. But he will be."

"But he isn't yet. Right?"

"Right."

"Okay. Has he fired you?"

"No. But he will. And then what am I going to do? I just bought this condo, and Greg's started orthodontia and—"

"Whoa. As of this moment you haven't been fired. Correct?"

"What does that matter? It's just a question of time!"

"That's exactly right," I replied. "You've still got time to set things straight."

One of the first things I do with clients and friends is to ground them in the present, the "now." This forces them to deal with reality, rather than become overwhelmed by the fears they mistake for reality. It also doesn't allow them to indulge in guilt feelings about what they should or shouldn't have done, because, at the moment, all that is irrelevant. Later one can go back and examine one's errors, to make sure that they aren't repeated. But when you accidentally drop a cigarette into a bush, you don't waste time thinking about the past ("If only I hadn't dropped this cigarette") or the future ("All of Southern California will burn to a crisp"). You pour a bucket of water on that bush just as fast as you can!

"Okay," I said to Sally. "What are your options?"

"I could borrow my boyfriend's motorcycle and drive off a cliff."

"Yes, you could. That's certainly an option. But assuming you decide to remain on the planet awhile longer, what are some other alternatives?"

We discussed the possibility of honesty—always the first option in my book.

"Why not call your boss back and tell him the truth? We all make mistakes, we all tell fibs once in awhile. We all have personal problems, and most of us fear other people's anger. If you explain the situation to Mr. Babcock in those terms, chances are he'll understand."

"Well," said Sally, "I'd like to be able to do that. But you don't know Mr. Babcock. He never listens; he just explodes."

"Okay," I thought for a moment. "How about faxing him a letter explaining the true situation?"

"A letter?"

"Sure. Then you'll avoid the pain of a face-to-face confrontation, and he'll have time to think about things after he blows up—if indeed he does."

"Hmmm," said Sally. "That might work. Any other options?"

"You could compound your fib and tell him you lost the disk the report was on. But if Mr. Babcock is the ogre you make him out to be, that kind of carelessness won't sit too well with him. And besides, the single thread of a lie soon becomes a tapestry of deceit."

"Okay," Sally sighed. "I've decided. I'm going to fax him a letter."

"Great. Let me know how it works out."

The following day, Sally faxed a letter to Mr. Babcock in which she stated, simply and honestly, that she did not have the report done. She explained the reasons why, and the reason why she had lied: because she feared Mr. Babcock's temper. She apologized for her actions and gently let Mr. Babcock know that when he is overly critical and quick to explode, she feels tense and scared. She ended the letter by telling Mr. Babcock the things she did like about him, how much she appreciated her job and that she hoped he would give her the chance to turn in an excellent report in a few days.

The happy ending to the tale was that Mr. Babcock called Sally to *thank* her for the letter. It turned out that he, too, actually welcomed the chance to communicate more honestly and, surprise of surprises, to discuss the issue of his temper, which was rapidly alienating him from more and more people, including his wife and children. As a result of Sally's letter, many positive changes in her and her coworkers' relationships with Mr. Babcock took place, and the department in which they worked became a happier environment.

Thus a situation that was potentially volatile did a 180-degree turnaround into one that was mutually advantageous, thanks to the "miracle" of open communication.

What are the ingredients of this miracle?

1. *The capacity, desire and intent to correct the situation.* Sally did not want this incident to escalate into a full-scale dispute. She was willing to do whatever was necessary to defuse the time bomb of impending conflict.

2. *Grounding in the now.* Don't look back ("I shouldn't have said . . . I wish I'd done . . .") and don't look ahead ("He'll be furious . . . I'll lose my job . . ."). Deal strictly with the present. What is the situation *as of this moment*? Don't mistake your fears for reality.

3. *Honesty*. Be willing to take the plunge and reveal yourself in all your humanness.

4. *Acknowledging your error.* If you're wrong, admit it. If you've got a good excuse, explain it as directly as possible, and apologize.

5. *Know the approach that's most comfortable for you.* All of us have different ways of dealing with direct communication that are most effective for us. Sally chose a letter. Others prefer phone calls or face-to-face meetings. Decide which approach works best for you, and don't feel guilty if another doesn't. The most important thing is to convey the information.

6. *Giving "I" messages.* If something about the other person caused you to react in the way you did, let them know about it in terms of *your* feelings rather than *their* faults. Don't attack them; instead, explain how their behavior affects you.

7. *Starting and ending with the positive.* Sally was careful to temper criticism of her boss with an acknowledgment of his positive qualities, and ended the letter by emphasizing her desire to continue working in a job she enjoyed. Such an approach minimizes the problem by putting it in perspective. I made a mistake; it's over. Let's move on.

In my sixteen years of professionally helping people to confront and prevent their disputes, I have found no substitute for open communication. There is simply nothing that I know of that can take the place of honesty, of the willingness to be human and vulnerable in an effort to help another person understand you and to be open enough to understand him or her.

I once heard the Dalai Lama remark that "We are all born with the capacity to achieve liberation and enlightenment." I would transpose that statement to read, "We're all born with the capacity to prevent and heal our own disputes."

All we really need is the willingness to be honest—the capacity, desire and intention to want the same for the other person as we do for ourselves.

UNEXPRESSED CONFLICT: THE SILENT DISPUTE

There is an important difference between a potential dispute and one that already exists in the mind of one or both parties to a disagreement, but that has not been formally articulated.

With a potential dispute, such as the one between Sally and Mr. Babcock, unexpressed *fears* play a dominant role. In a silent dispute, however, unexpressed *feelings* are at the heart of the issue. A potential dispute can be prevented by "taking the bull by the horns," facing one's fears and taking proper action to insure that they don't become reality. A silent dispute, however, is an *unexpressed conflict*—a situation where, if the truth about both people's thoughts and feelings were to come out and be presented, a conflict would clearly arise.

Here's a good example of an unexpressed conflict. Darla was a theater reviewer for a newspaper. Her editor, Mike, didn't agree with her opinions, but she was a fine reviewer and, as a critic, was entitled to her personal views.

Mike continued to use Darla, but he began to give her inferior assignments—B plays to review. Whenever Darla put in a bid to review a major play, Mike would either take the assignment himself or give it to another critic whose views more closely mirrored his own.

Naturally Darla was upset. She was bewildered by this turn of events and she began to resent Mike. But he was her editor and the keeper of her paycheck. She needed her position and didn't want to antagonize Mike. So she kept quiet. And Mike kept quiet. The result? A silent dispute.

Finally, things came to a head when Mike, short of reviewers, assigned Darla a big play to cover. She hated it and gave it a detailed, thorough thrashing. The following weekend, Mike went to see the play. He liked it. And the next day, Darla was horrified to find her review pulled, and Mike's in its place.

This sort of action was not only insulting and humiliating to Darla, it violated professional ethics as well. Shaking with rage, Darla phoned Mike and asked him why he had done such a thing, especially without first consulting her.

"Because I'm a bastard," he replied.

They then had it out. Mike accused Darla of faulty judgment and incompetence. Darla asked Mike why, if he'd felt that way about her work, he hadn't called her in to discuss it. When Mike couldn't come up with a decent excuse, Darla replied, "I'll tell you why. Because you're not only a bastard—you're a coward."

Needless to say, that was the end of Darla's tenure as a theater critic for that newspaper. Mike fired her, and the managing editor, who was Mike's old buddy from a former newspaper, felt obligated to stand by his friend when Darla appealed the case to him.

DISHONESTY: THE BREEDING GROUND FOR CONFLICT

It should be pretty obvious that had Mike chosen to be upfront early on with Darla—to call her in and express his concerns about her judgment as a reviewer—and had Darla been willing to confront Mike and ask him why he'd demoted her to second-rate assignments, the above unhappy confrontation could have been avoided.

There may still have been a conflict. Darla probably wouldn't have been able to tailor her opinions to suit Mike, and vice versa. But there would have been honesty, and the chance for a less hostile resolution of the problem.

But as easy as this sounds, it's tremendously difficult for many people, primarily because openness and genuineness have been conditioned out of most of us. Negative, critical upbringing, coupled with society's emphasis on putting up a front and maintaining a facade, effectively deadens our natural impulse toward spontaneity and honesty.

Young children respond with utter candor to the world around them. They shriek when they're upset; they crow when they're happy. While their parents wilt with embarrassment, they inquire of Ms. Smith how come she's so fat or of Mr. Jones why he walks funny. They are motivated not by cruelty or tactlessness, but by simple, nonjudgmental curiosity.

Of course, as we grow older, we learn that the blunt expression of such curiosity will not put us at the top of the popularity charts. We learn how to be kind, considerate of others' feelings, silent about their flaws, approving of their virtues. We learn how to get along in the world by "not making waves." In short, we become socially "acceptable."

There is nothing wrong with being tactful, with concentrating on the good rather than the bad in a person or situation, with keeping angry or hurtful comments to ourselves. But there *is* something wrong with denying a problem, glossing over a difficult situation, not expressing our true feelings when we need to. I would say that virtually every dispute I have come across has had, at its core, the inability or unwillingness of one or both parties to communicate their feelings honestly with the dual intention of articulating needs and truly understanding the other person's position.

It is only when we are willing to venture into the initially terrifying territory of honesty that disputes can either be solved or prevented altogether. What are some of the obstacles to honesty? And how can we overcome them?

1. *Fear of another person's anger.* Most of us grew up with authority figures whom we learned to fear and accommodate. These childhood patterns tend to repeat themselves in adulthood when we are dealing with bosses, spouses or anyone to whom we relinquish our own power out of a sense of helplessness.

A case in point is Mark, a writer who was coauthoring a book with a celebrity. Having had a father who tyrannized him with verbal criticism and temper tantrums, Mark learned to fear anger, especially in authority figures. The celebrity he was working with was extremely demanding and critical, and Mark had gotten to the point where he no longer wanted to work with him.

When Mark came to me, he was extremely upset. He didn't want to give up the project, which was an important one for him in terms of his career. But every time he had to meet with his coauthor, he was filled with anger and dread.

"Have you tried telling him exactly how you feel? that his angry and intractable behavior is alienating you and that you have difficulty in dealing with that behavior because of childhood experiences with similar figures?"

"No," Mark admitted.

"Why don't you?"

"Because I'm afraid he'll get mad!"

I convinced Mark to deal honestly with the celebrity, and to understand that his coauthor, too, was a victim of prepatterned reactions In his case, he dealt with people the only way *he* knew how to: by exploding.

Mark met with the celebrity and said to him, "I can understand your desire to have a top-notch book. But I have a personal problem. Because of the way my father treated me, I have a lot of difficulty dealing with other people's anger. When you get angry with me, I freeze. And I don't deal with things as rationally or honestly as I should. As a result, I'm having trouble continuing to work with you."

This admission took every bit of courage that Mark had. But it was worth it. Not only was the celebrity taken aback because he hadn't seen himself as being an "angry" person, but he also respected Mark's willingness to be vulnerable. And, of course, he respected Mark's talent and didn't want to lose him.

When I saw Mark again several months later, he

had just finished the manuscript and everybody was happy.

"How are things with your coauthor?" I asked.

"Great!" he replied. "He's been very careful never to lose his temper around me. And I've been much more aware of my feelings and how to express them in a nonthreatening way, *before* they get out of hand."

It isn't easy to transcend our conditioning, to break these types of deeply ingrained patterns. But it is possible. All it takes is the willingness to change. You don't need to change before things improve; all you need to begin with is the *intention* to change. If you tend, like Mark, to be paralyzed by other people's anger, first be aware of the reality of the situation and accept the fact that it's an internal impulse you need to play out. Second, realize that this impulse will change very slowly. Third, make a conscious decision to respond differently. And fourth, begin to practice changing that pattern.

Discover the method that will allow you to deal directly with the situation. Mark felt that he had to talk to the celebrity in person. In Sally's case, she was most comfortable with sending her boss a letter rather than confronting him directly. You may find a phone call less threatening, or you may even feel you need to engage the services of a third party in facilitating communication. Whatever you decide, just make sure that you are acting with the intention of opening up communication, of meeting rather than avoiding conflict.

And don't wait for conflict with a particular authority figure to occur before you embark upon changing your pattern of response to another person's disapproval. Allow yourself to take baby steps along the road to consciousness. Pick a relatively nonthreatening situation in which to practice new techniques. Instead of starting out with your boss or wife, you may want to confront a nasty store clerk or a bulldog receptionist. If you begin with a more "impersonal" situation, it's easier to act without fear of repercussions, and to gain confidence in the process.

Above all, maintain a positive attitude. You're engaged in an adventure—the adventure of improving the quality of your life and the lives of those around you. Treat the world as an opportunity to practice changing those things you need to change, and you're bound to notice an improvement in your attitude, from one of apprehension and anxiety to one of excitement and confidence.

2. *Fear of rejection.* Rita, an intelligent, lively woman in her thirties, is one of the most articulate people I know. She also has many wonderful friends. But she confessed to me that when it comes to close friendships, she has a great problem. If one of her friends does something that really irritates her, she finds it virtually impossible to confront them about it. Why? Because she's afraid that the friend will retaliate with some fault of Rita's that he or she has always disliked. And Rita simply can't take rejection or disapproval.

The fear of rejection or ostracism is a disease we all share. In fact, I think of it as a most infectious communicable disease. The fear of rejection prevents us from taking risks, in careers and relationships. It prevents us from experiencing life in all its fullness. Above all, it prevents us from achieving honest, open communication.

Like fear of anger, fear of rejection is an ingrained pattern that will take time and patience to change.

Begin by being approving of yourself and by committing yourself to a willingness to go within, to look inside yourself as objectively as possible. Note your virtues and flaws, suspending any feelings of judgment you might have. Do not attach any positive or negative conditions to what you discover about yourself; accept that fact that you're okay as you are and that there's room for improvement in everyone.

The following exercise will help you to formulate a realistic appraisal of yourself, and to become aware of how you respond to conflict or potential conflict situations.

EXERCISE:
Facing Yourself and Your Fears Without Fear

Take a moment now to assess yourself as objectively as possible. What are the things about you that you like and are proud of? In what areas could you use a little improvement? Write these down in the space below.

My Good Qualities   *Things I'd Like to Change*

_____   _____

_____   _____

_____   _____

_____   _____

_____   _____

_____   _____

_____   _____

Now, recall one or two conflict or potential conflict situations that you have experienced or are experiencing. How did or do you respond in the situation? Was fear at the root of your response? If so, what sort of fear? Describe the situation and your feelings about it in the space below.

If the conflict has already occurred, would you like to have responded differently to the situation? If so, how? If you have not yet reached the conflict stage, is there a way in which you might alter your response pattern to prevent a conflict from occurring? Write down your answers here.

Once you have faced yourself squarely, with as much unconditional love as you can muster up, you can begin to face others with equanimity. When someone criticizes you, it will become easier for you to evaluate their comments objectively. Rather than reacting in ways that block communication, by trying to defend yourself, attacking the other person or withdrawing in devastated silence, you can say, "Hmmm. There may be some truth in what you say." Or, "Well, I don't know. I've studied myself pretty well and I know my faults, but that doesn't seem to be one of them."

Until we face our fear of rejection and deal with it, our relationships with others won't attain the level of honesty and richness they deserve. By the same token, once we break through the fear barrier, we will find ourselves empowered with the creative energy that comes from a renewed sense of self and self-worth.

3. *Fear of listening*. I remember an interesting divorce case I was mediating. The husband and wife were going back and forth, and finally I said, "Hey. Wait a minute. All you guys are doing is arguing. You're missing each other completely."

They paused and looked at me, bewildered.

"It was my assumption, and one of our ground rules, that you were going to do your best to understand each other," I continued. "The quickest way to agreement is through understanding. In fact, it's the only way to real agreement. And if you're not willing to put in the effort to understand each other, I don't know what you're doing here."

To which they both replied, "No! I don't want to understand what he/she's saying!"

"I'm tired of listening to him," the wife added, for emphasis.

"You may want to look at that," I suggested. "You may want to look at how your wanting a divorce after five years of marriage may have been related to the fact that perhaps all along you didn't want to listen to him."

That was a pretty wild thing to say, but the wife was an intelligent woman. She thought about it for a second and then she said, "Maybe you're right."

In order to avoid a dispute or to reach an agreement, the willingness to listen to the other person is essential. A significant percentage of the people I see in my office are too frightened to really confront each other as to who they are. They are too intent upon "keeping the upper hand," maintaining "control"—in short, protecting their own fragile sense of self—to hear what the other person has to say, or to acknowledge what he or she may be feeling.

Remember: It takes two to tangle. Agreements can

never be reached when both people have a vested interest in being "right," or when they're out to hurt each other. If you're not willing to listen to the other person, to allow them their right to their own feelings, you won't ever achieve a satisfactory solution to the difficulty, if by satisfactory we mean a situation in which both parties get their needs met as amicably and productively as possible. And if you're not willing to listen to the other person, you probably won't get much out of this book, either.

Above all, accept where you're at. Embrace your errors as guideposts along the road to enlightenment. This attitude is perhaps the most crucial one of all in insuring that a potential dispute never becomes any more than that. Because in accepting ourselves and admitting our frailty, we take the first step to overcoming the fear of honesty that is at the heart of most disputes.

An important teacher of mine once said to me, "One wish I have for you is that you make at least one mistake every day. Just make sure it isn't the same one."

I pass that on to you.

3

So You Think You're Speaking English: Making Ourselves Understood

The most basic elements of successful communication are the intention to be understood and the intention to understand.

Unfortunately, the way most of us handle these intentions is by trying to "get" something from the other person. We want something—money, property, action, love. But we don't perceive that underneath the yearning for these external "acquisitions" is almost always the inner desire to be understood, appreciated and acknowledged.

Yet most of us never *ask* for these. Instead, we usually leapfrog over this most basic need, which is at the heart of all successful communication. How, after all, can we hope to get anything from anyone until our needs are understood? Communication is a one-step-at-a-time process. There's no leapfrogging; it simply doesn't work. If you try to do anything without first being understood, forget it. The probability of things going awry is 100 percent.

Why do we ignore this first step in communication? One reason is that our society has put such a high value on things and actions and such a low value on communication and understanding. We're used to "getting"; we want "tangible" proof of another person's intentions or feelings. Sue wants Brad to call her every day, even though that isn't Brad's modus operandi. In a bitter battle over a program that he says he wasn't paid enough for, Jack sues a computer software company for a half-million dollars in damages. What Sue and Jack really want is for their needs—love, respect, proper remuneration—to be understood by the other person. But instead of talking about that issue, demands are made that invariably put the other party on the defensive and diminish the possibility of communicating effectively and obtaining satisfaction.

Somehow we automatically expect others to understand us. But after fifty-four years of trying to communicate with people and watching others struggle with trying to make somebody else understand their point of view, I have come to a somewhat startling working hypothesis: When people actually understand each other, it's the *exception* rather than the rule!

Most of us don't realize how often we mistake "miscommunication" for "communication." We *think* we're communicating; we're convinced that the other person hears and understands what we're intending to say. Unfortunately, this is rarely the case. In fact, I have found that if you enter into a dialogue with the assumption that you're going to be *mis*understood (and that life is like playing telephone in the second grade), you're in a far healthier position than if you assume you're going to be understood. It's healthier for you because you're closer to the truth.

For instance, every one of us has probably witnessed the following scene. A tourist in a foreign country is trying to communicate to a shopkeeper. He knows a few words of the language, or worse, he doesn't know any words at all but thinks he does. He says something once and the shopkeeper doesn't understand. So what does the tourist do? Instead of using different words, or trying to convey his message in a different way, he says it *louder*. And he keeps repeating his demand, more and more loudly, getting everyone more and more frustrated and annoyed.

This little scenario is a microcosm of the kind of miscommunication techniques we all engage in. You don't need to be in a foreign country; every day I see people from the same culture—and often the same family—ostensibly speaking the same language, totally unable to successfully communicate. And if you compound this by cultural differences, language differences, religious differences, age differences . . . well, you've got an amazing tale of universal communication woe.

Here's a good example of how miscommunication occurs in everyday family life. One of my clients, Tanya, went back East to visit her mother. Because she was planning on staying for three weeks and because she wanted to begin an exercise and weight loss program, Tanya decided to buy a used bicycle. Here's the dialogue that occurred between Tanya and her mother:

TANYA: Mom, do you have the newspaper want ads?
MOM: What are you looking for?
TANYA: I want to buy a used bike while I'm here.

MOM: What for?

TANYA: I like to bike and I want to get some exercise. Besides, I used to love biking around here when I was a kid.

MOM (in an irritated tone of voice): And just how much is this going to cost?

TANYA (surprised): What do you care? I'm paying for it.

MOM: Yes, and you have the habit of wasting money.

TANYA: Mom, is there some problem with my getting a bicycle?

MOM: Yes, there is. I don't want it hanging around here after you leave. I don't want to be responsible for it.

TANYA: Okay. I'll sell it before I leave.

MOM (even more irritated): That's not the issue, Tanya.

TANYA: What is the issue?

MOM: I'm tired of your acting in irresponsible ways! I forbid you to buy a bicycle!

TANYA: Well, Mom, I've got some bad news for you. I'm thirty-eight years old, I've lived away from home for twenty years now, and whether you like it or not, I'm buying a bicycle.

MOM: You're doing it just to spite me!

TANYA: No, I'm not. I'm doing it because I'm going to enjoy riding around. Let's not discuss it any further.

Now, Tanya's mother's reaction may seem extreme to some of you and it certainly did to Tanya. She was shocked at how her innocent remark—"Mom, do you have the newspaper want ads?"—could have suddenly escalated into World War III. To any student of communication, however, the chain of events is no mystery. In fact, it's typical of the way most wars begin. One person says one thing and the other person hears something else.

THE PARTS OF THE COMMUNICATION WHOLE

How *do* we communicate? It might be useful here to break down the actual process of communication into its separate stages, which most of us experience unconsciously.

1. *First there is a feeling.* You could experience a tingling, a pain, a pulsation or you might get a glimmer—an inkling, a vision, an image, even a sense of confusion. This is the very beginning of communication: something that one of your six senses is picking up that you want to get into somebody else's mind and body in the way that you are experiencing it.

2. *Then there is an awareness of that sensation or thought.* You get an idea on the basis of that physical experience, or you feel a need that demands expression.

3. *This leads to the formation of words in your mind.* These words are an attempt to capture that sensation, or that idea or that glimmer that you are experiencing.

4. *These words and/or conduct are then put out to others.* Either communicated verbally, in sign language, through body language or on paper, they are your only means of mirroring to someone else the words that are in your mind.

5. *These words and/or conduct are then received and processed by the other person.* Your words must go to someone else's eyes, ears or both.

6. *The receiver then processes your words or conduct.* Whatever the receiver sees or hears will be reinterpreted into *their* own words. Furthermore, the receiver may have his own internal conversation and thoughts which are stimulated by his interpretation.

7. *The interpretation, internal dialogue and thoughts will in turn create feelings and images in the receiver's mind and body.* The receiver's ultimate feelings in response to the information you have sent out may be very different from what you were feeling or intending to communicate.

The reason we don't often successfully communicate is due to the common misconception that if two people speak the same language, i.e., English, each automatically understands what the other is saying. But the truth of the matter is that everything we hear and see is processed through the filter of our own personal history and our own perceptions of a situation. People don't always take in at face value what they hear or read. Someone who's dyslexic, for instance, will read something one way and take it in backwards. Well, many of us are *aurally* dyslexic—especially in the heat of intense emotion. Even when there is the intention on the part of the receiver to understand the sender, real understanding is difficult. But as soon as we encounter tension and anger, the difficulty is magnified. The receiver is so busy listening for flaws, arguments and reasons to disagree that the desire and ability to listen is virtually disabled.

The receiver experiences his or her own set of responses to our words, independent of the face value of the words themselves. Let's go back to Tanya and her mother. What were the real dynamics of that dialogue?

Because I had worked with Tanya, she was quick to understand—after she had experienced her own anger—that her mother was expressing anger not about the bicycle, or even about Tanya's "irresponsibility," but about another issue entirely.

"My dad had recently passed away and my mother was going through a period of real loneliness and mourning," Tanya reflected. "When I stopped and took the time to think about the interaction, what at first seemed bizarre—that my mother should actually try to prevent her grown daughter from buying a bicycle—became crystal clear. My mom wasn't angry about the bike per se. She was afraid that I'd be spending my time riding around, instead of being with her. She was, in short, afraid of being abandoned again."

This is a perfect example of an aurally dyslexic response. Tanya had been enthusiastic about the prospect of exercising, losing weight and reliving some of her childhood memories through the acquisition of a bicycle. But Tanya's mother heard her "backwards," filtering her daughter's words through her own fear and anger. As so often happens in the process of human interaction, an innocent statement gets blown out of proportion and the result is a fight. Fortunately, in this case Tanya was able to prevent things from toppling over into the absurd by her willingness to go beneath her mother's words in an attempt to discover what was really bothering her. She directly addressed her mother's fear, they talked about it and Tanya's bicycle is still sitting in her mother's garage, waiting for her next visit.

It may seem sometimes as though satisfactory communication between one person and another has about as low a probability for success as the old second-grade game of "telephone," where the teacher tells a child in the front row a story and expects it to be the same story by the time it gets to the kid in the back. Given this sobering observation, some people get so pessimistic that they refuse to try to communicate at all. But this is directly contrary to what I'm trying to help you achieve. In assuming that you won't be understood, I'm not telling you to assume that you *can't* be understood. I'm merely giving you what I perceive as a realistic picture, so that you can maximize the effectiveness of your communications.

The negative reaction that a lot of people have to the observation that communication should never be taken for granted is similar to the way many outsiders react to the Eastern view of suffering. A Westerner will often regard the Far Easterner as pessimistic because they usually accept the fact that all human beings suffer. If life is suffering, the Westerner replies, then why bother at all?

But if you look deeper into Eastern philosophy, you find that the emphasis is not on suffering. The emphasis is on studying the *nature* of suffering, so that you can find a way out of it. Once you accept suffering as reality, you have a chance of doing something about it, moving beyond it so that you don't have to suffer if you don't want to. But if you go unconsciously whistling through life, you may never realize that your illusions are the very bones from which the soup of suffering is made.

This analogy is applicable to the science of communication on two levels. First of all, it's a good example of the way in which two people often hear the same word but give it totally different meanings, a common cause of conflict. Second, the "suffering of communication" is similar to the Buddhist definition of suffering in general, in that the cause of suffering is "attachment"—in this case to one's ideas, one's own worldview.

Attachment to our ideas and views is tempting because most of us have a need to be "right." Being right validates us. Being "wrong," on the other hand, is terrifying, challenging to the entire foundation of our thought. Unfortunately, most of us believe, in effect, that in order for us to be "right," someone else has to be "wrong." This is a beginning of conflict and often the end of successful communication.

Attachment to our position may seem to be the best way to get us what we want. But in fact, it often prevents us from getting the thing we want the most: to be understood. It is often difficult to risk becoming vulnerable, to speak from the heart, to express hurt rather than anger, need rather than want. If someone else disagrees with something in which we strongly believe, *why* do we grow angry? Because they are stupid and "can't see the light?" Because they have insulted our perceptions? Or because they are not respecting and valuing our perspective—our need to be understood?

Conscious Communication

How do we define successful communication? Very simply: *Successful communication can be said to occur when the thoughts, images and feelings that are gener-*

ated in the receiver are the same ones that were intended by the sender.

This doesn't mean that the receiver has to *agree* with or even like these thoughts and feelings, but simply that the sender was so powerful and clear in getting his message across and the receiver was so open to it, that what was felt and thought was received as intended.

How can we maximize our chances for successful communication? By being willing to enter into the state of *conscious communication.*

Conscious communication involves ten basic elements: (1) commitment; (2) self-observation; (3) honesty; (4) going beneath the surface; (5) separating intention from conduct; (6) separating facts from feelings; (7) using "I" messages; (8) listening; (9) having the willingness to admit that you don't know everything; and (10) having the willingness to admit your mistakes.

1. *Commitment.* There can be no real understanding between two people if there is no commitment to the intention to achieve that understanding. That commitment might come out of intention. "I intend to resolve this dispute amicably; therefore I'm committed to understanding your point of view."

2. *Self-observation.* In order for someone else to understand you, you must first *understand yourself.* This involves staying awake to what you feel, think, do and say. Do you make snap judgments about the other person? Do you feel inadequate or powerless? Do you fail to listen to what the other person is saying because you're already justifying your position in your response?

It can be most instructive to really stop and listen to yourself. Very often we speak automatically and unconsciously, from an internal "script." When we throw the script away and begin to respond in the moment, we are forced to listen to ourselves. The result does wonders for effective communication. Suddenly we're in the other person's position and can appreciate how he or she might hear what we're saying.

3. *Honesty.* An eleven-year-old girl said to her teacher, "The trouble with telling the truth is that nobody believes you."

"That's not true!" retorted the teacher.

"Truth" is a difficult concept for many of us to deal with. Life holds out an infinite variety of opportunities for engaging in untruth, from the white lies we manufacture to explain a missed appointment or evade an unwanted request to the partial truths we tell in order to shield others from hurt or discomfort.

Dishonesty is often sanctioned by societal etiquette or business tactics. "Politeness," considered a primary social virtue, involves, more often than not, a delicate measure of deceit when someone else's feelings are at stake. Negotiating a successful business deal often involves a not-so-delicate measure of deceit on the part of those who believe in the entrepeneurial philosophy of the ends justifying the means.

Many of us do not realize that honesty is an option in *all* of our dealings with others. Not simply an option, in fact, but in most cases the only truly effective and humane option.

Many of us are so used to living in denial that we find it more comfortable than confronting and dealing with the truth. But as anyone who's gone through the agony of periodontia will tell you, the momentary discomfort of having a cavity filled is far less painful in the long run than the prolonged misery that comes from avoiding the dentist for ten years. The inner discomfort of dishonesty can easily become as nagging as a chronic ulcer. But the momentary discomfort of telling the truth is replaced by the peace of a clear conscience, and the satisfaction of knowing that we've acted with integrity.

But honesty does not simply involve telling someone else the truth about themselves. Honesty involves honoring your own inner truth, accepting your own feelings, being willing to be vulnerable. And it also involves being open to another's pain.

Dino DiFillipi, a Los Angeles consultant who trains people and organizations in honest communication, tells the following story. A prospective client sounded sad while discussing business matters with him. After a brief internal battle, Dino decided to ask the man why he seemed so down. The man began to cry, and the intimate story of a family difficulty poured out of him. At the end of the conversation the man told Dino, "I really appreciate this. I get the feeling you're just like me, and I'd like to do business with you."

Honesty is a risk. In holding out for a deeper truth, we may alienate or lose those people in our lives who prefer to live in denial. On the other hand, we may find, like Dino, that the other person may be infinitely grateful for the chance to be honest. Whatever the result, without honesty there is never even the possibility for genuine communication to transpire.

1. *Going beneath the surface.* As a mediator, I'm aware of the fact there's always more than meets the ear.

Very often people make statements that are not indicative of what they really want to say. Rather than take such statements at face value if you're trying to communicate with someone, it's important to trust the communication process and to believe that the other person has something valuable to say, even when his or her statements do not immediately support that assumption.

Real communication often involves digging beneath the superficial veneer of a statement in an effort to get to its true source. This is especially important when there is confusion about what someone means. But it is equally necessary in the midst of apparent clarity.

Tanya's attempt to confront the fear that was at the bottom of her mother's anger is an excellent example of going beneath the surface. When one person or party in a disagreement or conflict is willing to search past the other side's defensive or inflammatory words or actions to the discover the underlying fears and real needs, true communication really begins.

This was the case when, in 1977, I was asked to form and direct the Neighborhood Justice Center of Venice, California. This was one of three federally funded experimental organizations in the country conceived by then Attorney General, Griffin Bell, that was intended to help communities handle and resolve disputes that were either inappropriate for the courts or the resolution of which would save the city and state a lot of time and money.

Some of the most important work we did at the Center involved bringing the two rival neighborhood gangs together to work out their issues peacefully.

Now, in gang situations—as in other areas of life that aren't quite so violent—one of the big concerns is that actions will be taken by one side based upon what that side believes is true information about what the other side did to them. And a high percentage of the time this "true" information is really misinformation. So we began a three-pronged effort at the Center. First, we instituted an information service—a "rumor control line"—that anybody could call to find out whether or not something they'd heard was true. We did our best to verify that information with the community, the police and anyone else of relevance.

Second, we offered our office as a meeting place for the leadership of both gangs to come and talk about what was going on. We had them come in and sit down at different sides of a table. We didn't ask them to shake hands with each other initially, although they were required to lay down their arms at the door. We kept the discussion away from specific "provocative" incidents that each side felt the other had been involved with, and dealt instead with generalities. We asked each side to talk with the other about their intentions—how things were, and how they would like them to be. Whenever finger-pointing began, we diverted it by saying, let's deal with those incidents through an investigation. We carefully kept things focused on intention, philosophy and visions.

So, our negotiating tactics were centered not on the *external* actions of the gangs, but on the *motivations and fears behind them*. In the process, we discovered that the real issues with which the gang members were concerned were not the shootings or retaliations per se, but rather how they could best protect themselves, their families and their territorial identities. They were not out to wield power or crush the enemy; in a nutshell, they were afraid. Both sides realized that things had gotten out of hand, and that they would not have even come into that room unless they were looking for a way out.

Through a series of dialogues, the rival gang members eventually worked out a cease-fire, in which members of one gang would not go into the territory of the other. We even drew up the demarcation lines. As to the third phase of our effort, it involved an investigation into those incidents that both gangs insisted had provoked the escalation of the warfare. We agreed that a handpicked delegation from both sides would meet with one of our people who would do his or her best to investigate the allegations, write a report and submit it to both sides. We did not look into gang-related killings themselves, which was the domain of the police and the criminal justice system; we only dealt with the supposed provocations that led to the violence.

Our negotiations were successful for a number of reasons. First, we *accepted* the gangs. If the Tao is concerned, first and foremost, with reality, then the gangs were the Tao of the neighborhood! They were a fact—a way—of life. And in order to deal with them effectively, we had to acknowledge and respect their existence.

Second, we fostered real communication by *digging beneath the surface incidents and accusations*, into the underlying needs for acceptance, understanding and validation—as well as sheer survival.

Third, we dealt with the issues of pride and prejudice—who provoked whom, who deserved what—through the mutually respectful vehicle of an objective investigation, in which both sides participated.

The result was far better communication between the gangs, and a more peaceful environment for both them and the neighborhood. While our efforts did not put an end to the gang problem, or even necessarily make friends out of enemies, we did succeed in making the world of these two gangs safer for, if not democracy, at least day-to-day existence.

5. *Separating intention from conduct.* We've all caught ourselves saying one thing and meaning another. Or, doing something and realizing our action was not taken in the way we meant it.

If you suspect that you're being misunderstood, stop and clarify your intention. You may be surprised by the results, especially if your intention was not clear to begin with. By the same token, check the other person's intention when you're having trouble with his or her conduct. Perhaps the intention is consistent with your desires, but the conduct doesn't measure up.

Here's an example of checking someone else's intention.

SHERRY: I was really hurt when you didn't invite me to your party. What was going on?

DOUG: I'm really sorry, Sherry. It had to do with your boss.

SHERRY: What about her?

DOUG: Well, she's one of my closest friends. But I knew the two of you weren't getting along. I guess I didn't want you—or any of us, for that matter—to be uncomfortable. But I should have talked to you about it instead of just not inviting you.

SHERRY: Yes, I would have appreciated that. But at least I understand now.

6. *Separating facts from feelings.* Some people consider a "feeling" a type of "fact." If you have a stomach ache (because of a difficult conversation), or you feel happy (because you got a new job) or you're angry (because your car was stolen), these are certainly facts. But they are separate and distinct from the situations that gave rise to those feelings.

Making the distinction between facts and feelings helps you and the other person address what's actually happening between you. A common difficulty in getting caught up in your feelings is that there's no room left in which to maneuver. You become the victim of your emotions, and the result is usually anger and lashing out.

Let's say your boss has just informed you that you're being laid off. Your initial reaction is a jumble of emotions: rage, hurt, fear, helplessness. If, however, you are able to distinguish between the facts of a situation (you're being laid off not because of personal issues but because the company took a major loss) and your feelings ("That son of a bitch! I hope he falls off a cliff and into a manhole!), you can deal with the situation from a less emotional, and hence more rational, perspective. At the same time, the mere attempt to separate facts from feelings demonstrates respect for the other person and his or her position.

7. *Using "I" messages.* When we want our needs to be met and someone else to understand us, we sometimes resort to an "attack" mode of communicating.

"You made me feel horrible," or "You've got bad breath" may be the truth, but the recipient of the information isn't likely to respond warmly to what sounds like an accusation.

Learning to speak about yourself rather than about the other person, and to speak *for* yourself and not for the other person, is an important step in conscious communication. "I felt really badly when you said that," or "It's hard for me to be close to you when you don't brush your teeth," are more open ways of communicating the same truths and are far less likely to put the other person on the defensive.

The simple but profound practice of the "I" message encourages communication by reducing blame. When you take responsibility for your own feelings and actions, you're allowing yourself to be honest and vulnerable. In so doing, you invite the other person to be equally open.

In addition, you can check into what someone else may be feeling by stating what *you* observe first and then confirming it with the other person. Instead of saying, "Don't get upset," say, "It seems to me that you're upset. Am I right?" In clarifying other people's feelings rather than denying them the right to have them, you give others the opportunity to open up rather than close down.

8. *Listening.* Listening is more than simply listening. It can actually be a healing event. Just permitting someone else to feel heard can go a long way toward mutual understanding and agreement.

There are two kinds of listening: passive and active. Passive listening involves just that: listening without offering any advice or observations. Passive listening can be an "ear-opening" experience, particularly for the listener, who must transcend his or her own ego in the willingness simply to experience, as closely as possible, what the speaker is saying.

Here's a good passive-listening exercise that you can do with someone else. One of you speaks for five minutes without the other one saying a word—or frowning, nodding or otherwise reacting in any way. Then exchange positions. While this sounds simple, it is often quite difficult. You'll probably find yourself blurting something out before you've had a chance to catch yourself. The goal of this exercise is to make each of you feel "received" when you are expressing something, as well as to make you aware of how you sound when you talk continuously for five minutes, and how it feels to simply listen without interfering.

Active listening takes this process one step further. When you listen actively, you paraphrase out loud what the speaker is saying, so that he or she has a chance to correct you if you have misunderstood something. Active listening is an attempt on the part of the listener to clarify the speaker's intention.

An example of active listening would be the following dialogue between two people in the process of divorce:

STEVE: I'd like to get this mess over with as quickly as possible.

BEVERLY: What I hear you saying is . . . you really want me out of your life.

STEVE (clarifying his intention): No, that's not what I meant. I meant that I want to get the finances in order.

BEVERLY: In other words, you want to know how much money you'll have to pay me.

STEVE (again clarifying): Yes, I want to finalize the divorce and settle the finances so that we can move on with our lives.

BEVERLY: You want an end to the proceedings so that you can be done with it all.

STEVE: And I want us both to feel good about the decision.

BEVERLY: You want the divorce to be over with and you want us both to be happy with the outcome.

STEVE: Yes.

This exchange was used to clarify Steve's initial and potentially incendiary statement, "I'd like to get this mess over with." It helped Beverly to understand the intent behind the words, and it helped Steve to clarify that intent.

Active listening is like preventive medicine: It keeps a simple miscommunication from developing into a terminal illness.

9. *Having the willingness to admit that you don't know everything.* We all share an underlying dread of "not knowing," and thus "looking stupid." Because in our culture there is little or no support for seeming uncertain, we learn early on to act like we know what's going on, even if we really don't have the slightest idea.

If you're engaged in a dispute with someone and you don't admit your limited knowledge when you should, the possibility for honest communication is drastically reduced. The other person may discover your dishonesty, however unintentional, in which case you could lose credibility. Or, the other person may respond in kind and fake it also, in which case both of you lose contact with what's real, becoming involved in an escalating deception.

Because we are reinforced by society when we "know" things, it can seem like an enormous risk to admit it when we don't know something. In reality, however, this admission puts us in a powerful position. It can disarm the other person, opening the way for him or her to admit his or her own vulnerability. It frees both parties to ask intelligent questions and reduces the possibility of attacking-defending, avoiding, accommodating or stalemating, the four most common ingredients in a "win/lose" confrontation.

10. *Having the willingness to admit your mistakes.* I once came across a very funny greeting card. On the front was a photograph of a big, fat, sullen-faced baboon, with the statement, "I'm sorry. I was wrong." When you opened the card up, it said, "Not as wrong as *you* were. But I was wrong."

Like admitting it when you don't know something, admitting a mistake is difficult. It is also essential if successful communication is to be encouraged. When we admit our mistakes, others feel freer to admit theirs. We take two important burdens off them as well as off ourselves: the burden of having to be right and the burden of blame. When this happens, everyone has the freedom to be open and honest without fear of attack.

Soon after beginning work on this book, my coauthor Mary Beth discovered the power of admitting a mistake when she tried to park a rented car on a busy street and inadvertently backed up into a motorcycle, knocking it to the ground.

Mary Beth described the incident: "I was driving this car, which was much larger than the one I was used to, and which had a wicked blind spot. So I bashed into this cycle. Well, about six people immediately gathered at the scene. When I asked if any of them was the owner, one of them said, 'Nope. He's inside the bank. And he's six-foot-six and mean looking.'

"At first I thought the guy was joking. But when I went inside the bank, sure enough, there was this six-foot-six dude with a snarly look on his face!

"I was scared, all right. But I also was brought up on the exemplary, if sometimes naive, philosophy that honesty is the best policy. So I marched right up to him and told him just what had happened. Whereupon he let out a string of expletives and began to inquire of the entire bank if they'd ever seen 'such a stupid b—!' Then he stormed out to inspect the damage.

"At this point I seriously considered getting into my car and backing up once more, into him as well. I was really angry that he wouldn't listen to my explanation and that he chose instead to publicly embarrass me. I was just about to tell him what a jerk I thought he was when I saw him bending over his cycle as if it were his own kid, shaking his head in misery. Suddenly it hit me that he wasn't so much angry at me as sincerely unhappy about what I'd done to his most cherished possession.

" 'Look at those scratches!' he yelled at me. 'Do you know what that does to the resale value? Nobody'll want it now!'

" 'I understand exactly how you feel,' I replied. 'If

it were my bike, I'd feel the same way.' I took out my wallet and handed him my card. 'Here. Please call me and I'll pay for the damages. And I'm really sorry. I had no business driving a car I wasn't comfortable with.'

"He stared at me, and then at my card. And suddenly, his anger dissolved.

" 'That's okay,' he mumbled. 'I know you didn't mean to do it. And it won't cost that much. I was just upset.'

" 'I know you were,' I said. 'And like I said, I'd be just as upset if it were me.'

" 'Thanks,' he said. 'And thanks for coming into the bank and telling me. I appreciate your honesty.'

"That was it! For a couple of weeks I was terrified that I'd get a phone call telling me I'd have to pay $1,000 in motorcycle repairs, but the guy never called me. Admitting my mistake not only defused a volatile situation—it saved me a heck of a lot of money too!"

In this case, successful communication could be said to have occurred, thanks to Mary Beth's willingness to go beneath her adversary's anger and to forego her own anger as well. She understood what he was saying—"I'm really hurting because I love this bike and you smashed it up"—and he understood what she was saying—"I'm really sorry, I didn't mean to do it." The result was that each of them got what they wanted out of the interchange. The owner of the cycle got heard and understood, which was much more important to him than money or revenge. And Mary Beth got off the hook!

Conscious communication isn't easy. It doesn't matter whether the person you're trying to communicate with is your four-foot-high niece or nephew or a six-foot-six biker—being honest, open and vulnerable takes the same amount of courage. But if we can remember that all we want, and all the other person wants, is to be understood and respected, we've automatically maximized our chances for communication success.

4

What Do We Really Want, Anyway?

In difficult or dispute situations that I've been called in to deal with I've discovered that, on the surface at least, everybody claims to know what they want. From the moment talks begin, somebody's right there with, "I want the house, the car, the kids and eight million a month," or "I want my share of the business tomorrow morning" or "I want to see that guy in jail!"

But as the sessions progress, my clients are usually quite surprised to learn that in most cases they have no idea what it is that they're really after—that what they *think* they want and what they *really* want can be two very different things.

Most of us have never stopped to clarify our true wants, either to ourselves or to others. There's a good reason for this: Most of us learned in childhood that it was unacceptable to discover and articulate our deepest wants. Instead, we were told what our wants *should* be by parents, teachers, the media and other invincible authority figures.

So we grew up either consciously or unconsciously subscribing to the "keeping up with the Joneses" theory of what the "proper" kind of external life should be. We wanted money because in our society it's the measure of a person's true worth. We wanted to look like *Cosmo* girls or *GQ* boys, because that's our culture's definition of attractiveness. We wanted to be doctors or lawyers or marry doctors or lawyers because then we'd have prestige, power, security, approval.

These may not have been the things we really wanted down deep. But usually the desire to acquire them was instilled in us at such an early age that soon it became very difficult to distinguish our own wants and aspirations from those of the people upon whom we were dependent for our emotional and physical survival.

In addition, most of us were brought up with the belief that you have to know what you want or you won't "succeed" in life. "What do you mean, you don't know what you want?" an irate father thunders to his college son. "What's wrong with you? Do you think I'm putting you through school for my health?" It seems to be an important mark of mental stability in our society to have a firm idea of your goals and ambitions and to pursue them with unwavering persistence. As a result, there's a great deal of shame associated with uncertainty. Many people believe that if they don't know what they want, there's something terribly wrong with them. At the very least they're confused. At the very worst they might be failures or, God forbid, even insane!

It's no wonder, then, that most of us approach dispute situations clinging to fixed concepts of what we think we want rather than exploring *why* we want something and what alternatives are available to meet that need. Sometimes, in tense situations, people will arbitrarily blurt things out because they fear that appearing not to have a clear idea of what they want will make them look foolish. And because in disputes, emotions are usually exaggerated, wants often become exaggerated as well, escalating from mere desires into demands and legal "rights."

This concept of "just desserts" is really a cornerstone of our society, which has always lived by the rule that every apparent wrong should have a right attached to it. We want the house because it's our "right." We want a million dollar settlement because it's our "right." But all too often, we become attached to something we think we should have or believe we're entitled to, at the expense of reality, reasonableness or peace.

We cling to these beliefs as tenaciously as a dog to a bone, a child to a cherished toy, unwilling to explore other options, other ways of meeting our and the other person's needs. Rarely do we stop to reflect upon our wants, to dig deeper, below the surface of our material demands to the core of our real needs.

Admittedly, the whole concept of knowing what you want and getting it is, on the surface, a paradox. On the one hand, you certainly have to know what you want in order to get it. On the other hand, it's often necessary to let go of cherished beliefs about our wants in order to adjust them to reality.

The bottom line is: *It's okay to not know what we want.* In fact, it's usually in not knowing what we want that we approach true wisdom. Admitting this is the first step toward opening ourselves up to a nonadversarial response to a dispute situation. It's the same process we'll be talking about in information gathering (chapter 5). The first step is self-assessment, going past our surface emotional reactions in order to discover what it is we really want and need from the other person.

NEEDS VERSUS WANTS

Most of us use the words "need" and "want" virtually interchangeably—almost in the same way we confuse "arbitration" with "mediation"! But wants and needs are as different as arbitration is from mediation. And interestingly enough, arbitration—the process of having an impartial third party acting as judge to impose a decision in a dispute—can be said to be concerned first with rights and then with wants, whereas mediation— the process of having an impartial third party *facilitate* an agreement to a conflict—is really attuned to needs. Arbitration is an external "remedy" for a dispute, whereas mediation is concerned with the internal process of conflict resolution.

There are all kinds of needs. And there are all kinds of wants. There are the basic needs we have as human beings, for air, food, water, clothing, shelter. There are the equally important emotional needs we have, for support, friendship, love, family, community. Then there are the compulsive needs we acquire, that take the form of addictions: to money, drugs, food, sex, people, marathon running—whatever it is that we think we can't live without.

Wants are usually adaptations or distortions of needs. You *need* to eat; you *want* Chinese food. You *need* to be loved; you *want* a certain man or woman to fulfill that need. You *need* respect; you *want* a powerful position that you feel will gain you that respect.

Very often, however, wants become indistinguishable from needs. We *project* our needs onto other people or things, becoming convinced that once we acquire John or Mary or a ten-room Spanish villa on twenty-five acres, we'll be happy at last. But as many of us have undoubtedly learned, this is rarely the case. Our happiness can't be bought; our peace of mind cannot be dependent upon external forces.

When we confuse wants with needs, dispute situations become even more difficult to resolve. When our wants are consistent with our needs, however—when we can say, "I want love" or "I want to be understood" rather than "I want the house because you had an affair" or "I want all your assets because you screwed me over," we're far better able to arrive at terms that are mutually satisfactory and beneficial to both parties.

LEARNING TO ASK FOR WHAT WE REALLY WANT

In dispute situations, how do we clarify what it is that we really want? And how do we successfully communicate this to another person?

The first thing to take a look at is whether or not you have trouble *asking* for what you want. Many of us find it difficult to honestly express our innermost desires because it isn't something we learned to do. How many parents do you know who inquire of their children what it is that they really want and give them a chance to express it? Aside from letting the child choose between a tuna and egg salad sandwich, or a Quarter Pounder and a Big Mac, there isn't usually much room for a genuine sharing of the decision-making process. The reason for that is simple: We weren't given permission, as children, to value our real desires. So, until we learn how to give ourselves this permission, we won't give it to our children. And the legacy of self-alienation will continue to be handed down, from generation to generation.

Asking for what we really want is often a scary thought. It involves becoming vulnerable, exposing our innermost selves and opening ourselves up to the possibility of rejection. When a young boy sees his first ballet and announces that he wants to be a dancer, and his father snorts, "That's ridiculous! That's sissy!" the boy quickly learns that unless his dreams coincide with the wishes of those from whom he needs approval, he's better off keeping them to himself or forgetting about them altogether.

We all have uncomfortable memories of this kind of rejection and ridicule—memories that paralyze us when it comes to being able, as adults, to have the courage to express our deepest desires. How do we get past the roadblocks of the past, into the frame of mind that gives us permission to be who we truly are?

First of all, we must learn that we *deserve* what we want. The technique of affirmation is quite useful here. I've found that it's very effective to write down a list of positive statements about yourself—"I'm a beautiful, loving person;" "I can get what I really want and I deserve it;" "It's safe to ask for what I really want"— and repeat them every day while in a relaxed state. This is a powerful tool for reprogramming the sub-conscious. There are many audiocassettes available as well, on self-esteem and self-affirmation, which are extremely effective. Or, you can make your own tape, tailored to your specific needs. Whichever means you choose, remember to employ it on a regular, daily basis.

Studies have shown that in trying to create a new habit, a new outlook, the new idea must be repeated anywhere from thirteen to twenty-one times in order to become fixed in the subconscious mind. After several weeks of doing daily affirmations, you'll notice a marked difference in your attitude toward yourself and toward those things you used to regard as unattainable.

Another excellent technique is to break down, either through self-talk or two-person dialoguing, the fear associated with asking for what you want. In the same way that we can observe the motivating forces behind addictions and our hidden agendas, we can explore the beliefs that prevent us from expressing our real needs.

EXERCISE:
Why I Have Trouble Asking for What I Want

This simple exercise is designed to help you to become more aware of unconscious or unexamined fears you may have associated with asking for what you want. In the space provided, write down the first thought that comes to mind in response to the statement "The reason that it's so difficult for me to ask for what I want is . . ." Repeat the incomplete statement to yourself, writing down your subsequent immediate responses. The dialogue might go something like this:

The reason that it's so difficult for me to ask for what I want is . . . I won't get it anyway.

The reason that it's so difficult for me to ask for what I want is . . . I don't deserve it.

The reason that it's so difficult for me to ask for what I want is . . . I'm afraid of being rejected.

Continue to come up with possible conclusions to the statement.

1. The reason that it's so difficult for me to ask for what I want is: _____

2. The reason that it's so difficult for me to ask for what I want is: _____

3. The reason that it's so difficult for me to ask for what I want is: _____

4. The reason that it's so difficult for me to ask for what I want is: _____

5. The reason that it's so difficult for me to ask for what I want is: _____

6. The reason that it's so difficult for me to ask for what I want is: _____

Note: You can also make this exercise a two-person dialogue in which someone else begins the statement and you finish it immediately, with the first thing that comes to mind.

Now, examine each one of your responses carefully. *Why* don't you get what you want? *Why* don't you deserve it? *Why* are you so afraid of being rejected? You may learn that you believe you won't get a good relationship because your mom was divorced three times. Or that you think you don't deserve to be rich because somewhere deep down inside of you is the belief that money is evil. Or that you can't seem to advance in the company you work for because unconsciously you fear the responsibility associated with a promotion.

After you've done this work on your unconscious, turn to your affirmations. Rewrite your negative beliefs into positives. "I can have a beautiful relationship because I'm a beautiful, loving person. I have the power to create my own reality." Or, "Abundance and spirituality go hand in hand. I deserve financial security because God wants the best for me."

Personal Affirmations that Will Allow Me to Begin Asking for What I Really Want

Take a look at your responses to the preceding exercise (page 89). Now, for each "negative" response, write down a positive response, or affirmation, that will counteract it. For example, if you responded to "The reason that it's so difficult for me to ask for what I want is . . ." with "I'm afraid it will be taken away (because when I was ten my father lost his job and we had to move and I lost my friends, my house and everything I loved)," turn this belief around now, into a positive one. For example: "I find it easier and easier to ask for what I want because I am now an adult with the desire and power to control my own life and make it what I truly want."

Replace the statements and responses in the previous exercise with the following:

1. I find it easier and easier to ask for what I want because: _____

2. I find it easier and easier to ask for what I want because: _____

3. I find it easier and easier to ask for what I want because: _____

4. I find it easier and easier to ask for what I want because: _____

5. I find it easier and easier to ask for what I want because: _____

6. I find it easier and easier to ask for what I want because: _____

In a fairly short period of time, you may discover a change slowly taking place. You'll be able to ask for what you want without feeling guilty or fearing other people's responses!

Jeanne, a woman in her late thirties, wasn't getting her needs met in her relationship with Tom, a man who had a great deal of trouble being truly intimate. Jeanne felt that if she asked for "too much," Tom wouldn't be able to give it to her and would retreat in fear.

"He's doing the best he can," she reasoned. "It isn't right for me to push him."

But gradually, through the process of self-talk and affirmations, Jeanne began to see how she was actually setting herself up for not getting what she wanted with Tom. Her own father had been distant and uncommunicative, and she had spent her childhood trying to please him. She saw that her father, her primary male role model, was influencing not only her choice of partners but her expectations from relationships.

Eventually Jeanne was able to discover her real needs, for intimacy, commitment, communication, honesty. When she began to feel as if she truly deserved these things—that indeed, a relationship wasn't a relationship without them—she was able to express her desires to Tom.

Unfortunately, or fortunately as the case may be, Tom was not able to give Jeanne what she needed. Her initial fears proved correct: He did retreat. But the important thing wasn't Tom's response. It was that Jeanne had honored herself and her own needs. Through this process, she discovered that Tom wasn't the right person for her, and that because she now knew what she really wanted from a relationship, she was in a much better position to get it.

Remember, it's the *intention* followed by the *action* that counts, not the *result* of that action. Once we become aware of the behaviors, and the unconscious motivations behind them, that inhibit us from living fully and joyously, that's half the battle right there. Taking the concrete action of turning a negative belief system into a positive one, and learning to honor our deepest selves without fear of reprisal is the most effective step we can take in getting our needs met. Whether or not a particular person responds positively is unimportant. Eventually we'll create the appropriate situation to fulfill our needs.

ADDICTIONS: WHEN WANTS BECOME NEEDS

In her book *A Nation of Addicts*, Anne Wilson Schaef observes that as members of American society, we are all addicted to something. Sex, drugs, food, relationships, work, exercise, anger, love . . . Because we as a culture place such a high premium on external rather than internal gratification, we find ourselves becoming psychologically and/or physically addicted to expectations associated with key activities or emotions in our lives.

An addiction is a false need. When you're addicted to something, you're convinced that you need it, to the point that it becomes a consuming need—usually the predominant need—in your life.

If we are involved in a dispute situation, we have to examine ourselves very closely as to any addictions we might have that are associated with the problem. Addictions play a crucial role in creating and/or perpetuating disputes, because (1) they are usually related to the inflexible demands or expectations that polarize the parties, and (2) they undermine the sense of personal power and self-love that we have to maintain if we are to honestly and successfully explore the "big picture" and the role that we've played in it.

One of my clients, Don, was the manager of a famous rock star. Because this was a lucrative job, Don and his wife became used to living on something like $40,000 a month. But when the rock star went to another manager and Don's business took a nose dive, he was suddenly faced with having to cut back on his monthly expenditures. And he and his wife nearly went crazy. They had become so attached to living on $40,000 a month that they found it all but impossible to get their expenses below $25,000 a month! Most people, of course, would consider even Don's reduced monthly income a sign of extreme wealth. But to Don and his wife, it was poverty. They had grown addicted to a much higher income and a different lifestyle, to the point that they honestly felt they absolutely *needed* $40,000 a month in order to survive.

Or, take the case of Sharon, a writer who uses food to stimulate her into completing her work. Often, when she's on deadline, Sharon will want coffee and something sweet to get her through the night and the project. Soon, Sharon becomes addicted to having coffee and sweets in order to do her work. She may not "need" these substances per se—in fact, her body definitely doesn't need them. But her mind has discovered a successful way of coping with a high-stress situation.

And because her addiction "works" for Sharon, she confuses wants with needs.

How do we deal with addictions? Well, often we attempt to "fight" them, to "overcome" them. We go on strict diets. We reprimand ourselves out of taking a drink, a piece of cake, a fix. Or, we end up substituting one addiction for another—exercise for overeating, food for cigarettes, cigarettes for food, drugs for alcohol, alcohol for drugs.

But in dealing with addictions, the only thing that really works is first becoming aware of them—admitting them, taking responsibility for them, finding out what's behind them and working *with* them, not against them.

Although it may sound surprising, I'm not necessarily recommending that people stop their addictions. Addictions may not *be* genuine needs, but they *fulfill* needs. As such, the most important thing is to become aware of the addiction and the role it's serving for us.

So, the next time you reach for a cigarette or a doughnut or a drink, pretend you're a Patriot missile catching the Scud of desire the moment it comes over the horizon. Stop and think about your state of mind, your state of "want." How are you feeling as you reach for your "fix"? Scared? Depressed? Bored? Exhilarated? Are you feeling some pain that you need to suppress? Are you feeling a joy that makes you uncomfortable? Do you need some reward in advance, to be able to do something? And if you're not willing to look at what's behind the action, *why* are you not willing to look at it?

This process is intended to be entirely nonjudgmental. It involves the willingness to be totally honest and totally objective. You're not out to condemn your addiction—you merely want to observe it, to learn from it. Again, you become a researcher, an information gatherer. It's the "scientific" approach to self-awareness.

Once you become aware of your addiction and the immediate function it's serving, you then have two choices. You can take the practical approach, saying, "Aha! Okay, I'm smoking a cigarette because I'm nervous about tomorrow's report. What are some alternative ways of meeting my immediate need to relax?" Or, you can shoulder a mental shovel and start digging deeper, going below the addictive behavior and the immediate need it fulfills, into *why* you're nervous about tomorrow's report. Are you unprepared? Is there tension between you and your boss or coworkers? Are you a perfectionist, always afraid of not being good enough? And then, keep digging. Why are you unprepared? Did you dislike the nature of the assignment? Why is there tension? Are you unhappy at your job? Would you be happier doing something else? Why do you feel the need to be perfect? Is it because your father or mother always expected it?

As you can see, the simple act of reaching for a cigarette is not the problem. It's merely the doorway to the problem. It's as if the addictive behavior is a kaleidoscope, through which we can view the infinite facets of our inner selves. As such, the addiction becomes not our enemy, but our friend and guide, helping us to unravel the mystery of why we act the way we do.

Addictions are sneaky things. Often the thing we're addicted to may not be as obvious as cigarettes or alcohol or drugs or food, but may instead be a belief system, intention or motivation that we are either not aware of at all, or are not aware of as being an addiction. Such "invisible" addictions may come under the classification of *hidden agendas*.

HIDDEN AGENDAS

As we saw in chapter 1, many disputes are the result of a simple miscommunication, where one thing was meant and another understood. "You said you wanted to be rid of me!" "I did not! I said I just needed some space!" Or, there are disputes that arise when two people have opposing aims. One business partner wants to expand, the other doesn't; one screenwriter wants the project to be for TV while his partner says it's a feature film or nothing. Some disputes are the result of *other* people's disputes: Family feuds come in this category. And some disputes are caused by third-party mischief, in which the chief adversaries have become estranged or hostile not in and of their own accord, but because of a meddlesome relative, a gossipy associate, a well-meaning friend.

Then there's that other class of disputes that we touched upon: those that involve a *hidden agenda*, in which one party has an undisclosed intention or motivation.

We saw that hidden agendas come in two categories: conscious and unconscious. Let's examine the unconscious variety in more detail.

Joe and Marion had been married for forty-five years and had been fighting about the same issue for all forty-five of those years: Marion's messy housekeeping. Joe wanted a clean house, but that, unfortunately, didn't seem to be Marion's priority. The more Joe ranted and raved, the more Marion balked at cleaning. Interestingly enough, however, neither of them ever stopped to look beneath the surface "dirt," if you will, into the underlying hidden agendas involved.

It turned out that Joe had rejected Marion sexually soon after the birth of their first child. Coming from a generation that didn't openly discuss sex, Marion was confused and guilt-ridden. She felt that Joe's unresponsiveness was somehow her fault. She grew depressed, which in turn led to her being apathetic about things like housework.

But Marion was also terribly angry at Joe. She had married him because he was handsome, charming, protective and an ideal authority figure. But she also resented his domineering, know-it-all attitude and his refusal to discuss their sex life with her. So, she unconsciously "rebelled" against him by keeping the house untidy.

As for Joe, he had had an extremely problematic relationship with his mother, a tyrant who alternated between beating him and coming on to him sexually. Needless to say, when his own wife became a mother, he grew terribly conflicted. He loved Marion, but he began to transfer, subconsciously, the rage he felt toward his own mother onto her. He grew impotent, which only worsened the situation. Now he was terribly ashamed because he was no longer the all-powerful, all-knowing man he was supposed to be. Unable to discuss his fears and feelings with Marion, he focused on the house as a "safe" subject through which to vent his anger and disappointment in himself.

If we take this particular situation apart, we see not just one or two hidden agendas, but level upon level of them. Marion keeps the house messy to "pay Joe back" for his rejecting her. But she also keeps it messy because she's depressed. And she's depressed because she has such a low sense of self-esteem. It's as if the messy house is a metaphor for Marion herself. "I'm a no-good slob," it's saying. "I'm not attractive. No wonder my husband doesn't make love to me."

Joe is angry at his mother and angry at himself for being her victim. When he loses his libido, he becomes even more angry at himself for "not living up" to his responsibility as a man. Hidden under the anger is another unconscious agenda, of shame and guilt. And hidden under his blustery, know-it-all attitude is a terrible insecurity, a fear of "being found out," of the world suddenly discovering that Joe isn't the in-control man he pretends to be.

This kind of scenario is, unfortunately, a common one. Whenever we act out against another person, we are not facing, on some level, a similar truth about ourselves. The bottom-line issue that was central to both Joe and Marion's problem was low self-esteem, and each of them "blamed" the other for their own feelings of worthlessness. This is why unconscious hidden agendas are so confusing, and so destructive to relationships. There's no way one person can "win" if the real problem exists within the other too. An accommodator will soon find that trying to change his or her behavior to suit the attacker-defender will be a futile task, for the attacker-defender will always find something else to criticize. An attacker-defender will be more and more frustrated by a stalemater, an avoider or an accommodator, who will keep him or her stuck in their angry rut through a barrage of passive-hostile tactics. When two attacker-defenders lock horns, the chances of discovering and resolving hidden agenda issues become almost nonexistent, as each projects his or her own unhappiness onto the other, refusing to take responsibility for the situation. And the saddest thing about it is that in avoiding our hidden agendas and defending our need to be "right," we are preventing ourselves from enjoying life-affirming relationships of trust, support and true intimacy.

Now I'm not saying that in order to successfully respond to disputes that involve hidden agendas, we all have to go to therapy for twenty-five years. What I am saying is that if you really want to understand the source of a dispute, you've got to go inside of yourself. You don't have to take the "blame" for the problem. But you must recognize that you had something to do with creating the situation and drawing it to yourself.

If you are involved in a "personality dispute" type of situation, stop. Draw back from the battlefield for a minute, an hour, a day, a month. Look at the pattern, at your participation in the problem, in the same way that we discussed looking at addictive behaviors. Do some self-talk: What am I doing? How do I feel when I'm doing it? What do I get out of doing it? Get beneath the surface dispute, into your own hidden agendas that may be contributing to it.

What was Marion really accomplishing by not cleaning the house? Was there a certain amount of satisfaction involved in making Joe mad, in "controlling" him by making him a slave to his anger through passive-hostile tactics? Was her sloppiness really a demand, to be accepted for who she was, a refusal to change in order to please others? The list of possibilities is endless; there will always be more than one reason for a seemingly unproductive behavior.

Until we are ready to admit our own responsibility

for *our part* in a conflict situation, and until we are willing to become aware of our hidden agendas and the hidden agendas behind *them*, we will always be fighting ourselves in the guise of fighting someone else. As the great French essayist Montaigne observed, "We seldom possess well the thing that possesses us." Similarly, we seldom successfully respond to the external dispute situations that only mirror our own internal conflicts.

MAKING OUR WANTS REALISTIC

Ed and Bernice are in the middle of divorce proceedings. Their only asset is the house. There's no money to speak of, there are a couple of kids and Bernice says, "I want to keep the house."

"Well, I want the house too!" Ed replies. "I work out of it. What am I going to do if you take it?"

"I don't care what you do," Bernice snaps. "I'm getting the kids—I want the house. Period."

I encounter the above "dialogue" all the time. A couple comes in to see me. They each know what they want. And there seems to be no room for discussion. It's an either-or scenario, and it involves a central "unrealism": a total unwillingness to take into account what the other person needs or wants.

First of all, let's define "realistic" as it applies to dispute situations. As I see it, a realistic demand is something that is truly possible and that maximizes the benefit for all parties involved. A realistic demand involves an honest appraisal of what we genuinely deserve, not simply what we think we deserve based on feelings of anger or hurt. A realistic demand does not come from the intention to "ruin" the other person, nor does it deny your needs—it simply takes into account the other person's needs as well.

In the case of Ed and Bernice, how could they make their wants realistic, according to the above definition? Well, there are a number of options. They could, of course, sell the house and split the proceeds. This may be a satisfactory solution or it may not, depending on the market, the fees involved and a number of other factors. They could decide to have Ed live in the house and give Bernice a promissory note, which would be paid off over a period of time. They could even work out an arrangement—not an unheard of one, by the way—where Bernice lives in the house and Ed lives on the property, say in a guest house, both sharing equally in the equity of the property. Or, Ed or Bernice might decide simply to give the house to the other as a gift: "It's yours, I'm leaving, goodbye."

The point is that options *always* exist. We are never stuck; we are never really in the position of "no choice but." As soon as any statement comes down in the form of "I have no choice but to . . ." you know it's either a lie or a manipulation. Because there are always choices, options in every situation. And if they aren't immediately evident, we can create them. The universe is a constantly changing, ever-expansive entity, and as far as I'm concerned, there is no situation that can't be altered or improved.

But often we have to be willing to adjust ourselves to a larger idea of reality, one that is empathetic instead of narcissistic. We have to be willing to say, "Okay. I want the house. But what I really need is the security that the house gives me, or the space to do my work, or whatever. How can I get those basic needs met without possessing the actual physical property of the house itself?"

Again, this involves the process of separating the wheat from the chaff, the want from the need. Once we look at the need that underlies any want, we are in a position to explore other avenues through which we can meet that need.

And, if those other avenues don't seem to immediately exist, how can we create them? Let's say Ed needs the house because it's where his office is. Can he move to a small apartment and rent an office with the money he might make from the sale of the house? Or, if Bernice is completely unwilling to sell the house because of the children, can she agree to share some of Ed's expenses in renting an office? And, if Bernice has no money whatsoever, how can Ed increase his income to meet his basic need for an office and living space?

There are *always* options. Sometimes we have to be willing to create those options ourselves, without relying on the support of another person. But they exist. And the more of them we discover, the freer we become.

COMMUNICATING FROM THE HEART

Above all, in getting our needs met we must be able to articulate them in a way that the other person can truly understand and respect.

When I use the term "understand" in this context, I'm referring not simply to the mind but to the heart. It's not until you can create a picture and a feeling within the other person that resonates to your own emotions that you have successfully communicated what it is that you truly want and need.

Let's take the following example. A man is paralyzed from the waist down in an auto accident. He sues for six million dollars. What the other party hears is, "I want six million bucks; I'm going to soak you for whatever I can get." And their lawyers respond accordingly, and there's a legal battle.

But what if our accident victim meets with the other person (usually an insurance company adjuster or lawyer) and says, "What I really want is to be compensated for the loss of the use of my lower body. For the loss of being able to live like a normal man, to have a normal sexual relationship with my wife. True, a large amount of money can't buy me back the full use of my body. But it can support me and my family without any of us having to worry for the rest of our lives. It can give us a more satisfying lifestyle. It can even help me to start my own business, to be productive again."

When put in these terms, the other person can truly *understand* the need behind the six million dollars. Now, negotiations can take place from here. The marketplace and prior settlements or court judgments in similar situations must be taken into account, of course. But once the other person genuinely feels where you're coming from, in the center of his or her heart, the chances of peacefully resolving a conflict situation are immeasurably improved.

5

I Spy, You Spy, We All Spy: Effective Information Gathering

Mr. A, a top defense attorney, has a client facing a murder charge. His client pleads innocent. What's Mr. A's next step?

Shirley and Marge are coworkers who don't get along. Marge accuses Shirley of trying to undermine her behind her back. Shirley pleads innocent. Marge, who has seniority, threatens to go to the boss with an "It's either her or me" ultimatum. What should Shirley's next step be?

Becky and Larry have been dating for nearly six months and Becky is ready for a commitment. Larry, however, shies away from making the "big M" decision. Becky is hurt and frustrated and accuses Larry of not really loving her. Larry pleads innocent. Where do they go from here?

While they seem to be different on the surface, all three of these situations have two things in common.

One, they happen every day. And two, they involve conflicts or potential conflicts that require the same necessary first step in being resolved.

That step is: *Information Gathering.*

When Mr. A embarks upon a case, the first thing he does is to begin compiling information. Information about his client, past and present; information about the incident; information about the plaintiff; information about the witnesses—information about everything relevant to the case. A lawyer would no sooner enter a courtroom without being prepared than you or I would arrive at our jobs dressed in our underwear.

Yet as obvious as this observation may seem, when it comes to the conflict situations we encounter in our everyday lives, most of us go into them wearing our underwear. In other words, most of us do not understand the importance of advance preparation and information gathering as a first step to resolving any kind of conflict or potential conflict.

CONFLICT RESPONSE AS AN INTELLIGENCE PROJECT

In their best-selling book, *Negotiate Your Way to Success*, David Seltz and Alfred Modica make the following surprising statement.

Preparation is probably the single most important part of successful negotiations. . . . Yet despite the obvious importance of preparations, an astonishing number of business people enter into their negotiations fully prepared to "wing it"—that is, to ask for what they want without anticipating that the other person will say anything but yes! . . . In many cases, the result of these free-wheeling, shoot-from-the-hip sessions is a complete stalemate; most of the time this means either a job termination or the permanent discontinuance of a business deal or even a business relationship.

Time and time again I have witnessed people going into an actual or potential dispute situation determined only to see things from their own perspective, not even bothering to sit down for five minutes and think about just who the other person is, what they might be thinking and why, and what it is that *they* really want.

The way that agreements are made and the way that disputes are prevented or resolved is through *information*. And it's the process of gathering, evaluating and using this information that determines whether or not your objectives will be realized. In his book *Power Shift*, Alvin Toffler talks of our Information Age, and how, in these sophisticated times, the ability to collect and process information is a far more powerful skill than brute force, political power or money. So, it's those of us who have the most information, *and* who know how to distill this information and synthesize it to our advantage, who are, in truth, the most successful members of society.

The Research Frame of Mind

When you view a conflict or potential conflict as a research project instead of a war, things immediately change.

Instead of assuming that the other person shares or should share your value system, which is one of the most common errors of miscommunication, your approach undergoes a 180-degree shift. You begin to come from the position that says, "Gee. Maybe there's something going on here that I don't understand. I know what I want, and I have a view of what I think has happened already and what I want to happen now. What I know, I believe to be the truth. But maybe I don't know everything that needs to be known. Maybe there are some other truths here too, in terms of facts, actual conduct and other people's feelings, which may be different from my feelings."

Getting into a research state of mind is a preliminary step to conflict solving. Yet it's the step that most of us invariably leap-frog over or completely ignore. We want to get into action immediately. As soon as we see that we're in a conflict situation, we perceive a threat and our "fight or flight" response goes into gear. But unless you're facing the kind of conflict scenario where somebody's pointing a gun at your head and you have to make an instant decision, it is absolutely foolhardy to jump into the realm of action before researching, as thoroughly as possible, all of the aspects of the problem you'd like to resolve.

THE "CIA" APPROACH TO CONFLICT SOLVING: BECOMING A SPY

When we think of a spy, the image that immediately comes to mind is a guy in a black trench coat, slinking along dark alleyways, furtively glancing around with both pairs of eyes, the ones in front and the ones in the back of his head, as he goes about his dangerous business of "stealthing" information.

But this isn't what I mean by being a spy. And, except in a relatively small percentage of cases, it isn't what the CIA means either.

The CIA is in the business of gathering information. And contrary to popular belief, most of their information sources are public or quasipublic knowledge. If you take a close look at their budgets, which are mostly public knowledge, you'll find that most of the money that the CIA and some other intelligence agencies spend has little to do with surreptitious intelligence at all. They read newspapers and magazines. They talk to people. Many times it's as simple as that.

When I was working as a research analyst for RAND, I would read, on a regular basis, at least five daily newspapers, twenty magazines and the CIA briefing reports. Even those reports were gleaned primarily from public sources, which were just edited. And even when I was gathering information in Vietnam, I invariably found that the most useful information that came to me was out there for the asking. I didn't have to engage in any covert activities to find out what I wanted to know. I simply went to the source directly and asked.

So, by using the analogy of spies, I'm actually referring to the ability to obtain the information you need, as well as the ability to analyze that information and make the best use of it that you can. The important thing in any research project is not simply the raw data. It's knowing what to look for, how to process that data and how to select from it those facts that are most important to you. And then, we must be aware of both how to use the information we've selected, and how *not* to use it.

Learning How to Read Information

During the years I worked for RAND, I learned "how" to read. Of course, when I came to them in 1963, I assumed that I already possessed that skill. I was twenty-four years old, with an undergraduate degree in electrical engineering and three years of graduate school in operations research and industrial engineering.

But the first project I did for RAND had nothing to do with engineering. Instead, it was writing a paper entitled "Buddhist Crisis?" and it involved analyzing both the public and not-so-public sources of information that were available in Vietnam concerning the government and the growing Buddhist opposition, including self-immolation by monks.

This was a fascinating project, not only because of the subject itself but because what it turned out to be was really an analysis of what was "real" and what was being reported, and learning to see the differences between the two. On the one end of the spectrum there was what David Halberstam of the *New York Times* and others were reporting, and on the other end there was the information being reported at the official level. And you could have been talking about two different worlds, two different countries.

So, out of that process I taught myself how to read a newspaper, how to read a magazine, how to read any piece of information, whether it was a CIA report or a *New York Times* report. And I discovered some interesting "tips," which I have applied, ever since, to any situation in which I need to gather information.

1. *Believe everything and believe nothing.* By "believe everything," I don't mean "be gullible." Rather,

have an open mind, as to the possibility that the information you're being confronted with is valid. But at the same time, "believe nothing" in the following sense: Do not take anything you read as a fact simply because it appears in print. It is merely somebody's belief, opinion, guess or wish, or it is misinformation that they *want* you to believe.

2. *Take the "Watergate" approach to information gathering.* "What did he know and when did he know it?" Once you have the information, the next step is to determine who wrote it, why the story is there, who wanted it there, the previous history of the person who wrote it, his or her bias, the bias, if any, of the publication and any other relevant questions.

The sophisticated way of looking at any piece of information is to *know all the circumstances surrounding it, so that you have a context for that particular story and that particular piece of information*. Until you know *why* a story is there or *who* wanted it there and *what* it means and what the *biases* are, you really shouldn't believe the information. You can see the smoke, but you can't tell if there's a fire until you've adequately assessed the context in which the information appears.

3. *Never believe a number in a media report.* Never. Because the probability that it's wrong is so high that you can't really depend on it. Whatever the number refers to, whether it's dollars or months or people or cows, it has to pass through so many hands that by the time it makes it to print or on the air, the probability for error is enormous. We know from research that

when people are simply asked to copy figures from one column to another, one in every 155 digits is going to be wrong. Multiply that figure by hundreds when figures are being transmitted, through a variety of hands.

How do these tips relate to the average everyday person who's facing a conflict situation at work, at home, in love? In this way: Simply that in learning how to get information about another person or a situation, you must view that information within the context of all the surrounding factors. Who's saying something and why? What's his or her personal bias? What's his or her background? How many people did the information filter through before it got to you?

Decision Making: The Power Continuum

In gathering information and using it to our best advantage, our first job is to observe just what kind of power structure is being dealt with and just who makes the decisions within it.

After all, if the first rule of life is to know thyself, the second and third rules should be to know those around you and to know the environment.

Taking out your spy glass and donning your research cap, *find out what the game is.* How are decisions made in the group or organization in which you're involved and by whom? Where is the seat of decision-making power?

This may not be readily apparent, because decision making may be different at different levels of the organization. At the top, the philosophy of pure autocracy may prevail, whereas somewhere near the bottom, it

The Power Continuum

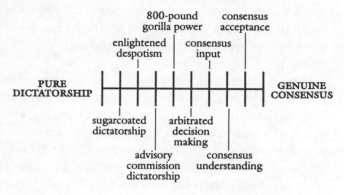

could be an apparent consensus or majority rule. In other words, the rules of the game may change depending upon what level you're at.

Remember the "Conflict Continuum" in chapter 1 that provided a means of examining the degree of harmony or disharmony in your personal relationships? Well, there is a corresponding continuum for decision making that applies across the board to any system, country, group or family. I call it the "Power Continuum," and it's designed to help you key in to the type of decision-making process operating in the groups or organizations of which you are a part.

THE POWER CONTINUUM

At one end of the Power Continuum is what I call a *pure dictatorship*. At the other end is *genuine consensus*. Between these two extremes are numerous variations on the themes of autocracy and democracy.

In a pure dictatorship, one person or one group has, either individually or collectively, absolute power in the realm of which they're in charge to say, do and accomplish what they want. The opinions and input of anyone else are unnecessary in the decision-making process. We're familiar with dictatorships in the context of governments; they can also operate within any organization where one person or group has unlimited power. The president of a company may wield absolute authority. Or, in a family, the father or mother may easily assume the role of dictator, handing down decisions and rules that, if opposed or broken, incur heavy consequences.

One step down from pure dictatorship is what I refer to as a *sugarcoated dictatorship*. This is simply a dictatorship in disguise. There may be a puppetlike legislature or a puppet council of advisors. But one person, group or ideology still makes all the decisions.

After the sugarcoated dictatorship comes *enlightened despotism*. In this type of decision making environment, the dictator is assumed, like God, to be benevolent in his/her authority. The enlightened despot theoretically has the desire or intention of doing good for others. Yet, according to the structure of the organization, he or she still makes the decisions as to what is actually good for other people.

Next we have the *advisory commission dictatorship*. This differs from the sugarcoated dictatorship in that it's not a case of window dressing. There is actually some built-in mechanism that provides for a group of people other than the top authority figure to have some public input into the decision-making process. The President's Advisory Commission on AIDS, for instance, is a good example of this. The commission itself has no real power. But its members get to write a white paper, and their opinions are recognized publicly. The final decision, however, is still in the hands of one person or group.

Then there's the *800-pound gorilla power*, which is a take-off on the question, "Where does an 800-pound gorilla sleep?" The answer, of course, is "Any damn place it pleases." In this instance, decision making is proportional to money power or vote power. The person who can afford the best lawyer, or who runs a political action committee or who has the most money in the poker game can call certain decision-making shots.

Now, this may smack of pure dictatorship, but it's more temporary in substance. It may be that the gorilla wandered into your living room because it was hungry, and once you fed it, it left. *Eight-hundred pound gorilla power*—which can also be thought of as the "money/elective dictatorship"—is essentially limited in nature. Its primary effectiveness has to do with single-issue politics. The insurance lobby, for instance, is exceedingly powerful when it comes to insurance legislation, but it will not have corresponding clout in foreign policy issues.

Now we move from the realm of dictatorship to *arbitrated decision making*. This can be summarized as the "rule of law," where the decision making is based on some supposedly objective standard which in turn is being interpreted by one person, either a judge or an arbitrator. Now, the judge or arbitrator is bound by law to listen to both sides and abide by certain rules of evidence. In effect, however, he or she is an autocrat. Although his or her decisions are theoretically appealable, the probability of such judgments being overturned is actually quite miniscule.

The next level of decision making involves *consensus*

input. This is where there is no final decision until everyone involved in that decision has had the opportunity to provide input into it. This is a kind of democracy in which everybody has an opportunity to at least *say something*, whether we're talking about politics, marketing or the homeowner's association meeting on what color to paint the entire condo complex.

Following consensus input, we have *consensus understanding*. In a situation of consensus understanding, the group will not announce a final decision until everyone *understands* what that decision is. They may not necessarily agree with it, but they understand how and why it was arrived at. One of the things I'll often do in a divorce mediation, for instance, is to make sure that if one party wants the divorce and the other doesn't, the person who is resisting it is at least able to say in good conscience that they understand why his or her spouse is requesting it.

Understanding a decision that you don't necessarily agree with makes it much easier to swallow the pill and move from anger, hurt and bewilderment to acceptance. Which brings us to the next level of *consensus acceptance*, where no final decision or action is taken by the group until everyone is *accepting* of the outcome. Again, this doesn't necessarily mean that everyone *agrees* with the decision. Rather, it means that everyone is able to at least say, "Well, I don't agree with this but I accept it."

With this we come to the final extreme of the Power Continuum, which is *genuine consensus*. This is a situation in which there the final decision or action is taken only when everyone *agrees* with the outcome. Genuine consensus may seem, on one level, to be a rarely realized ideal. But in actuality, it's the basis of our criminal jury system, where every member of a jury, for instance, must agree on the verdict before there can be a conviction.

See if you can locate along the Power Continuum the decision-making power in the groups, organizations or situations in which you're involved. Is your boss or supervisor a pure dictator? An enlightened despot? A believer in consensus input, acceptance or agreement? Is there a commission at your workplace that can suggest policy or listen to grievances? Are decisions in your family made by a single authority figure or a genuine consensus?

Understanding the prevailing decision-making dynamics is an important element in determining the most effective way in which to gather—and utilize—information in your various environments, especially when you're involved in an uncomfortable situation that could become one of two things: a full-blown conflict or a harmonious working relationship.

DOING RESEARCH AND MAKING IT PAY OFF

Steven has been a project manager at an aerospace company for eight years. His record is excellent and he's gotten along well with all of his supervisors. Then, one day, he gets a new boss, Sylvia. Immediately there's trouble. Sylvia's aggressive, domineering personality conflicts with Steven's more easygoing demeanor. She's used to getting things done fast; Steven's approach is more methodical and thorough. Sylvia piles work on top of Steven while criticizing him for his "slowness." Soon, Steven begins to fear that he'll be getting a bad evaluation and that his job is in jeopardy.

When Steven came to me, the first question I asked

him was, "Is this a conflict situation, or merely a case of 'I don't like you and you don't like me?' "

"What's the difference?" asked Steven.

"If it's a personality clash, that's one thing," I replied. "But if there's a real conflict in terms of goals and expectations, that's another."

"There sure seems to be a conflict here," Steven said.

"Okay," I nodded. "What's the basis for the conflict?"

"That b——— wants to get me fired!" Steven exploded.

"Let's backtrack a minute. Is that an actual fact? Do you have unimpeachable information on that score? Or is it a feeling, a reaction on your part to Sylvia's working methods?"

Steven had to admit that while he felt that Sylvia was trying to make his job so difficult for him that he would be forced to either quit or be fired, he had no actual factual evidence for that assumption.

"Let's go on," I said. "What do you want out of this situation?"

"I want to keep my job."

"What else?"

Steven thought for a moment. "I want to be allowed to work at my own pace, and to be treated with respect."

"Anything else? How about wanting to get along with Sylvia?"

Steven agreed that while that would be lovely in theory, it hardly seemed promising given Sylvia's unpleasant disposition.

We then discussed ways in which Steven could accomplish his goals. He had the following action options: He could remain in his present position and try to change his working methods to suit Sylvia. Or, he could try to negotiate with Sylvia, for mutual understanding and respect.

Since he'd always gotten his work done and had received superior evaluations, Steven didn't feel that changing his own personal style was either necessary or possible. "That's me," he said. "I'm a plodder and a perfectionist. But I'm meticulous, I work extra hours and I get things done." So, he decided to embark upon a plan of action that involved sitting down and talking with Sylvia.

Step Number 1: The Subject in Info-gathering: You

The first step in gathering information about a situation is to get in touch with *your* own realities. This involves the willingness to step back and observe yourself, in both the past and the present.

Pick a conflict or potential conflict situation in your life and write it down. It can be one from the past or one that you're currently encountering. What role are you playing in this scene? Which "conflict personality type" are you—an attacker-defender, an accommodator, an avoider, a stalemater or a combination of the above? Is this a first-time conflict for you, or have you encountered it at other times in your life? What are your feelings about the situation, the other person or people involved? Are you feeling angry? hurt? scared? guilty? If so, why? How would you like to see the situation resolve itself?

Then, sit with all of that for a moment. That moment may be five minutes or five days or five weeks or five months—whatever the length of time it takes or you feel you have to get some clarity about your feelings, and to separate those feelings from the facts of the situation.

If you want to be able to gather reliable information, you first have to be able to take a good, hard look at yourself and answer the most basic question of all: Do you actually want to obtain this information and resolve the situation calmly and in a way that's mutually beneficial to both parties? Or do you just want to continue to feel upset and angry?

This is really a baseline consideration. While your immediate response to this question will probably be, "Of course I want to solve the problem! Why wouldn't I?" the truth of the matter is that a lot of people would rather be angry than channel their energies into gathering information on the situation. It's a lot like the famous old Taryton cigarette ad from around thirty years ago that featured a man with a black eye and the proud caption, "Taryton smokers would rather fight than switch!" Whether it's because of early childhood issues or fixed patterns in our lives that we don't feel we can alter, most of us will tend to gripe and complain or tenaciously defend our positions rather than take responsibility for changing an uncomfortable situation.

So this is our very first consideration, to ask yourself whether you have a sincere desire for things to be different, or whether you're simply using this situation as yet another opportunity to complain about someone else and feel victimized.

Look at the conflict situation you've written down. If you can honestly say that you would like, or would have liked, things to be different, the question then becomes, different in what way? Do you want a peaceful, amicable resolution to the problem? Or do you want to bring the other person to their knees? Write down some very honest conclusions to the statement, "In this situation I want . . ."

After your feelings have become clear, you can decide what it is that you really want from the other person. Do you want him or her to know something? Think something? Feel something? Do something?

Once you've clarified what you want from the other person, you can then move to the next stage of information gathering, which is finding out more about him or her in order to maximize your chances for success.

Step Number 2: A White Magic or a Black Magic Intention?

When we gather information about a person or situation, we may be motivated by one of two intentions. We may sincerely want to show our goodwill and bring about a lowering of tensions and an increase in understanding. Or, we may, either consciously or unconsciously, be info-gathering for less-than-honorable purposes, such as manipulating the other person or using the information we obtain against them.

It's a little like the difference between white magic and black magic. It has to do with ethics—the choice to use information for helpful versus harmful ends. To those who believe in magic, both kinds "work." But their results are at opposite ends of the spectrum, because they are dependent upon the heart and mind of the person involved. It has nothing to do with a level of expertise, or the ability to process information or "power."

So, if the intention of the person gathering the information is an honest and peaceful one, that will most likely be the way in which the problem is resolved. If, on the other hand, their intention is to manipulate, dominate or hurt someone else with the information . . . well, their strategy may "work," in the sense that they may achieve their adversary's "surrender." But since their intention is not coming from a healing place, they'll eventually discover that the situation wasn't really resolved, in the sense of gaining clarity and understanding. And when we don't approach a conflict situation from a healing place, we're likely to encounter similar situations again and again, until we really understand *why* they occur and *how* they can be prevented.

Here's an example of what I mean by a "white magic" versus a "black magic" state of mind in the info-gathering process. Let's say our beleaguered aerospace employee, Steven, runs into Beth, an associate and former supervisee of Sylvia from another department. Without Steven's having taken the time to embark upon his difficulty with Sylvia as a research project and clarify his intention by gathering information about her, he and Beth proceed to obtain and share information the way many people do: by responding to a negative situation through tactics of gossip and back-biting. The scenario would most likely go like this:

BETH: Hi, Steve! How are things going?

STEVEN: Ugh. Don't ask.

BETH: Why? What's wrong?

STEVEN: Sylvia.

BETH: Oh, right. She was transferred to your department. Isn't she a pain?

STEVEN: I'll say. She's undermining everything I do! Did she do that with you too?

BETH: Not just me—everybody who let her roll all over them.

STEVEN: Listen, is there anything you can tell me about Sylvia? You know, that might be good to know for the next time she comes at me?

BETH: Well . . . You remember Linda Smith?

STEVEN: Over in data processing?

BETH: Yeah. Well, as you know, Linda doesn't take any you-know-what. And when Sylvia tried to sit on her, look out! She'd met her match! Linda marched her off to Mr. Jenkins for a three-way "talk!"

STEVEN: Jenkins? Sylvia's boss? No! What happened?

BETH: Sylvia got transferred!

STEVEN: To my department. Thanks a bunch, Linda!

BETH: Well, Steve, you've got my sympathy. Sylvia is *such* a witch.

STEVEN: What do you think I should do?

BETH: Well, my advice to you is either to ask for a transfer or go into the ring with her.

STEVEN: Well, I'm not exactly the confrontational type. Anyway, I'd better be going. Listen, Beth, keep this little conversation confidential, if you know what I mean. Okay?

BETH: Don't worry. Good luck, guy. Keep me posted!

You see, although most of us aren't aware of it, we're always gathering information. We're always either talking about others or finding out about them. The problem is that when we really need that information to resolve a difficult situation, we have little or no idea of how to go about getting it "scientifically."

This interaction is a good example of the misguided way most of us go about getting—and giving— information about another person. Steven was frustrated and angry and used the encounter with Beth to both vent his own unhappiness and defend himself at Sylvia's expense. Beth, who was also probably carrying a lot of unresolved anger against Sylvia and who wanted to sympathize with Steven, responded by eagerly engaging in a bit of "friendly" gossip.

But when they were finished "laying Sylvia out," what had Beth and Steven really accomplished? Did they come away with any real insight into Sylvia and the conflicts they'd encountered with her? Did Steven have a better idea of how to deal with Sylvia and possibly resolve his own situation? Did Beth learn anything about how to respond to an unreasonable employer that might help her in the future, should she encounter the same kind of situation again?

No. What Beth and Steven did succeed in doing was to become more firmly entrenched in their positions "against" the adversary—Sylvia—and less able to view her behavior objectively and productively. After he left Beth, Steven probably felt more defensive and angry toward Sylvia than before. And Beth probably felt that she'd helped Steven by taking his side against the "enemy."

This is what I call coming to the information gathering process from a "black magic" frame of mind. Now, this doesn't necessarily mean that we intend to obtain information dishonestly or to use it purposely to harm someone else. Most of us don't participate in such conversations out of malice or evil intent. We're simply angry and hurt and don't have a very good idea of how to deal honestly with the person whom we view as inflicting pain upon us.

Now, let's turn the above scenario around. Let's say that Steven has engaged in the first step of information gathering—internal examination—as consciously, objectively and honestly as possible. First he discovers that he's angry at Sylvia and would like to get revenge against her. Then, after doing some self-talk about his feelings, he discovers that what he really wants is to keep his job and have Sylvia's respect. He's now gone past the anger stage, into one of sincerely wanting to resolve their difficulties in as amicable a way as possible.

Now he can go into phase two of the info-gathering process, which is to learn as much as he can about Sylvia. What's her past like? Where did she work before? What does she respond well to? What does she respond poorly to? When's her birthday? What kind of flowers does she like? What's her home environment like? Is she married? widowed? divorced? dating? Does she have children? Are there any difficulties in her personal life that might provide a clue to her unkind behavior?

Here Steven becomes a little bit of a spy. But it's okay, because he knows he's going to be using the information he receives for productive, not destructive purposes. He's got a "white magic" intention.

Steven decides that the best way to get the information he needs is to talk to someone who knows Sylvia and who has worked with her before. So, he calls up Beth and asks her to meet him for lunch. Let's listen in.

STEVEN: Beth, I invited you to lunch because—and I hope this won't be a total surprise to you—I'm having some difficulties with Sylvia Jones.

BETH: Sylvia, huh? Poor baby.

STEVEN: It's gotten to a point which is beyond where I think it's healthy for me and healthy for my job performance. And I imagine Sylvia must be feeling a lot of frustration too about this. So I'm just wondering whether you're willing to take a little time to hear what's going on.

BETH: Sure.

STEVEN: I'd like to bounce some ideas off you, and it would be great if you could give me some helpful information from your vast storehouse of experience with her. Is that something that sounds okay to you?

BETH: I'd be glad to help.

STEVEN: Now, I wanted to let you know that my purpose in meeting like this is not for you to tell me something that I might use against Sylvia. I mean, there was one time, especially in the beginning, when she came in like she was riding on a Sherman tank—

BETH: Yes, she does that!

STEVEN: I felt like I wanted to kill her. But I think I've gotten past that. Now I'm really wanting to figure out a way to work with her where I'm not feeling frustrated and I can be effective. And I'd like the same for her. But I want you to understand that I'm not asking you to reveal any information that you got in confidence, or that you're not comfortable sharing with me.

BETH: Thanks. I appreciate that.

STEVEN: So . . . Tell me about Sylvia. What about her good qualities?

BETH: Well, actually, my experience with her was that she was really tough to take in the beginning, but that when you realize that she's basically insecure, it's not all that bad.

STEVEN: Insecure in what way?

BETH: She recently went through a divorce—I don't know if you knew that.

STEVEN: No, I didn't. When was this?

BETH: Last year. It was one of those long marriages. And she's having a lot of trouble trying to raise her kid herself.

STEVEN: How old is her child?

BETH: Let's see, her daughter must be nine now. So, she's had a pretty stressful time, and you know what it's like, working at this company. It's really tough; you're always afraid of your position. So, whenever Sylvia gets transferred somewhere she just gets very uptight until she feels more secure about her territory.

STEVEN: I've been having a kind of personality clash with Sylvia over my working methods. I tend to be very methodical, slow and accurate, and she's more of a racehorse type, a workaholic who wants everything in yesterday. Now, I want to show her that I can do a good job. And I've always gotten excellent evaluations. But it seems to me that she's trying to force me to adopt her modus operandi. And I can't change who I am. So, I'd like to talk to her about this but I'm not sure of the best way to go about it. Can you give me some input?

BETH: What you have to do is catch her at a moment when she's relaxed. Which, by the way, happens to be just after she's had her morning coffee. Do *not* try to talk to her before that! And then, I would tell her pretty much exactly what you've told me. Because Sylvia is actually pretty straight, when it comes right down to it. I think she's got a good heart—there were times when she was really sympathetic to my problems. But I don't think she really realizes just how she comes across sometimes. And she's so worried about her own position, and getting stuff in on time to her superior, that I don't think she trusts you enough. And maybe you want to bring that out to her.

STEVEN: Let me see if I understand what you're saying. The best time to catch her is after she's had her coffee, in the morning. And then I should basically just lay out my dilemma?

BETH: Yeah.

STEVEN: Would you suggest I just walk into her office? Or should I send her a memo ahead of time?

BETH: You could send her a memo, if you're more comfortable doing that. But I think it's safe just to stick your head in her office after she's had her coffee and tell her you'd like to talk to her when she has a moment, about something important.

STEVEN: Are there any other incidents you can remember, experiences you might have had with her that you can think of that would be helpful to me?

BETH: Hmmm. Gee, I'm just trying to think. Well, this isn't the first time this has happened with Sylvia. She got into it with Linda Smith, over in data processing.

STEVEN: What happened there?

BETH: Linda actually had to go to Mr. Jenkins and he acted as kind of a mediator between them.

STEVEN: What do you think Sylvia's lesson from that was?

BETH: Well, it doesn't look to me like she's quite learned her lesson yet. I mean, that was part of the reason she was transferred to your department. But anyway, I remember that incident unnerved her because she's so worried about how she appears to her superiors, and she really freaked out when Linda sent a memo to Mr. Jenkins, requesting a three-way meeting.

STEVEN: Hmmm. What that tells me is that it would be better not to send her a memo, because that's liable to touch a raw nerve. She might feel threatened that I'd do what Linda did.

BETH: You've got a point there.

STEVEN: So I'd probably want to say something like, "I'm feeling very anxious and concerned about my performance here, and I'd like to talk to you and nip any differences in the bud before they get out of hand for either of us."

BETH: That sounds good to me.

STEVEN: Great. Listen, Beth, I really appreciate your doing this. And by the way, this isn't likely to happen but if Sylvia were to come to you and ask something about me, you have my permission to tell her about this conversation. I just want you to know that I'm not trying to do anything sneaky or secretive here.

BETH: I know. And I hope it works out. Keep me posted!

Step Number 3: Just the Facts, Ma'am

Obviously, this conversation is quite a bit different from the earlier example I used. Here Steven has actively engaged in a strategy that will help him in his final phase of information gathering, which will occur when he meets Sylvia face to face. What were the different components of his strategy, and what were the results?

1. *Being upfront about his intentions.* By clarifying his intentions at the outset and letting Beth know that he wanted to be aboveboard, Steven reduced the possibility of putting her in an uncomfortable or awkward situation and maximized his chances for getting the kind of information he wanted.

2. *Giving Beth the option to either respond or retreat.* By making it clear that Beth did not have to share any information with Steven that she wasn't comfortable sharing, Steven continued to be nonthreatening and to maximize his chances for getting useful data.

3. *Being as objective and fair as possible in his assessment of the situation.* By trying to understand Sylvia's position as well as his own, and by refusing to attack her, Steven encouraged Beth to respond in kind. Thus, he allowed Beth to give him more objective information about her experience with Sylvia, rather than information that would be more biased and heavily weighted against Sylvia.

4. *Asking for facts rather than feelings or opinions.* If you'll notice, Steven consistently asked only for information of a factual rather than an emotional nature. He

wanted to know about Beth's actual experience with Sylvia, actual incidents that had occurred, facts about her personal life and working style that might prove helpful to his gaining a more accurate picture of who he's dealing with. Thus the conversation was prevented from descending to the level of gossip or conjecture.

5. *Asking about Sylvia's good qualities.* Again, Steven needed balanced information in order to make as accurate as possible an assessment of his options. Knowing about Sylvia's good qualities not only encouraged Beth to take a more balanced approach to her, but helped him enormously in seeing Sylvia as a human being and approaching her from a positive rather than negative position.

6. *"Checking in" with Beth.* Steven regularly "checked in" with Beth, to make sure he was understanding her correctly. By repeating what he thought she said or meant, and giving her a chance to corroborate it, he not only gave Beth the security of knowing that her statements would not be misread or misinterpreted, but he gave himself the security of knowing that the information he was receiving was as accurate as it could be.

The result of this type of information gathering, versus the type of information gathering we saw in the first scenario between Steven and Beth, is somewhat like the difference between mining fool's gold and the real thing. In his first encounter with Beth, all Steven came away with was data gleaned from gossip and Beth's negative perspective of Sylvia. This type of information is at best biased, at worst inaccurate. As such, it is pretty much worthless as far as constructive use goes.

But in his second meeting with Beth, Steven has unearthed a veritable goldmine of useful information. The knowledge that Sylvia is basically good-hearted but insecure and that she's gone through a tremendous amount of personal and work-related stress goes a long way in helping him to sympathize with her and reduce his defensiveness. The information that Sylvia is most relaxed after her morning coffee tells him when to approach her. The information about Sylvia's confrontation with Linda tells him that the activity of memo-sending, as far as Sylvia is concerned, could be a red flag. And the information that Sylvia has, in the past, been sympathetic to the needs of those she supervises tells him that she's not totally unreasonable and he's got at least a fighting chance of amicably resolving his problems with her.

MAKING RESEARCH PAY OFF

You've officially become a spy. You've gathered a bulging attaché chock full of mouthwatering tidbits about the other person. You know when they get up in the morning, when they go to bed, their favorite color, whether or not they take cream in their coffee or sugar in their tea. You know their strong suits; you know their Achilles' heel. You're ready to move in now—to meet them, talk with them, see if you can settle your differences amicably based on the data you've accumulated.

But research in and of itself is not a guarantee of success in resolving conflict. Of equal importance is knowing what to do with the information you've received. How much of it do you use? How much is expendable? And how do you make sure you're using it most effectively?

Think of the analogy of nutrition. In the same way that we are constantly receiving and processing information, we are also fueling our bodies and processing that fuel, in the form of what goes into our mouths. In order for our bodies to be operating at maximum health capacity, we can't simply eat anything and everything we see. We must go through a process of selection, to decide what is helpful to our health and what isn't. Then we must decide when to ingest these items, and in what quantities. If we eat too much, we get fat; if we eat too little, we starve. It is only when we balance our nutritional information wisely that we maximize our chances of functioning at an optimum state of well-being.

We are all inundated at every turn with information in our everyday lives. Instinctively we have to be selective; if we really allowed every fact that's reported to us in the newspapers or on TV to be taken in, valued, *felt*, we'd be basket cases within a few minutes. So we've learned to allow just a tiny fraction of 1 percent of all the information we receive to affect us. This is a form of necessary self-protection, one that we can carry over into the selection of appropriate information to use in the process of preventing and resolving disputes.

When selecting information, it's of utmost importance to always remember what your intention is to deal with the conflict at hand. Go back to our criteria in the previous chapter. Do you want the other person to know something? think something? feel something? do something? What is it that you yourself want the information to achieve? A cessation of tension and nothing more? a monetary settlement? a job promotion? a friendship? a reconciliation?

The Process of Selection: Deciding What Information to Use

As in any research project, you'll never use all of the information you've amassed. You might read a whole book for a paper, yet only be able to use one or two lines from it. Or, if you're a photographer, you know how many rolls of film you can go through before you've gotten the two or three shots you want. Well, it's the same with preparing to enter into conflict solving. The more skillfully you're able to refine and distill the essentials out of the information you've gotten, the better equipped you'll be to dialogue with the other person.

Selecting appropriate information involves making decisions as to what is necessary, what is expendable and what should be withheld in the best interest of all concerned.

When going through the process of selection and elimination, ask yourself the following questions. What does this particular bit of information tell me about the situation and the other person? Is it relevant to the goals I want to achieve? How can I use it to my best advantage? And if I use it, will it hurt the other person or people in any way?

Information that Helps: Clarifiers

Generally speaking, after you've done some research into the situation and/or the person or people you're dealing with the information you'll want to keep will serve to clarify things and move them ahead toward peaceful resolution of hostilities or impending hostilities.

Some kinds of information may be interesting but may not actually add new dimension to anything. If, as in our earlier example, Steven had discovered that Sylvia's favorite breakfast cereal was Kellogg's Froot Loops, he may have considered the possibility that Sylvia might be suffering from hypoglycemia and could kill him in a moment of sugar-powered rage. On the other hand, since he really would have no substantial evidence for that hypothesis, he'd probably have to conclude that this particular bit of information, while interesting, was not of particular value to the issue at hand, which was how to resolve the tensions in their working relationship.

When Steven went info-gathering about Sylvia, he got a lot of information from Beth. What did he decide, in the final analysis, to use? And how did he decide to use it? Here's a hypothetical construction of how he conducted his meeting with her.

At 9:25 A.M. on Monday morning, Steven sees Sylvia disappear into her office with her cup of coffee in hand. After allowing five minutes for the elixir to take its effect, Steven takes a deep breath, delivers a last-minute prayer to the God of aerospace engineers and goes to Sylvia's office. The door is open.

STEVEN: Knock knock!

SYLVIA: Yes?

STEVEN: Hi, Sylvia. May I come in?

SYLVIA (suspiciously): Okay.

STEVEN (sitting down): How are you this morning?

SYLVIA: Well, as usual at this time of day I'm just having my coffee and outlining my schedule. So that's the way it is. Now, what can I do for you?

STEVEN: I don't want to take up too much of your

time. But I was wondering if you might have a few minutes to talk.

SYLVIA: I always have a few minutes. You know it's company policy here to have an open door, and I am a good company person. Shoot.

STEVEN: Okay. Lately, Sylvia, I've been feeling a tension between us that seems to focus on my working habits. I sense that you have some reservations about the way I work.

SYLVIA: Now that's a fact. You're absolutely a hundred percent accurate. And I'm glad you're getting it!

STEVEN: I was wondering if you could expand on your feelings and expectations a little.

SYLVIA: Happy to. I'm a manager who wants to do a good job, and I want to make sure that everybody in this section is working at maximum efficiency and effectiveness and that our reports get out on time. Because that's the way I work and that's really important to me, okay? And one of the things I noticed right away was that, compared to the others in this section, you seem to be dilly dallying. And I'm concerned that if this continues, the whole department is going to suffer and I'm going to look like yesterday's newspaper.

STEVEN: Well, I can appreciate how you got that impression based on the desire that you have to get your job done. However, I've been here at this position now for six years. I've gotten excellent evaluations. And I come in with excellent work. It might take me a little longer than somebody else, but that's because I tend to be more thorough than most people. So the kind of work you get from me you can really count on. And I guess what

I'm feeling right now is a lack of trust on your part. This is making me pretty anxious, and I wanted to talk to you about it to see if we could resolve the situation to both our advantages.

SYLVIA: Well, I appreciate your coming in here. I'd like to make it clear that in the short time that I've been here, I have nothing to criticize about the quality of your work. My beef has been over the quantity and timing of things. And as far as quality goes, I assume the quality is going to be superior. It has been with everyone else.

STEVEN: Can you tell me how you'd like to resolve this situation?

SYLVIA: Sure. I want to know that your slowness isn't going to give me an ulcer. I want to know that the work I give to you, which is no different in amount than what I give to everyone else, is going to be on my desk when I want it on my desk. You know, I just hate to get nervous over things.

STEVEN: So what you're saying is that if I bring my work in on time there won't be a problem between us.

SYLVIA: You got it. And for extra clarification, I do not want you bringing me your reports at the last minute. I need a chance to look things over before they get forwarded.

STEVEN: Maybe I wasn't taking that into account. The previous supervisor and I had a different working relationship. So, I will try very hard to get you the work when you need it. Now, there's something I need too, which is not to feel that I'm under abnormal pressure. I feel now that you've been giving me a lot of extra work. This probably goes along with your expectations of getting things done quickly—if somebody can whip things out, then they should be able to do twice as much. But I get very stressed out in that type of situation.

SYLVIA: Hmmm. I'm sure that I'm giving you the same work as I give everybody else. But maybe I have been a little hard on you. I don't know; I haven't been intending to. What I'll do is this: I'll look at what I've asked other people to do and what I've asked you to do. And I'll compare the two. If it turns out that you're right, I'll make some adjustments.

STEVEN: That sounds fair.

SYLVIA: But I'm not promising anything! If it turns out that that isn't the case, we're going to have to settle things.

STEVEN: Another thing I wanted to bring up was last week's meeting. I felt that you came down on me in front of everybody.

SYLVIA: I never did! What did I say?

STEVEN: Well, you—

SYLVIA: You'd better be able to back up a statement like that. I consider myself a very good supervisor, and a good supervisor doesn't go around doing things like that. You're probably just being over-sensitive.

STEVEN: Several other staff members commented on it to me afterwards, so I don't think it was just me.

SYLVIA: Hmmm. I'll tell you what. Along with the open-door policy I have an open-mind policy. So let me rethink that and go over my notes from that meeting. But I want to assure you right now that I wasn't intending to insult you or put you down. I believe in frankness, that's all.

STEVEN: That sounds fair to me, Sylvia. Well, I don't think we need to go on and on. I just wanted you to know that I really do enjoy my work and I want to do a good job. I also want the department to benefit, and I want us to get along.

SYLVIA: Then we're on the same wavelength, because that's just what I want too. Have some coffee?

MEETING THE OTHER PERSON: THE PROCESS OF NONCONFRONTATIONAL DIALOGUE

When we want another person to understand and respect us, and when we're willing to do the same for them, the chances of resolving or preventing conflict are maximized. Engaging in a dialogue with the intention of honoring both yours and the other person's feelings in an honest, nonattacking manner is the most effective way to accomplish this.

At first glance it may seem as though Steven and Sylvia were not equal partners on the journey toward conflict resolution. After all, it was Steven who single-handedly did all the information gathering, developed a strategy and initiated the meeting between the two of them. Sylvia certainly didn't go out of her way to be an active participant in the process.

The conventional wisdom has always been that it takes one to start a dispute and two to resolve it. But as we know already, the reverse is actually true: *While it takes two to keep a dispute going, one person alone can initiate and guide a process that can resolve the dispute.*

In a conflict situation, both parties do not need to actively engage in the research and planning stages of resolving their differences. If one person is really doing his/her homework, has a strong intention to work things out and is persistent, he/she can often overcome the other's unwillingness or resistance to play the same game.

Of course, it's a lot easier if both people are willing to actively seek a peaceful, coexplorative solution to the problem. But it's not an absolute necessity. You don't have to give up simply because someone isn't initially as open to you as you are to them.

In the case of Steven and Sylvia, Steven proved that his own willingness to try and understand Sylvia's perspective and to approach her from an honest, upfront position himself was an effective means of opening Sylvia up to the same nonconfrontational process. At first she was on the defensive. But as their meeting progressed and she realized that she wasn't being attacked and that Steven really did have a strong desire to do his job well and have a friendly working relationship with her, Sylvia relaxed and was able to respond in a more supportive, open way herself.

One of the most important things to remember before engaging in a meeting of this type with someone is that we really don't know what the other person is thinking or feeling. While this may sound obvious, it isn't; in a conflict situation, most of us usually fall prey to the danger of over-believing that we really do know about the other person: their thoughts, their intentions, their motivations, the actions they're sure to take. Although we may know the other person's past history, all too often we act based on the parade of horribles we usually project onto the other person, which involve our own fears, fantasies and insecurities.

How many times have you found yourself saying, "Oh, he'll never go for that . . . She won't listen to

reason . . . These guys are just jerks . . ." It isn't often
that we are willing to go beneath the surface of another
person's exterior—and our own exteriors as well—in
order to discover the real person behind the mask. It
isn't often that we are willing to put aside our own
reactive emotions of anger, hurt and fear in order to
help the other person to put aside theirs.

Had Steven gone into his meeting with Sylvia without doing his research—had he approached her from
his old, defensive position that said, "She's impossible,
I'll never be able to talk to her, she just wants to get me
fired"—chances are that that's just what would have
happened. When we believe we know what another
person is going to say and do, we often create a self-
fulfilling prophecy. Expecting the worst, we prepare for
it. We go in on the defensive, the other person senses it
and becomes equally defensive. And chances for honest, meaningful dialogue diminish by the minute.

Now it's true that we can predict a person's behavior
pattern based on past experience. It was the great trial
lawyer Louis Nizer who said, "If you want to know how
a man's going to act in a given situation, look at his past
actions. This is what I call the 'law of probability.' " This
is undoubtedly an accurate observation—people do
tend to act and respond to certain stimuli the way
they've always acted and responded—*until the pattern
is broken*. And my point is that in the case of conflict
solving, by breaking our own patterns we take the initia-
tive in helping the other person to change his/her behavior as well. Once we analyze our own pattern, as an
attacker, accommodator, avoider and/or stalemater,
and refuse to succumb to the temptation of those unproductive roles, we at least give the other person a chance
to move out of *their* unconscious pattern of response.

Now, they may not choose to do that. They may resist the discomfort they feel in the new and unfamiliar territory of honesty and openness. *But we have no control over someone else's response.* This is a very difficult fact to accept in a dispute situation—that we really have only limited control over its outcome. We may think we're in charge, but we're not. Which means that when we enter into the coexplorative process, we must be willing, like the members of those Twelve Step Programs, to take the first step of surrendering to a higher power, to admit that we're not in control of anything except our own actions and responses. And many of us are not even in control of these.

It's the "good" news and the "bad" news again. The bad news is you're not in sole control; the good news is that when you adjust yourself to that reality, there's a lot of flexibility that you can bring to every conflict situation, and a lot you can do to maximize your chances for successful mutual understanding.

Misusing Information: A Time to Speak and a Time to Refrain from Speaking

Along with selecting and using information comes an important aspect of conflict resolution that must be emphasized: the *misuse* of information.

Every one of us has information that could be hurtful to ourselves or someone else. For instance, I know things about virtually everyone in my family, and many of my friends, which could be devastating to them if I chose to confront them with my knowledge. Forget about passing that information on to other people— that's a whole other can of worms. But how many of us stop to realize the power that goes along with the information we have about others, and the *responsibility* we have to use that information wisely?

A very high percentage of disputes are caused by people misusing confidential information. In business, family, friendships, office situations, government, the misuse of information regularly leads to all sorts of conflict situations that range from misunderstandings and resentment to divorces, employment terminations, even wars.

Basically, we can misuse information in one of two ways. We can either withhold important information when we should release it, or we can divulge information that we should have kept to ourselves. Either way, we're engaging in an abuse of power that is far more potent than most of us realize.

The Buddhists have a principle known as "right speech." According to this principle, you don't want to say anything that isn't true, and you don't want to say anything that is true if it's not necessary and you think there's a high probability that it's going to hurt someone. Right speech does not only mean speaking wisely and honestly; it also refers to the conscious effort to *refrain* from engaging in "wrong speech," all the way from gossip and useless or idle chatter to more serious "sins" like abusive language, lying and slander.

The principle of right speech is basic to any honest, well-intentioned attempt at conflict solving. We have to know when it's appropriate to speak, and when it's appropriate to remain silent in everyone's best interest. The goal of right speech, according to one commentary, is to learn to communicate in a way that is "gentle, cultivating harmony and unity between people." In a coexplorative dialogue situation where we feel wronged by the other party, it's often very difficult to refrain from saying things we know that may be true but may be hurtful to the other person. And yet, in many cases it's absolutely essential.

Just because information is "truthful" doesn't mean we're at liberty to hit someone else over the head with it. In conflict resolution the truth is not enough—it's one of the necessary but not sufficient conditions for saying something. In order to make the conditions sufficient, you have to go into your "white magic" space, where you can determine whether or not divulging the information you have would be to the good of everybody concerned.

Let's take our example of Steven and Sylvia. Through the office grapevine, Steven knew that Sylvia had locked horns with Linda Smith and had been called into Mr. Jenkins's office. He also knew that her transfer to his department was a direct result of that unpopular incident. Now, Steven could have let Sylvia know that he had this information. He could have said, "Look, Sylvia, I know that you've had problems with your employees in the past, that I'm not the only one who's been abused by you. And as a matter of fact, I know that the very reason you're in this department is because of what happened between you and Linda Smith. And I doubt if you'd like Mr. Jenkins to get another memo about the same thing. So let's clear our little tiff up before it gets out of hand, okay?"

Yes, Steven could have said that. But he chose not to. Why? Quite simply because it would not have been in line with his intention, which was to resolve their differences peacefully and have a good working relationship.

Had Steven decided to be an "attacker," had his

intention been to give Sylvia "a dose of her own medicine" and talk to her "in the only language she understands" so that she's out for the count and he's the new champion, he probably would have used this information against her. And he might have "won," but at a great price. They would probably never have a good working relationship—Sylvia would have resented him until the end of time. And she very well might have put a note in his file, to the effect that he tried to blackmail her—never a helpful hint on anyone's references.

Fortunately, Steven accomplished what he set out to achieve without having to resort to using hurtful information. Now, had his initial strategy been ineffective, he might have been justified in taking a more "direct" tack with Sylvia—but only as a last resort. And even then, the *way* in which he lets Sylvia know that he knows what he knows is crucial. Instead of attacking her with the information, he has the option of saying, "Look, Sylvia, I know that you've had these problems with employees in the past. I have reason to feel that I'm not the only one that this has happened with. But I'd like to make it work between us—I'd like it to remain right here in this room. Because I respect you and I want very much to get along with you." That's a very different way of divulging potentially damaging information—it lets Sylvia know what Steven's intention is, and it gives her the option of trying to resolve the situation not because she's threatened, but because she realizes that Steven truly wants to have a friendly, productive working relationship with her.

What we're really talking about here is learning how to communicate information *skillfully*. Communication, after all, is a skill that requires practice like any other skill. And knowing when to use and not use information is a vital part of sincere communication.

STATEMENTS VERSUS QUESTIONS

Another aspect of skillful communication is the technique of making statements rather than asking questions in order to get the most useful response from the other person.

I've often said that "the best questions are those that are never asked." In other words, in most cases it's far better for someone to volunteer information than to be asked for it. Why is that?

Well, questions tend to have a quality of "theft" about them. One of the reasons that people often get defensive when they're being asked questions is that viscerally they feel that they're being stolen from, invaded or manipulated. This is a primary reason why journalists are often seen in such an uncomplimentary light—because they're the "question askers," the "truth seekers" of society, and people instinctively react with suspicion and hostility when they're confronted in this manner.

"But what about innocent questions?" you ask. To which I would reply, there's hardly any such thing as an innocent question. Because a question, no matter what its intent, is either consciously or unconsciously manipulative. It demands an answer, even when someone else may not be ready to give one.

The most effective way to elicit information from someone else is first to share information yourself. By this I don't mean simply sharing ideas or opinions. I mean sharing what it is that you want and, in terms of feedback, why you want it, what you're going to do with it and what benefit it might be to the other person if they give it to you.

Let's go back to Steven's conversation with Sylvia. If you look closely, you'll notice that Steven asked Sylvia only one direct question during the entire interaction. He was careful to make statements about his feelings, intentions and observations, but he didn't put Sylvia on the defensive by asking her for information point-blank. Instead, Sylvia was made aware at the outset of why Steven wanted the information and what he intended to do with it. As a result, she felt safer to respond from her "feeling" level, rather than having to come up with the "right" answers to questions that could have put her on the spot.

What we want to do above all is to create a safe environment that frees both parties to be as honest as they can. It behooves us to consider carefully the things that we might be doing, either unintentionally or unconsciously, to put someone else on the defensive. Do we make accusations, "you" statements rather than "I" statements? Is our body language either attacking or defensive? Do we shake our fists, wag our fingers, stand there with our hands on our hips? Do we "move in" on the other person, infringing upon their space? Or do we "distance" ourselves with protective, defensive gestures like folded arms, crossed legs and indirect eye contact?

Coming from a position of honesty, vulnerability and compassion isn't always the easiest thing in the world, especially when we ourselves are feeling hurt or threatened. That's why the process of information gathering is vital in terms of lessening discomfort all the way around and building an atmosphere of mutual trust.

THE ART OF FLEXIBILITY

The process of gathering and using information involves a certain paradox. On the one hand, you want to do your research as "scientifically" and skillfully as possible, in order to maximize your chances for getting the result you desire. On the other hand, you realize that you can't "overcontrol" the situation, in terms of its outcome or the other person's response. So, you have to maintain a balance between becoming uptight and anxious over what you want and what the other person may or may not do, and simply sauntering into a meeting without having done any preparation whatsoever.

What we're talking about, then, is really the comfortable middle ground between "winging" it and "clinging" to it. I'm reminded here of the old Indian story told by the Buddha: A king ordered a certain man to carry a vessel of water on top of his head and to move rather quickly. But if he spilled so much as one drop of water, his head would be cut off. So, the problem becomes, how does he walk? If he's too stiff and nervous, he won't be able to respond with enough flexibility to avoid that bump in the road or the oxcart in front of him. If, on the other hand, he's so loose and relaxed that he's not really paying attention to what's happening around him, he's bound to spill some water sooner or later.

The point of the story, of course, is that the appropriate attitude to take along the road of life is one that's equally balanced between awareness and flexibility. We must learn the art of being both attentive and relaxed, of watching without worrying. Once we have achieved this balance, we won't be in danger of "losing our heads" through hasty or ill-timed action.

In going into a conflict situation, then, we must understand the elements that are within our control—how we prepare for it, and how aware we are of our own intentions and response patterns—and those that are not. We must be able both to define what we want and take action toward achieving that goal, while at the same time releasing ourselves from any attachment to the outcome.

Once we have taken responsibility for our own actions and needs and allowed the rest to unfold in its own way and time, we have created the best possible atmosphere in which to respond to a conflict peacefully and amicably.

6

Inner Conflict: Your Relationship with Yourself Mirrors Your Relationship with Others

It was just a little matter of the Tiffany Lamp.

When Shirley and Edna's mother died, they set about dividing her things between them. All went smoothly until they came to mom's Tiffany lamp, a valuable family heirloom. Both sisters had set their sights on that lamp, and neither was willing to relinquish it. Finally Shirley simply declared that, since she was the oldest, the lamp was hers. Period. She took it and left for home.

That was thirty years ago. Shirley and Edna haven't spoken since. Should they chance to collide at a family gathering, they simply ignore each other. For all intents and purposes, Shirley doesn't exist to Edna, and vice versa.

Let's take another example of nonrecognition. A certain country does something outrageous. Other countries withdraw their ambassadors and refuse to "recognize" the offender, making it a pariah in the international community.

On the surface these seem to be two separate and distinct examples of conflict situations. One is a personal dispute. The other is an "impersonal" international dispute, many times removed from the kind of intimate daily conflict situations that most of us encounter.

Yet if we look very closely, we'll find that both of these situations are really very similar. In fact, it's as though we're looking at the same conflict, only from different angles. Why? Because each involves disownment, of one person or entity by another. And on a deeper level, they all involve disownment of one or more parts of the "self."

OUR DISOWNED SELVES: WHERE CONFLICT BEGINS

What is a "disowned self"?

Just as our bodies have numerous components, so our psyches consist of various parts or selves. We are not, after all, just "one" person; we are many different people, in the sense that we have many aspects to our character that reveal themselves at different *times* in our lives, in different *situations*, and sometimes *simultaneously*.

We may be aware of some of these aspects or selves. We may have, for instance, a funny side, an introspective side, a melancholy side, a compassionate side, an opinionated side. These components of our personalities may be quite evident, to ourselves as well as to others.

On a deeper level, however, we have less immediately recognizable selves, selves that are hidden deep within the recesses of memory. We have a "needy child" within us, who requires nurturing and freedom of expression. We have a "critic," who passes judgment, on ourselves and others. We have a "loving self," that is open and vulnerable. We have an inner "parent," who makes decisions and takes on responsibilities.

These are only a few of the less conscious selves that live within us, and that motivate our actions and responses to situations and stimuli as we move through life. Often unaware of their existence, we may or may not listen to what they are telling us. In our belief that we are, or should be, mature, realistic, "grown up," we may repress or neglect our inner child. If we believe that it's "not nice" to be critical or confrontational, we may silence our inner critic. Similarly, if our stance in the world is an aggressive one built on a desire for power and control, we may not acknowledge the more loving, tender, vulnerable side of our nature.

When we refuse to acknowledge one of our many selves, we are said to be "disowning" that self.

Most of us are familiar with disownment in the legal sense of the term. We've seen the typical scenario endless times: An irate father, insistent that his daughter marry a prominent lawyer, threatens to disown or disinherit her should she go against his wishes and elope with the town ne'er-do-well. Or old Mrs. Moneybags, upon learning that her favorite nephew is gay, disowns

him and wills the family fortune of six billion dollars to
Jezebel, her cat.

Why would we disown a part of ourselves? And what
happens to us when we do?

In his book *The Psychology of Self-Esteem*, psycholo-
gist Nathaniel Branden explains the process of disownment and its consequences.

> When a person represses certain of his thoughts,
> feelings or memories, he does so because he regards
> them as threatening to him in some way . . . wrong,
> or inappropriate, or immoral, or unrealistic, or indic-
> ative of some irrationality on his part—and as *dan-
> gerous*, because of the actions to which they might
> impel him . . .
> Consider the case of a man who represses his *ideal-
> ism*, i.e. his aspiration to any values beyond the level
> of the commonplace.
> When he was a boy, no one understood or shared
> his feelings about the books he read or the things he
> liked; no one shared or understood his feeling . . .
> that he should achieve something difficult and great.
> What he heard from people was, "Oh, don't take
> yourself so seriously. You're impractical." . . . Now,
> as a middle-aged Babbitt, he listens with empty eyes
> and an emptier soul while his son speaks of the great
> things he wants to do when he grows up, and he tells
> his son to go mow the lawn, and then, sitting alone,
> why, he wonders, why should I be crying?

The man in question has disowned his idealistic self.
This disownment has a number of tragic consequences.
Not only has he denied himself the chance to explore
and enjoy life to its fullest; he is in the process of
denying his son that same chance, of passing on the

terrible legacy of repression. And his inner conflict, between his parental, authoritarian, critical self and his idealistic self, will be mirrored in the conflict he will have with his son, who will most likely either rebel against his father or put aside his dreams and harbor deep resentment against him.

Too often we tend to view disputes or conflicts as the fault of either the circumstances or the other party. But the reality is that *external conflicts are often merely external projection of the conflicts that are going on inside of us*. Interestingly enough, disownment in its legal form is usually the conscious manifestation of an unconscious process. When a father disowns a daughter for marrying against his wishes, he is, in effect, disowning that part of himself that longs for romance and freedom. When an aunt disowns her nephew because he's gay, she is also disowning that sexual self within her—gay or straight—that has never been allowed either its legitimacy or its freedom.

In other words, you can be sure that if you're involved in a dispute with someone, you need to look inside yourself to discover the disowned part of you that either may have been a large contributing factor or that played an important role, either consciously or unconsciously, in fanning the flames of disagreement.

Let's relate this to our opening example of Shirley and Edna. When Shirley "seized" the lamp, Edna was so enraged that she cut off communication with her. On the surface it may seem as though Edna was justified in her anger; after all, didn't Shirley act like a selfish pig, a mean and nasty older sister who was still doing power-play numbers on her helpless younger sibling forty years later?

But let's take our mental shovel again and dig a little

deeper. Now, Edna always considered herself to be a kind, reasonable person. In fact, she never would have entertained the possibility of taking a crude action like swiping something somebody else wanted and walking off with it.

But there was a part of Edna that really wanted that lamp, and that wished she'd grabbed it first. Edna didn't want to consciously acknowledge that part of herself because she found it distasteful—or, as Nathaniel Branden puts it, "wrong, inappropriate, or indicative of some irrationality." At the same time, she was angry at herself because she had let Shirley "get away with" her outrageous act of piracy.

So, Edna transferred to Shirley the anger at the "greedyguts" she'd disowned in herself.

Now, you may argue that Shirley certainly "had it coming." But my point is that Edna, while perhaps justified in her anger, did not have to let the situation escalate into a full-fledged Thirty Years War. In fact, had she not been so conflicted on an inner level, she would probably have been able to forgive Shirley once her initial hurt and rage had passed. But as long as Edna refuses to "own" the possessive child self within her that wanted to snatch that lamp and to hell with anybody else . . . well, she can hardly forgive Shirley because she hasn't yet forgiven her own disowned self.

DISCOVERING OUR DISOWNED SELVES

The problem with disowned selves is that very often we are simply not in touch with them at all. We haven't the slightest conscious inkling that they exist. This presents, of course, a real difficulty: If we don't know that something exists, how can we deal with it?

Well, first of all you have to make the discovery. In my mediative role as adviser/consultant/coach, I had a client to whom I started to explain the concept of the disowned self. It was particularly relevant because of a difficulty she was having with a coworker who kept "pushing her buttons." The only problem was, my client could not find the buttons. She was not yet in touch with the part of her unconscious that her coworker represented. So, we did a dialogue in which we tried to contact this disowned self. This is how it went.

JOEL: Okay. Tell me about something or someone that really pushes your buttons.

BARBARA: Hmmm. Let's see. Okay, here's something that really bugs me: pushy people. Pushy people bug me a whole lot.

JOEL: Perhaps pushy and domineering people would not bug you if you didn't have a part of yourself way down deep that was like that, and that was abhorrent to your other selves. It's as if an inner committee comprised of all your different selves decided that it did not like this part that could be pushy. And the spokesperson for the committee—your Inner Critic—says, "Yuck! We don't like this pushy part of Barbara. And whenever we see it in other people we shake our finger and say, 'Oh that jerk! Do you know what he/she did?' "

BARBARA: So this doesn't necessarily mean that we have acted in the way we dislike in others. It means that we haven't allowed that part of ourselves to come out at all.

JOEL: That's right. We haven't allowed that part to be given its rightful place. We are so busy putting it down, kicking it in the shins, that we have to continue our internal subjugation on an *external* level as well.

BARBARA: This is fascinating, because I'm not at all in touch with that part of myself, that "pushy" part. It's absolutely unconscious. So how do I make it conscious?

JOEL: Okay. What we're going to do together is a process that was refined by Hal Stone and his wife, Sidra Winkelman, two psychologists whom I admire and with whom I studied briefly. It's known as "voice dialoguing." Now, move over on the couch a little and assume a physical position that you would imagine that pushy part of yourself might take.

BARBARA (sitting up and putting her hands on her hips): Okay.

JOEL: And let's give a name to this nasty, pushy part of you that you don't like.

BARBARA: Doris!

JOEL: That's my mother's name!

BARBARA: Oh no! Is she pushy?

JOEL: As a matter of fact, no. Now, I'd like to talk to *your* Doris. Is that okay?

BARBARA: Sure.

JOEL: Doris, tell me a little bit about you. What's life like for you?

BARBARA: I don't even know how to talk like Doris because I don't feel like her.

JOEL: Just allow yourself to get into the place where you're feeling pushy and angry and you want to get your way at all costs.

BARBARA: Wow. That takes some doing. That's the problem in my life. I get into a lot of problematic situations because I don't stick up for myself. I don't seem to know how.

JOEL: You don't seem to be responding as Doris, but as your "controller." We were trying to gain access to Doris, that part of Barbara that is really pushy and annoying. How do you feel about Doris, Barbara?

BARBARA: Well, if I met her face to face she'd probably really piss me off.

JOEL: What would she do to piss you off?

BARBARA: She'd be obnoxious and grasping. She'd order me around.

JOEL: Do you ever order people around, Barbara?

BARBARA: No, I mean, not really. Well, if I have an organizational job where I'm managing people, I give them duties. But in a nice way.

JOEL: Is there anyone you can think of who might think of you as pushy?

BARBARA: Well, come to think of it, a guy I almost married. But he was so passive-aggressive that anyone would have been pushy to him. I had to make all the decisions because he wouldn't make them. And if I wanted to do something he was pretty much always willing. It wasn't until two years into the relationship that he exploded with all this pent-up resentment, at how "domineering" I was.

JOEL: Um hmmm. How did you feel?

BARBARA: Terrible. Like a bitch. And I never thought of myself as a bitch.

JOEL: There's a part in all of us, a demanding child that wants what we want when we want it. Somehow you've decided that that demanding child in you is "bad" and not only needs to be punished— its very existence needs to be completely denied.

BARBARA: You know something? Whiny kids really push my buttons! If I see a child whining in a store, doing the "I want this, I want that" number, I get really angry.

JOEL: Did you ever whine as a child?

BARBARA: Sure. In fact, I used to throw public tantrums!

JOEL: How did people respond to you when you did that?

BARBARA: Not too well! My mother would be beside herself. The neighbors would call me a "bad little girl." And my dad would wallop me.

JOEL: Perhaps you don't want to be reminded of one of the ways that you were as a child because that whiny part of you was put down so much. Is that possible?

BARBARA: Yeah. Sure.

JOEL: Now, you said that one of your biggest problems is getting yourself into situations where you don't stick up for yourself. Can you tell me a little more about that?

BARBARA: Well, in my work I've gotten involved in some collaborations with people who tend to be domineering. I "give in" a lot, they take advantage of my flexibility, and pretty soon I'm hating them and the project. But I'm not good at confronting them, so I sort of whine and moan about them.

JOEL: Can you feel Doris yet?

BARBARA: No. I really can't. I'm not in touch with her at all.

JOEL: That's exactly the definition of the disowned self. You've so disowned Doris that you can't even feel her. But you are feeling *something*. You're feeling the shadow of Doris.

BARBARA: The shadow of Doris? It sounds like a B horror movie! *The Shadow . . . of Doris!*

JOEL: Well, Doris is casting a shadow over your life in the following way. You know that you're angry whenever you're in the presence of or are affected by someone who is being pushy and obnoxious. You don't simply say, hmmm, well there's a pushy, obnoxious person. You have an emotional reaction to him or her; it sets you off. And this shadow affects your whole life.

You see, there's a rule in life that applies both to the intrapsychic as well as to the external world on every level: Whatever you avoid, disown, are unwilling to deal with is going, sooner or later, *to run your life.* This rule of the universe can't be avoided. It's like gravity. You can hate gravity and spend your whole life refusing to get up out of bed. But your hatred of gravity isn't going to make it go away. It's just going to make your relationship with the world all screwed up, because you have to go to such lengths to avoid the thing you hate. And in the same way, when you avoid a part of you, you make changes and compromises and contortions that will almost certainly get you into conflict with yourself and therefore with others.

At the end of this session, Barbara still hadn't been able to "feel" Doris. But she was aware of her existence, and the effect it had had on her life. And as always seems to happen, when we finally confront the thing that's causing us pain, its power over us is considerably diminished and we find, miraculously, that it doesn't seem to bother us as much. A few weeks later, Barbara reported to me that one of the "pushy" people in her life whom she had so detested telephoned her. It wasn't until after they'd hung up that Barbara realized she was no longer rubbed the wrong way by this person. "We actually had a nice conversation," Barbara recalled with wonder. "She just didn't bug me the way she used to."

EXERCISE:
Examining Your Pet Peeves

In discovering the parts of yourself that you've been neglecting or denying, a first step is to make an inventory of your pet peeves. What things in other people really annoy you? Make a list.

_____

_____

_____

_____

_____

_____

_____

_____

After you've written these down, look inside of yourself. Do you have any of these annoying qualities in your own makeup? If you have discovered that you do, write down which ones and the types of situations that cause them to surface.

Techniques for Getting in Touch with Your Disowned Selves

If you were unable to find in yourself any of the qualities that annoy you in others, you may be involved in conflict situations where they seem to come up all over the place—always, of course, in the other person.

Try to get in contact with the self in you that possesses a quality you firmly dislike in others. Give it a name. Try to talk with it. If you can't feel it or sense it at first, try the following meditation exercise.

1. Find a quiet, comfortable place in which to sit or lie down. Make sure you'll be free of distractions, and that any others in the household are aware that you do not want to be disturbed.

2. Choose the position in which it's easiest for you to relax completely. If you like to sit in a chair or cross-legged on pillows, fine. If you prefer to stretch out on a bed or mat, do so.

3. Close your eyes and breathe deeply for several minutes, until you feel any tension beginning to leave your body. Notice the rhythm of your breathing; get into it. Become aware of precisely how you are breathing. Are you taking shallow, short breaths from your chest? If so, make sure that you're breathing from your diaphram: Suck your breath slowly up from your belly into your chest, and exhale slowly and calmly. *Note*: You may want to put on some soothing music—or you may prefer complete silence. Do whatever feels best.

4. Relax each part of your body, one by one. Start with your feet; breathe deeply and as you exhale, feel all

the tension leaving your toes, your arches. Imagine that a magic wand is touching your feet and instantly relaxing them. Now, do the same for your legs, pelvis, stomach, chest, arms, neck, face—even your scalp. Continue to breathe deeply and calmly.

5. When you feel very relaxed, think of the most restful and wonderful place you can imagine. It might be a place you already know, like a cabin in the mountains or your favorite hotel on the sea. Or, you might want to create it right now. Once you have the image of this place, think of yourself in it. Imagine it as vividly as you can, contacting it with all of your senses. What does the air smell like? What does the sky look like? What can you touch around you? What noises do you hear?

This is your "safe" place. Whenever you're feeling tense or upset, or whenever you'd like to do some meditation and self-exploration, you can always relax and "go" directly to your safe place in your mind.

6. Once you're comfortable in your safe place, think about the disowned part of yourself that you'd like to contact. What does he/she look like? Picture this disowned self as clearly as you can, noting all features and personal characteristics.

7. When you can see your disowned self, picture him/her coming toward you. Greet this self; invite him/her to sit down beside you.

8. Ask this self his/her name. (You may or may not get a name immediately; don't worry if it doesn't come up in this meditation.)

9. Ask your disowned self how he/she is feeling, and what, if anything, he/she would like to tell you. Try to talk with this self, to discover why you have disowned him/her. Ask it questions. Why was it disowned in the first place, and when? How does it feel when it's neglected or denied? What beneficial part could it play in your life if you gave it the chance? (Hal Stone and Sidra Winkelman's books, *Embracing Ourselves* and *Embracing Each Other* are highly recommended reading for the process of contacting and integrating your disowned selves.)

10. As you become familiar with your disowned self, you can bring in other parts of you—the members of your "internal board of directors"—to talk with that self, and among themselves. This may sound a little like the famous "Sybil" case, in which one woman had sixteen different personalities. But it's really not at all the same. Sybil was a case of a pathological manifestation, where there was absolutely no communication between her different selves, and no awareness of these different selves. But here we're talking to a person—you—who can be and is aware that at different moments, or even simultaneously, there are different parts of you that are having some influence, some power over your thought processes and feelings.

11. When you feel ready to end your meditation, thank your disowned self for being willing to talk with you. Breathing deeply, count down from ten to one, gradually leaving your safe place and, by the count of one, opening your eyes.

You may not encounter your disowned self in your first meditation, or even your second or third. Don't worry about how much time it may take, don't try to speed up the process, and don't become discouraged. Just allow things to develop in their own time. Continue to do this meditation, and eventually the two of you will connect.

Another useful technique for becoming aware of when one of your disowned selves is attempting to be heard is to give it a nickname. A couple I once worked with found this to be quite effective. When the husband admitted that when he was angry he had a tendency to become very cold, almost to the point of "freezing" his wife, they nicknamed that part of him "Old Iceberg." The next time he found himself growing cold and distant, his wife suddenly said, "Oh oh. We'd better duck. Here comes Old Iceberg." Both of them began to laugh, and Old Iceberg eventually became a member of their family who could always be counted on for comic relief.

As you do these exercises, you may find that the conflict or problem situations you've been encountering in your life will begin to be defused. Even more importantly, the chances of their recurring will be substantially diminished. Why? Because you won't be "reacting" so intensely to the external stimuli that once pushed your unconscious buttons.

Not only was Barbara no longer bothered by several aggressive coworkers who had once driven her up the wall—she made the vital connection between the disowned "pushy" part of her and the difficult situations she often encountered as a result of her being *afraid* to be seen as pushy. Invariably, her unwillingness to acknowledge her assertive side *drew demanding and controlling people and situations* to her. And these people and situations were "controlling" her life.

I'd like to emphasize, as I have in previous chapters, that the most important thing is not "solving" the problem—in this case the problem of the disowned self. It's *becoming aware of and in touch with the problem*. Once there's simple awareness—once the light's been turned on—you can see the things you previously couldn't. From there it's merely a matter of the willingness to be observant, and to realize that in choosing whether to act "reactively" or "consciously," we have much more control than we realize over the conflict situations in our lives.

7

Making Negative Emotions Work for You

Anger. Envy. Depression. Hate. The very words conjure up an image of the various rungs of Dante's *Inferno*, where those who indulged in such unbecoming feelings during their lifetimes found, in hell, an ingenious variety of posthumous punishments befitting their earthly crimes.

Thanks to our cultural and religious conditioning, which tends to be highly judgmental and critical in nature, most of us have been taught that it's "bad" to be angry, or envious, or anything else that causes us to feel ill will toward someone else. To be anything less than continuously cheerful and positive, after all, runs counter to certain biblical teachings; if we're worried or upset or frustrated or despairing, we aren't putting our trust in God. And what's worse, we aren't being properly grateful to Him for the daily joys we receive.

While I'm all in favor of counting blessings, I find

that this sort of attitude is actually quite counter-productive, as it tends to pass judgment on our emotions, often causing us to deny or disown those which are considered "negative" by the more liberal proponents of the cheerfulness doctrine and downright "evil" by others.

I have a bit of a problem with the idea of "negative" emotions, primarily because I have a problem with the very word "negative." "Negative" is a label we generally give to qualities or experiences that are commonly considered to be undesirable and nonaffirming. The opposite of "negative," after all, is "positive." That seems to say it all right there. Or does it?

Not really. When you stop to think about it, many of the things in life that we automatically term "negative" are actually positives waiting to be born.

We probably all have discovered, at some time or another in our lives, the treasure hidden beneath a seeming misfortune, the silver lining behind the cloud, the blessing in disguise. Through a relationship that doesn't work out, we accidentally meet the person who's right for us. We get laid off from a job, only to find another that was far better suited to our talents and needs. We break a leg, end up in the hospital for two weeks, and are able to catch up on all the reading, resting and visiting that we'd never had time for until our "terrible" accident.

In other words, an event or experience can be either negative or positive, depending on how we choose to view it and learn from it. And the same is true for our emotions.

While this may seem, at first glance, to be fairly obvious, it isn't. In the previous chapter we talked about our "disowned" selves, those parts of our personalities that we refuse to acknowledge and accept and that we inevitably criticize in others. Disownment is not always obvious; in fact, by its very definition it is an unconscious process. When we take this concept of disownment further, we find that it extends to the very emotions that are such a natural part of human existence—emotions that we tend to view as negative.

There is nothing wrong with any emotion. There is nothing wrong in feeling anger, or jealousy, or hatred, or despair. Feelings are simply that: feelings. To react with rage when we're hit, or hurt when we're insulted or sadness when our dreams are shattered is as natural to our existence as being hungry when we haven't eaten or exhausted when we haven't slept. *Every feeling we experience is normal and valid in the panorama of the human condition*.

So, emotions are neither negative nor positive. They just *are*. It's interesting to look at the words "negative" and "positive" through the eyes of the physicist, who views both states with scientifically calculated objectivity. In dealing with energy, the term "negative" simply refers to a minus direction of said force, whereas "positive" is the plus end of the scale. Both are equally valid, and equally necessary; neither can exist without the other. It's exactly the same with all of the emotions and feelings that form the complex package known as a human being.

That's why even terming an emotion "negative" is making a judgment on it which is prejudicial to its utility. When I speak about negative emotions, then, I'm being descriptive rather than judgmental. I am not implying that there's anything wrong, bad or unhealthy about these emotions; I'm referring, rather, to the general societal view of them, which is that they should be suppressed or disowned rather than accepted and dealt with as a natural part of life.

FEELINGS: SEPARATING THE FACT FROM THE EXPRESSION

I began this book by observing that in and of itself, conflict—which most people view as a negative experience—is actually a natural, healthy and inevitable part of life. If approached constructively, it can often be a *positive* experience for all concerned, leading to increased self-awareness, empathy for others and the development of intra- and interpersonal skills that can help to prevent future conflicts from escalating, or from occurring altogether.

We've been seeing that the successful prevention or response to conflict involves, first of all, the ability to separate our feelings or fears about a person or situation from the reality of the circumstances. We need to "step back" from our emotions in order to get a calmer, more objective view of the situation and to see how large a part our feelings and fears play in distorting or magnifying the facts.

In the same way, neutralizing negative emotions such as anger or fear involves being able to separate the *fact* of the emotion from its *expression*—and from its hold on you.

This separation can be broken down into three steps: the feeling itself, the awareness of that feeling and the expression of that feeling.

1. *The Fact of the Feeling.* When you have a feeling, it's real. Feelings generate palpable, measurable currents of energy throughout our nervous systems. In the

1930s, in an extreme example of this phenomenon, a man known as "Tom" allowed doctors to observe his inner workings through a hole in his stomach, an ostomy through which he'd fed himself since childhood, when he'd gulped down scalding chowder and irreparably damaged his esophagus. Over a period of twenty years, physicians interested in the body's response to stress were able to observe Tom's gastric mucosa, or stomach lining, through his ostomy, and to measure, as one physician put it, "the critical relationship between emotions and visceral function." This relationship was undeniable; Tom's mucosa would turn from its normal pink when he was calm to pale and dry when he was depressed or frightened or to bright red when he was angry, shifting minute by minute along with his emotions.

Feelings are, first of all, involuntary physiological responses. And the *way* in which we react to people or situations is pretty much built into our early childhood conditioning and our DNA. Research has shown that our tendencies toward hot- or even-temperedness, or melancholia or cheerfulness, or nervousness or mellowness, are our birthright and that our initial *reactions* to stimuli will not change throughout our lives.

What can change is how we become aware of and choose to *respond* to those stimuli.

2. *The Awareness of the Feeling*. The next step of the process of separating feelings from their expression involves the awareness of the feeling. While the first step—the actual feeling—cannot be stopped, we begin to have control over what we're feeling at this second stage, when we make the decision either to become aware of it or to deny it.

When confronted with a feeling that causes us discomfort or pain, however, many of us will not even allow ourselves to experience it. We're taught, after all, to bear up under suffering, to "turn the other cheek," to keep a "stiff upper lip." Remember the old maxim, "Sticks and stones may break my bones but names can never hurt me?" We know today that verbal abuse can be even more devastating than its physical counterpart. Many of us who were brought up with this insidious myth learned to deny the pain we felt when we were hurt by criticism or ridicule. The result was that we conditioned ourselves against these feelings, repressing them until we disowned them entirely.

This mechanism of denial is usually so unconscious that we may honestly believe we're not angry or hurt, when indeed we are full of rage and pain. Other people may see it in us, noticing our tight voices, the stiff way we hold our bodies, the cynical or sarcastic way in which we view the world. On a deeper level, denial of our emotions goes hand in hand with illness. Disowned or unexpressed anger has a devastating effect on the immune system; "I'm sick over this" or "He makes me sick" can be self-fulfilling prophecies. Sooner or later our feelings must be owned; if they aren't, they will all too often manifest in the form of dis-ease.

This second step is a critical one in terms of our development as whole, self-actualized, successfully integrated human beings. If we allow ourselves to become aware of our feelings as they come up—not to judge them but simply to be aware of them— we can then move on to the third stage, which is the appropriate expression of those feelings.

3. *The Expression of the Feeling.* At this final stage, we've experienced a feeling, we've had awareness of the feeling and we're ready to express it in some form.

The way in which we express our feelings depends upon the situation. Sometimes if we're angry at someone, it may be entirely appropriate to show that anger directly, as long as we don't hurt or otherwise abuse the other person. Other times it may be more appropriate to pound a pillow or howl when you're alone in the car on the freeway. If someone has hurt us, we may need to burst into tears on the spot. Or, we may need to crawl into bed and have a good cry all by ourselves. The point is that we can choose how we want to express our feelings, or whether or not we want to express them at all.

In the healthiest possible scenario, we will proceed through all three of these steps in dealing with our feelings, allowing the cycle to complete itself and allowing ourselves to move beyond it. When this is the case, interestingly enough, conflict prevention is often the result. But when it comes to negative emotions, most of us do not reach this stage of completion, either because of denial of our feelings or an unwillingness to express them. And the result is repeated conflict, both inner and outer, in our lives.

ANGER: A POWERFUL MECHANISM FOR GROWTH

When it comes to natural feelings and responses, anger is at the top of the list. To say that there "shouldn't" be anger in the world, or that we "shouldn't" get angry is about as sensible as saying that there shouldn't be sand on the beach or fur on a cat.

Anger is a fact of life. It's neither good nor bad; it's

simply energy. In its most basic form, anger is a wonderful indicator of aliveness. It generates an excitement, a current, a creativity. Anger can spur us on to great heights of achievement; some of the greatest works of art have erupted out of rage, and I had some of my best drives in golf when I pretended the ball was the person in my life I most wanted to wallop.

Thus, anger becomes a positive or negative experience depending upon the way in which it's expressed. Like other forms of energy, anger can be used either creatively or destructively.

What's the best way to deal with anger? Well, there is no best way because every situation, and every individual, is different. A humor writer friend of mine once remarked that when she was mad at somebody, she created her finest works of wit and satire. Some people are better off directly confronting the person or situation at the root of the anger. But I can safely say that whatever form it takes, the *expression* of the anger is essential.

As a mediator, one of the most important lessons I've had to learn with clients is to allow anger to take its natural course. While it may be tempting to try to "reason" with the person (to acknowledge their anger in an attempt to get them to calm down and proceed "rationally"), it's usually far better to let the volcano explode if it's going to explode. Of course, I'm always "controlling" the situation; if it looks like the other person can't take the heat, I'll step in to make sure that the recipient is able to receive both the intensity of the anger and the information (or hurt) underneath it. But as long as the other person doesn't attempt to walk out or become violent, the expression of intense anger can be incredibly cathartic and rejuvenating.

Recently I sat calmly in my office while a wife went at her husband with cannons blazing. She was petite, bright and thoroughly charming; he was the proverbial "nice" guy. But suddenly she exploded, accusing him of being "insanely jealous, verbally abusive and potentially violent." When he tried to defend himself, she proceeded to let loose, on and off, for the better part of an hour, with a barrage of yelling and screaming that almost shook the paintings off my walls.

Since she was definitely on a roll, I decided not to interfere. But I watched her husband carefully. Many times he was on the verge of getting up and walking out, but he sat down again. And what happened was that after she finally unloaded, she was able to talk rationally, and even affectionately, about how she saw her husband, and what the real problems were in their relationship and in her own upbringing that had brought them to the doorstep of divorce. When they left my office they were both smiling with relief, and looking forward to their next session with me.

After they left, I thought about many of the observations the wife had made toward the end of the session. They were insightful and honest; it was as if the anger had sharpened her mind. And the expression of the anger allowed her to become more precise about exactly what it was that was bothering her.

This is one of the transformative values of anger, and one of its great utilities. When anger can be expressed in a safe, controlled environment, perceptions that were formerly clouded by rage can become crystal clear. The mind becomes keener as the blunderbuss is traded for a scalpel.

Now in promoting "freedom of anger," I'm not advocating uninhibited abuse, either physical or verbal.

This situation, after all, was a mediated one, and would probably not have been nearly so successful had the couple in question been by themselves. Nuclear reactions need control rods; the expression of anger needs to be monitored as well, so that it doesn't destroy that which it ultimately seeks to understand.

It's very difficult to vent your anger on another person in a noncounseling or mediated situation. The angrier you are, the less in control of your anger you'll tend to be. The mere *unleashing* of anger does little to promote growth. It may make *you* feel better, but chances are it's going to make the object of your rage feel worse, causing them to react fearfully, defensively or just as angrily as you are.

Jake, who's the head of a public relations firm, has a notoriously "short fuse." Whenever he's upset, which is often, he unleashes his volatile temper on whoever happens to be nearby. Then, like a flash flood, it's over and the sun's shining again. Jake feels lots better—but everyone else feels terrible. His employees are afraid of him, and the office atmosphere is understandably tense.

In this instance, the release of anger is not sharpening Jake's mind. It's merely a temporary release of frustration. Until Jake can go inside of himself and discover the real source of his anger, he will continue to use it destructively rather than constructively.

If anger is a regular part of your life—if you either hold it in or unleash it in wild eruptions that you can't seem to control—it's essential for you to do some inner research. What kinds of people and situations tend to enrage you? Why do you think you react the way you do? How do you think you can change your life so that (a) the trigger people and situations in which you find yourself are minimized and (b) you can deal with your anger in a positive rather than harmful way?

Many times we are angry because we have been hurt. We may be conscious of what or who has hurt us, or we may have repressed the source of the pain. Once we can get in touch with the hurt and the pain—through some of the exercises in this book and/or through therapy— we can choose to release our anger in any number of ways that are far healthier than having a temper tantrum at someone else's expense, or keeping a lid on your anger at the expense of your emotional and physical well-being.

Some Techniques for Becoming Aware of and Expressing Feelings

A friend of mine, Gloria, was involved in a problematic relationship with Sam, an older man whom she adored and whom she knew was in love with her. Although they did not have a sexual relationship, they had been each other's constant companion for over a year. But, being very insecure about the age difference between them, Sam had great difficulty facing the depth of feeling he was experiencing for Gloria.

One night Gloria took the bull by the horns and asked Sam how he felt about her. He replied that he thought of her as a "good friend."

"Good friend?" she said incredulously. "Sam, we've done everything together for more than a year. In case you haven't noticed it, we're madly in love with each other too. How can you just say we're 'good friends'?"

Sam grew very defensive. He denied that he was "in love" with Gloria; he even told her that if she wanted to see other men, that was just fine. "I've never tried to be possessive of you," he said.

Gloria did what many women would have done under the circumstances. She burst into tears. This made Sam even more defensive, and he left shortly thereafter, in high agitation.

In assessing the situation, Gloria said, "I know Sam is in love with me. The way he glows when he sees me, the way he calls me all the time, the chemistry in the air when we're together, the incredible closeness we've had—you'd have to be blind, deaf, dumb and brain dead to deny that! But I honestly believe that *he* believes that he's not. I know he's threatened by the age difference between us, and I suspect he may have some sexual problems that are behind his avoidance of physical intimacy. And I think he's talked himself into this absurd notion that we're just buddies, in order to avoid his real feelings. So what I'm wondering is, is he *really* in love with me if he's not letting himself be aware that he is?"

Well, that's a little like the old conundrum, "If a tree falls in the forest and there's nobody around to hear it, did it make any noise?"

The answer, of course, is that certainly the tree made a noise. Just because you may not happen to be in the forest, or you're deaf, or you're a half-mile away doesn't mean that a sound didn't occur. By the same token, just because Sam refuses to admit his love for Gloria doesn't mean that he doesn't love her. He's just a half-mile away, outside the forest of his true feelings.

We've talked about the three steps involved in the "feeling process"—the fact of the feeling, the awareness of the feeling and the expression of the feeling.

Sam may not be aware of his feelings. He may not be willing to express them. But because of how we human beings are wired, it's an absolute certainty that regardless of whether or not Sam has conscious recognition of his feelings, he's *having* them.

Now, through their particular early childhood conditioning, some people's "wiring" may actually inhibit their ability to allow themselves to be aware of certain feelings. Because it's considered "sissy" in our culture to cry or be "mushy," many men are taught to block feelings such as pain or vulnerability and tenderness. And it's not uncommon for women who have been molested as children to feel sexually "numb" toward their husbands or lovers. "I don't feel anything," such a woman will say. "I know I love my husband. But when it comes to sex, I don't *feel* anything for him."

Of course, when we're hurt, we feel pain. But for many people, the feeling may be so deep and terrifying that it is effectively blocked from consciousness. On a less extreme level, we may not be aware of many of the feelings that are engendered in us by a wide variety of everyday situations. We may not be conscious of the effect stress is having on us, or that we're overworking ourselves to avoid loneliness or dissatisfaction at home or that we're overeating because we're afraid to face the pain of a recent loss. Like Sam, we may not even realize that we feel happy and alive with a certain person, because the cacophony of our worries and insecurities is drowning out the sweet song of love.

So the question becomes, how can we become aware of what really is going on inside of us?

The following techniques may be useful in developing a conscious awareness of your feelings. If you're at home, pick a quiet place where you know you won't be disturbed. If you're at work, it will be somewhat more difficult to do this exercise, but you can probably find an empty office or conference room, or another spot where you can be alone for fifteen minutes.

1. *Deep breathe*. The technique of deep breathing in the *chest*, not the *belly*, is highly effective in helping us to connect to our bodies and the cues they are always giving us. At least three or four deep chest breaths are guaranteed to begin shaking things loose, to make us aware of areas in our bodies that are holding stress and tension or emotions that are being suppressed.

Begin by placing your fingers just below your collarbone. Now, breathe deeply into your upper chest. When you can feel your fingers being pushed up, you know that you're deep breathing into your lungs. (This exercise is even more effective if you're lying down.)

As you breathe, become aware of any physical sensations that may be occurring. Is your chest very tight? Do you feel a pressure in your chest that makes you want to cry, or laugh or yell? Are you aware of any muscular aches, any tension in other areas of your body?

Whatever comes up, simply observe it. Don't pass judgment on it, don't worry about it—just *be aware of it*. Eventually, through the deep-breathing process, you may begin to connect certain physical feelings with their underlying emotional promptors.

2. *Sit quietly*. This is more of a formal meditation technique that incorporates relaxed breathing with emptying the mind, as much as possible, of all thoughts. Focus on the natural breathing of your body without attempting to change its rhythm or

depth. As you focus on your breathing while letting your thoughts come and go, not holding on to any of them, there's a good chance that something will come up, because you're sneaking up on it in the silence.

The more mentally "still" you can become, the more easily you'll be able to tune into the inner whisper that is usually drowned out by the cacophony of sound in your mind. And when you tune into the whispering, you'll eventually hear the "silent screaming" of feelings and thoughts that you've neglected or repressed as they bubble to the surface.

3. *Ask and ye shall receive.* If you want to know what to look for in terms of feelings and inner body language, ask somebody. Put the following question to several people: If such and such happened to you, what would you be feeling? And where in your body would you be feeling it? If it turns out that two or three people say the same thing—"I'd be really scared and I'd get a sick sensation in the pit of my solar plexus," or "I'd feel really sad in my throat, just above my chest," then you have a place in which to start looking. Check your body in the places your friends have mentioned, to see whether you might really be feeling something and are just not aware of it.

Then ask yourself, "Is there anyplace in my body that I'm feeling hot or cold? Anyplace I'm feeling vibrations? Am I getting a headache? getting tired?" Put your hands in different places, particularly in the abdominal and chest region. The body always gives clues; you just have to become attuned to noticing them.

If you have discovered an area that seems hot, cold, tense or painful, concentrate on that area. Breathe deeply and try to relax in that particular place. As you are doing this, think of any emotions that could be associated with the feeling in this area. If something comes up—anger, sadness, fear, whatever—*stay with the feeling as long as you can*. Try to look at it simply as a form of energy that needs to be released through crying, yelling, talking or whatever form of expression seems appropriate, and recognize that pain or discomfort is often your body's way of telling you this.

The technique of Reichian therapy, developed many years ago by the noted psychiatrist Wilhelm Reich, approaches emotions through the body. This form of therapy is based on the theory that the body has a memory just like the mind, and that feelings associated with early trauma are stored in the areas of the body that directly experienced the trauma. Through deep muscle massage, the patient is able to connect to these traumas or fears that have, through years of repression, become unconscious memories.

Here's an example of how Reichian therapy works: Alicia, a woman in her forties, was undergoing deep muscle massage. It felt very relaxing—until her masseur began working on her lower left leg. Suddenly Alicia felt a searing pain, followed by intense panic. To her amazement, she began to cry, in pain and terror. Soon afterward she made the connection: At the age of two, she had been bitten by a dog on that exact spot. The deep massage had brought to the surface all of the pain and fear associated with the experience, which through the years had gone underground, into the deep recesses of her psyche. After the release of these feelings, Alicia experienced great peacefulness and a release of tension throughout her body. No wonder— she had expended a great deal of unconscious energy on holding in her emotions, and her body was now allowing her to let them out—and, in the process, to let them go.

The most important thing is to become *aware* of our feelings, and to be willing to accept them and learn from them. Anger, fear and other "negative" emotions can be invaluable friends and wise teachers, a source of tremendous energy and power. But we can't have friends unless we open our hearts to them. We can't learn from a teacher unless we open our minds to him/her. And we can't channel energy creatively until we realize that we ourselves are the true source of the power that can transform our lives.

8

Love Relationships: Karma or Common Sense?

You all know the scenario. Two people lock eyes across a crowded room. Both are drawn inexorably to each other. There is a sense of recognition, of slumbering past lives rising and stretching to meet the present. An inexplicable spark has been ignited—the spark that most people call chemistry, which in turn leads straight into the fire most people call love. And thus is a love relationship born.

But is it love? And is it a relationship? If it is, how can we maintain it? And if it isn't, how can we make it blossom into the kind of caring, sharing partnership most of us are seeking?

Love relationships probably form the basis for the most exhilarating—as well as the most painful—experiences we are likely to encounter in our lifetime. There is nothing like being "in love," in the state of ethereal bliss that causes feet to leave the ground and heads to collide with plate-glass doors. There is also nothing like the torture of unrequited love or of breaking up a love relationship. From the soaring lightness of the satisfied love state, we plummet down, down, down, into the dark cave of despair, where burdens are heavy and joy seems impossible to recapture.

Because love relationships bond us in such deep and unique ways to other human beings, they have often been explained as "karmic" reunions of souls. According to the past-life school of thought, these reunions can either be happy ones, leading to marriage and fulfillment in this life, or they can be painful lessons for growth. Either way, the souls have encountered each other for a purpose: to either pay or cash in on a karmic debt.

I'm not qualified to comment upon the mysterious, complex issues of soul connections and past lives. It could very well be that all of our relationships in this life are karmic ones. But that doesn't mean that they have to be endured if they're unhappy, or that we still don't have to work at them even if they're wonderful. Karmic or not, effective love relationships boil down to effective communication. And as my primary work focuses on helping people in relationships of all kinds to better understand each other, I can attest to the fact that it is, quite frankly, a miracle that human beings can communicate at all, let alone with understanding.

All of us are so different, with our thought processes molded by a myriad of cultural and family influences, that it is quite rare for us to truly understand precisely where another person is coming from. Although two people may be from Los Angeles, supposedly speaking English, I have often found that they might as well hail from other planets when it comes to true communication. As the Spanish writer Una Muno observed, "Every head is a world." We all have our own agendas, our own needs and expectations. We all receive information through the filter of past experience. And so, what we think we hear, or see or feel, may not be at all what the person we love is hearing, seeing or feeling. (This is a familiar phenomenon in business too—business partners also "fall in love," creatively speaking, and go through a "honeymoon" stage, as we'll see in chapter 11.)

Faced with such formidable obstacles, how *do* people get together? Well, this is one of the remarkable ironies of life. On the one hand, here we are, so different and so complex that it's a wonder the human race continues at all. On the other hand, since we are all born with the ability and the capacity to love and relate to everyone, the fact that we all aren't coexisting in perfect harmony is in many ways equally baffling.

Nonetheless, we do get together, do fall in love, do make our attempts, however bumbling, to peacefully and meaningfully coexist. But those attempts don't necessarily have to be as hit-and-miss as they often are. Precisely because each of us has within us the potential for universal love, it is indeed possible to maximize this potential in our intimate love relationships. We *don't* have to enter into relationships that spell disaster, and we *can* make troubled relationships work. All it takes is the *intention* and the *willingness* to discover what's going on inside of ourselves and each other, and to *process* that information, carefully and constantly.

THE LOVE TRIANGLE

The triangle is the most stable geometric form. By the same token, there are three key elements to any enduring relationship that, when present, form a triangle of love.

I have discovered that the overriding difference between those relationships that work over a long period of time and those that don't has to do with the presence or absence of the following characteristics:

1. *The "spark."* There is usually an almost intuitive, energetic connection between two people that is unexplainable on any logical basis. This connection can be instantaneous, or it can come with time. It is commonly known as "chemistry," and it is a necessary ingredient to any long-term love relationship.

2. *The intention and the willingness to be aware of and process everything of significance.* In order for two people to live and grow together, they must be in real, active human communication with each other. They must be willing to explore what's working and what isn't. They must have the desire and intention to resolve any disputes, or, on the more positive side, to make life wonderful for each other.

The other day I saw a bumper sticker that hit this particular nail on the head: "Love isn't a feeling; it's a commitment." Nothing could be truer. The "feeling" of love, of passion, of desire will quickly fade without the corresponding commitment to the growth and happiness of both the one you love and yourself.

3. *Commonality of purpose, values and interests.* In order for a love relationship to grow and deepen, certain common life themes must be shared. These themes can involve spiritual or religious matters, a philosophy of life, marriage and family, a business or profession or creative and artistic activities. Whatever the common ground, both parties have to till the soil, making sure that it doesn't become parched through neglect. Shared values or activities provide the basis for years of mutual enjoyment, interaction and growth, whereas if two people are too dissimilar and come together primarily out of sexual attraction, chances are that they will eventually drift apart.

When love relationships—or even business partnerships and family businesses—get into difficulty, it's usually because one or two of these three essential elements is missing. Instead of a cohesive, committed relationship, you get two people operating from their own perspectives without joining together in a true partnership.

When two people enter into a relationship with only one of the necessary ingredients binding them, there is very little hope for either love or marriage to endure. If they are simply drawn together because of chemistry, but share no common themes and have neither the interest nor the ability to explore mutual growth, a brief affair is often the result. If there are common interests but no spark and no commitment to partnership, you have a friendship. And if there is a mutual willingness to explore and process a relationship with no common interests and no spark, you have a very strange situation, to say the least!

Now, what happens when two out of three of these

elements exist? Well, that depends on which two we're talking about.

Of these three relationship requirements, by far the most important is *the intention and willingness to process*. This commitment to mutual growth and understanding is the primary quality that makes any relationship—whether it's business, friendship or love—continue and prosper. And this willingness to constantly explore and communicate is what this book is all about.

When the *intention and willingness to process* is one of the two-out-of-three elements present in a love relationship, the relationship has a chance to work. Without it, the chances are virtually nonexistent. When you combine chemistry with good communication, the lack of common interests can be overcome. When you combine common interests with good communication, chemistry may eventually result. But attraction and shared activities without the commitment to growth will probably result in a relationship that is, at its center, hollow and unfulfilled. In such a relationship, neither party is truly known to the other, and the possibility for misunderstanding and stagnation is high.

Unfortunately, lack of true and honest communication is a problem in many, if not most, marriages. We tend, after all, to marry for many reasons, from passionate addiction to the desire for security or the craving for the attention we never received as children. And in the process, we comfortably blind ourselves to all sorts of uncomfortable realities. A woman may find a man's overwhelming concern for his mother noble and admirable before marriage, whereas after marriage the same nobility suddenly and inexplicably becomes neurotic. A man may find his fiancée's inability to make up her mind adorable, until he is faced with this behavior day in and day out, at which point it becomes so frustrating that he finds himself wistfully drawn to women who have a strong sense of self. In a movie I saw recently, the main character, an unhappy wife in a stale marriage, summed up this state of disillusionment in the following observation about her husband: "He used to love me because he thought I was a nutcase. Now he just thinks I'm a nutcase!" In marriage, we too often go to bed as lovers and wake up strangers, wondering how it all happened, unwilling to admit that the signs were there all along. We were just reading them upside down—or not at all.

My friend Ronald and his former wife, Lena, really should never have gotten married in the first place. They were simply too different from each other. But as is the case with so many couples, their differences were what initially drew them together. Sparks flew from the moment they met; Ron found Lena absolutely fascinating precisely because she seemed to possess many qualities that *he* didn't have. What a remarkable, mysterious being she was! What a challenge it was going to be, to win her!

Ron was a very "feeling-oriented" sort of person who tended to be easygoing. Lena was a far more structured, "mind-oriented" personality who, at the same time, could be quite volatile. It wasn't until they were married that Ron began to see that the aspects of his wife's personality that were complex, challenging and exciting were not necessarily the best aspects to bring into a partnership with a more laid-back person like himself.

But by the time Ron came to terms with the fact that his marriage wasn't working, he and Lena had a child, a new house and a vastly more complicated life to contend with.

Now, you might say, "Well, how could Ron and Lena know that these differences between them were actually so great? Isn't that sort of realization a function of experience?" To which I would reply, "No." Intuitively Ron knew about all of the ways that he and Lena didn't mesh. He simply didn't want to pay attention to them. Instead, he preferred to allow himself to be carried away by the energy, the desire, the severely misguided perception that Lena had all the qualities that he didn't have, and that if he "possessed" her, he would somehow acquire them. By the same token, Ron had many of the qualities that Lena felt were missing in her own life.

In the beginning, both Ron and Lena viewed this gap between them as a positive thing. They were two halves of a whole, they thought. Ron's flexible nature could complement Lena's rigidity. He could make her more flexible; she could add a little focus to his life. He could calm her when she was angry; she could excite his passions with her intensity. He could take care of business—never Lena's forte—and she could be intellectual and creative, domestic and stimulating. Together they could both take care of each other forever.

Sound familiar? There's a popular term out there today for this insidious kind of behavior. It's called "codependency," and it seems to characterize the majority of relationships that commonly come under the classification of love. Now, the kind of codependency described above is generally more successful in business than in love relationships. It is often beneficial to have a "Mr./Ms. Inside" and a "Mr./Ms. Outside" in a business partnership. And a division of talents—various

VPs in charge of sales, human resources, marketing—works well when there is successful communication in a corporate atmosphere. Such an arrangement, however, is not generally successful in love relationships, because sooner or later both people tend to "wake up" and resent what they have given away or what has slipped out of their control.

I don't want to spend a lot of time going into the dynamics of codependent relationships, because there's plenty that's already been written on that ever-fertile topic. What I *would* like to discuss is how we can avoid, through proper awareness and communication, the conflicts in love that lead to the breakdown and eventual dissolution of a relationship.

TECHNIQUES FOR MAXIMIZING THE POSSIBILITY OF SUCCESS IN LOVE

1. *Do not become attached to the label or form of a relationship.* Don't immediately think, "This is the one! This is the one I want to marry, or go steady with, or have children with," or whatever it is your mind and hormones are conning you into expecting. As Mark Twain said about work, "Every time I think about it, I sit down until the feeling goes away!"

It's a crime against yourself to *label* a relationship at the outset, because it creates such craziness in your mind. Most of what we think we perceive at the outset of a relationship can all be boiled down to our own projections. We dream about the "perfect" person, the "perfect" job, the "perfect" life. Then we try to make the situation fit into the very narrow doorway of our expectations. This can take a great deal of squeezing and pushing, and in the end it is usually extremely exhausting. For just as there is no way to jam a square peg into a round hole, so there is no way to make someone else conform to your expectations of what they should or shouldn't be. And similarly, there is no way to totally control situations and circumstances. Too often we want to discover the elixir of the "perfect" life and bottle it. But when we bottle up life, it tends to eventually explode in our faces.

The great Tibetan lama, Chogyam Trungpa, had this to say about the self-deceptions engendered by expectation:

> As long as you regard yourself or any part of your experience as the "dream come true," then you are involved in self-deception. Self-deception seems always to depend upon the dream world, because you would like to see what you have not yet seen rather than what you are seeing. You will not accept that whatever is here now *is* what is, nor are you willing to go on with the situation as it is. Thus, self-deception always manifests itself in terms of trying to create or re-create the nostalgia of the dream experience. And the opposite of self-deception is just working with the facts of life.

In order for any relationship to be of maximum benefit to us, we must be willing to do two things. We must be willing to take reality by the horns, and we must be willing to surrender to the facts of life, moment by moment, day by day. We must be willing to meet a man or woman, "fall" in love with them, and not expect any more from them than what they are able to give. We must be willing to let the relationship grow into itself, at its own pace, rather than construct a scenario that may or may not be appropriate for it. Above all, we must be willing to accept the fact that the state of being "in love" does not necessarily imply anything beyond this. We do not "have" to marry someone with whom we are utterly enchanted. Instead, we can allow ourselves to have feelings, and hopes and dreams, without immediately assuming that marriage will insure that these dreams will come true. (And, as we'll see in chapter 11, the same is true for budding business partnerships.)

Every time we try to change a person or a relationship into something else, we're actually committing a form of theft. In criminal law, there's a term known as "conversion." Say I loan you my car with my permission and you go off and take the car out of state and keep it for a year. You have illegally "converted" our agreement and your action is a form of theft. Similarly, when in a relationship, you *take* something on your own, without consulting the other person, and move it into something else, it's as if you've stolen something from the other person. You've converted it into something it wasn't. And that's a crime that people do eventually pay for, in the form of failed expectations and disillusionment.

2. *Learn how to talk to yourself.* Now, maybe you've created something where nothing exists—or even worse, you've discussed your expectations with the other person and you both have agreed upon them, even when they are not appropriate within the context of the relationship. How do you deal with that?

The best way to become grounded in the actual reality of a relationship is to actively engage in the process of "self-talk." There are different levels of self-talk. One is observational—simply being aware of what's going on. What are you feeling? What are you thinking? What are the feelings in your body? You may answer, "I'm feeling a strong sexual desire for this person. My mind is resenting the fact that he or she is not responding to me. The frustrated feeling is being translated by my body into a knot in my stomach."

This sort of observation is absolutely basic. If you try to leapfrog over it, there's a high probability that you've blown it. You're trying to get to home plate without running the bases, and you're going to get called out. Those are the rules of the game. And first base is, "What's going on here and now?"

When you engage in observational self-talk, you do not attach judgments to your thoughts or feelings. You simply observe them. As in the methodology of classic analysis, where the patient talks and the analyst simply sits there, saying nothing, attaching no values to anything he's hearing, here you're both patient and analyst. You are *allowing* yourself to simply *be* with all your thoughts and feelings, however appropriate or inappropriate they may seem.

In conjunction with this form of observational self-talk is the instruction to let yourself feel whatever you're feeling, to really get into it. If you think you've found your true love and you know your feelings are running away with you, give yourself a paradoxical instruction. Tell yourself to actually *increase* those feelings. Go bananas, go wild. Just don't let your heart move into your head. Realize that it's just your heart, or your gonads or whatever. But don't try to stop the feelings, and don't let them mean anything more than they mean in and of themselves. It's like exorcising a demon. What happens to a lot of people is that they have a feeling and they're scared by that feeling. So they immediately change it into something else more "acceptable," out of a fear of really going with it or the notion that they have to make some sort of conclusion out of it. "This is true, therefore this has to follow." What I'm saying is, forget the "therefore" and go with the "this." Remain in the moment, not in a projection of the moment.

The second level of self-talk involves having your "thinking" mind talk to one of your feelings. You talk to your churning stomach, or to your fear that Mary will never love you as you do her and the relationship will end. This in turn leads to another level of self-talk where two disparate parts of you are actually having a fight and trying to work it out. "How come you're in love with her? She's not the right person for you!" "Oh yes, she is! I'm just not good enough for her." "Oh, no? You certainly are good enough for her!" "Why?" "Because you're kind and understanding and bright and you deserve better than what you're getting." And so on, until your perceptions become more balanced and less emotional.

There are other kinds of self-talk. One involves the "planning" mind, where your immediate mind is talking to your future mind. Here you may be preparing a conversation, practicing it. "When I see Mary, I'm going to tell her, 'Listen. This is the way I feel about you, and I'm not sensing a similar feeling on your part. Am I correct? Or are you feeling things for me and just not expressing them?' " Then there's critical self-talk, where you play the parent with yourself. "Gosh, I'm so dumb sometimes! Why did I say that to her? Why didn't I do this instead of this?"

These various kinds of self-talk are quite useful when dealing with conflicts, because conflicts begin in the mind and the way you talk to your mind is the precursor of the actual external dispute. So, if you can become the different parts of yourself and resolve the conflict *within*, you've got a much better chance of never even becoming involved in a conflict with the other person.

3. *Never expect the other person to change.* How many times do we fall in love with someone whose personality or personal circumstances are not quite up to our ideal? How many times do we get involved with such a person—even marry them—with the hope that they or their situation will change? And how many times are we disappointed, disillusioned, devastated?

It is a tragic mistake to assume that a man who's quiet and uncommunicative will suddenly come to life once you marry him, or that a woman who's a workaholic will suddenly metamorphose into a homebody once she's wearing your ring on her finger. It's an equally tragic mistake to continue in a dissatisfying relationship with someone who can't seem to make a commitment to you in the hopes that he or she will eventually "come to their senses."

If you don't want to check into the Heartbreak Hotel—which, as full as it already is, always seems to have a vacancy sign on the door—you must understand and accept the universal truth that in a relationship, *what you see is what you get.* In other words: Your married lover is married; your skittish boyfriend isn't ready to settle down yet; the woman of your dreams has an alcohol problem. That's the way it is, and your decision to either remain in or leave the relationship must be based on the assumption that the things you aren't happy with may never change.

In addition to the old truism that you can't change another person is the equally valid truism that you are highly unlikely to change yourself either. You probably won't be able to extinguish or eliminate your own feelings or ways of responding to the world. You can, however, change the *balance of forces* within you to allow you to better deal with a person or situation.

In order not to be driven crazy by events beyond your control in a relationship, you must begin to look within rather than without for answers to your dilemma. Becoming a keen observer of all of your subparts gives you the ability to emphasize some of them and deemphasize others. If, for instance, your beloved's refusal to propose to you is giving you a peptic ulcer, and you observe that part of you that is becoming so upset, you can say, "Okay. I'm allowing myself to acquire a peptic ulcer over this situation. Why?"

You may get an answer like, "Well, I can't live without him. I need him in my life to survive." You can then evaluate that answer as to its reality. Logically, you know you can survive without this person. But emotionally you may feel as though you will "die." You can then move into an exploration of what, precisely, "death" means to you, and, correspondingly, what life means. You may deal with the part of yourself that is terrified of abandonment. You may deal with the part that yearns to fulfill the dream of marriage and a family. You may conclude that, "Okay. I realize that it's all right to be terrified of abandonment, it's all right to want marriage and a family. It's just not all right to expect this other individual to fulfill my needs, or cure my hang-ups."

Now you have the choice of remaining in the relationship *as it is*, or leaving it for something that better suits your needs. You may find yourself able to accept the fact that you're not happy and need to find another man or woman. Or you may decide that remaining in the relationship is better for you, at this point in time, than leaving it. Whatever your choice, however, it will be a *conscious* one. (The same internal calculus goes on when you are deciding on job or career changes.) Remember: You can change how you deal with people and situations only to the extent that you can deal with the complex and ever-present forces within you.

And most importantly, how do we know when a relationship just won't work? Well, this is, of course, a very individual matter. But I don't feel that it's very healthy to fall in love, or to remain in a relationship with the hope of marriage or exclusive partnership, unless all three points of the love triangle are present. In my own life, I have found an interesting parallel to this philosophy in my work. What I say to potential clients is, "I don't even want to get started in a mediation case unless I feel it has a high probability of reaching a successful resolution." And that goes for my personal relationships as well. Now, I'm not telling you to refrain from relationships until your "perfect" partner comes along. All I'm suggesting is that you accept a relationship for what it is, and then make a conscious choice as to whether or not it's enough for you. Because as hard as you push and shove, you're probably not going to get any more than you now have. You can only change your response to it.

4. *Never attach too much importance to the words.* Carla, a friend of mine, is involved in an unusually

problematic love relationship. She is a thirty-six-year-old artist and the man of her dreams is a Catholic priest. Needless to say, not only are the circumstances not particularly conducive to the marriage she wishes for, but the differences in background and perception between her and John pose very nearly insurmountable obstacles to meaningful communication. Carla is open, bubbly and extremely verbal and articulate, whereas John is quiet and shy. Carla was brought up to gear toward relationships with the opposite sex; John has never touched a woman, and his strict seminary training has instilled in him a fear of the opposite sex. Carla longs for marriage; John's desire to remain a priest means that he can never marry.

Then why, you might rightly ask, is Carla involved with John? Well, that's easy. The two of them are "in love," if by "in love" we mean excited by and longing for the presence of each other. Thus, although Carla is well aware that her chances for not only marrying John, but having a marriage that would actually work, are comparable to winning the lottery, she is willing to explore other alternatives in her desire for a meaningful relationship.

I didn't discourage Carla from her difficult quest, because she obviously has something to play out here in terms of her own growth. But I did give her some tips on how to "read" John, admittedly a difficult thing to achieve given his shyness and degree of repression.

The first thing I told her was never to assume that what *she* is feeling is what *he* is feeling, or what he is saying is what she would mean if she made the same statement.

For instance, when John went on vacation to visit his family, Carla received a card from him, saying, "You are remembered daily." Since she missed him very much and thought of him every minute, her natural and immediate assumption was that John was conveying similar emotions, especially since the card had arrived so quickly.

But John is a priest. I deflated Carla's romantic balloon somewhat by sharing with her the story of a priest I knew, who told me that while I was in Vietnam, I was remembered daily in his prayers. I also pointed out to her that John had respectfully distanced himself from her by using the formal, passive form of "You are remembered," rather than the active "I remember you." In other words, John's choice of grammar was very telling. His statement could be read the way Carla wanted to read it: "I miss you, I love you, I think of you all the time." Or it could be interpreted the way a priest may have wanted her to interpret it: "Every time I say my prayers, I include you in them."

The point is, there was no way of knowing *what* John meant, unless Carla came out and asked him point-blank. The only information she was qualified to deduce from his card was that he was thinking of her. In what context, or to what end, only he could say, and even then, he might not be capable of articulating his deepest feelings.

Two weeks later, John called Carla. This was a major event. Although he didn't say, "I love you," or even "I miss you," Carla felt that it was implied, especially after he said, "I'll be back next week. It will be good to see you."

Carla was ecstatic. From a silent, withdrawn man like John, such an admission was tantamount, in her mind, to a proposal of marriage. She immediately began planning for their grand reunion, convinced that when they saw each other again, they would simply fall into each other's arms and the words they had both carried in their hearts for so long would be uttered at last.

I cautioned Carla not to view John's phone call as anything more than a phone call.

"But you don't know John," she argued. "It was a big thing for him to call me. Especially from his family's house."

"It may have been a big thing," I replied. "But it doesn't mean that it's going to go beyond what it was: a phone call. I'm not saying he isn't in love with you; what I'm saying is that, being a priest, he can be in love with you and never do anything about it. Or he can try to deny those love feelings entirely, when they get too frightening. Whatever he does, though, the chances are that what *you* mean by love and what *he* means are two different things."

I asked Carla what John's being "in love" with her meant to her.

"He thinks about me all the time," she promptly replied. "He fantasizes about me. He wants to be with me."

"That's what *you* mean by being in love with John," I said. "It doesn't necessarily follow that his interpretation of love is yours."

As we know from the earlier portion of this book, in order to understand what another person intends to communicate, we often must be extremely adept at gathering intelligence, i.e., obtaining information. We cannot afford to take words at their face value, for we invariably attach too many personal values to them. We have to get information in different ways. When

Carla asked me what my criteria were for someone being in love with someone else, I constructed a checklist. When all of the following elements coexist, someone may be said to be "in love," and ready for a more extended commitment.

- *The magic words,* whatever the appropriate words are for that couple. When a man or woman says, "I love you," "I want you" or makes similar admissions of desire, you may assume an intention to enter into a committed partnership. But that assumption can't be validated unless his/her voice tone, body language and actions support the words.

- *A voice tone that's consistent with those words.* When a potential client calls me for an appointment, I find myself listening far more to the tone of his or her voice than to what is being said, for this gives me far more accurate insight into the personality I'm dealing with and whether or not I want to take them on as a client. Similarly, in relationships it behooves us to become adept at listening to the "words between the lines." When you ask someone, "How are you?" and they reply, "Fine," in a flat monotone, you know they aren't. Being aware of such inconsistencies is crucial in communication. If someone says, "I love you" without the appropriate accompanying tone quality in their voice, beware. It would be like playing circus music at a funeral. Something isn't right.

- *Body language that's consistent with the admission of love.* Jennie was very much in love with Philip. And Philip always told Jennie that he loved her. The problem was, as he said the words he often jumped up in the middle of an embrace, or kissed her hurriedly and changed the subject. The fact was that Philip didn't love Jennie and was actually carrying on an affair with another woman. Unfortunately, Jennie clung to his words as "proof" of his love, ignoring the other vastly more revealing clues he was giving her.

If someone says, "I love you," what is their body saying? Is there an accompanying warm and caring embrace? Is there the willingness to be physically close? Body language must be consistent with words in order for a successful love relationship to blossom.

• *Conduct.* Do the person's actions support the words of love? There are many questions you will need to ask yourself here. What is the person's capacity, their ability to love? Are you up against some kind of block? Are they capable of carrying out what they say they will? Just as a paraplegic can't be in a foot race, so an emotionally crippled person will not be capable of fully loving another.

In Carla's case, the answers to these questions were clear, if not happy, indications that a love relationship between her and John was an impossibility. His ability to love her as a woman and a wife was virtually nil. Even if he said, "I love you," and meant it, he was prevented from acting on that love by the moral and physical obligations of the priesthood.

You will want to ask yourself how your love interest is using his or her resources. Are they putting their money where their mouth is? How do they use their time? If somebody vows eternal love to you but gives you 2 percent of their time, what does this mean?

How consistent is their present behavior with past conduct? If it's different, can you explain it? Is it an aberration? How real is it? If a man says he loves you but has broken up with three women in the past six months, what exactly does he mean by "love"?

In addition to this checklist is the checkup on yourself that you are obligated to perform. What is your own bias? What do you want or need to hear or see? How does this affect what you're perceiving in the other person?

Unless you consciously ask yourself all of these questions, there's a reasonable possibility that you're going to lead yourself astray in a relationship.

Finally there's the element of "intuition." Carla often said that she "knew," intuitively, that John loved her. "Even if he can't say the words, even if he's shy or scared, it's something I *know*," she insisted. "It's just there, between us, like a living, breathing entity. And it's not there with other men that I'm with."

I have no quarrel with Carla's statement. When all is said and done, our intuition is the single most important voice we need to listen to. But even though Carla's intuition was probably on target, it did not necessarily follow that because John loved her, he wanted to marry her.

Intuition is the label we give to the unconscious application of all of the information we've gathered. Ultimately, your conduct should be guided by your intuition. But in order to use intuition efficiently, you have to put it in its proper place. In Carla's case, the question to ask was not "What does my intuition tell me about whether or not John loves me?" but rather, "What does my intuition tell me about the possibility of John leaving the priesthood, marrying me and becoming a satisfactory husband?" When I asked her to answer that, she sighed.

"It tells me we'll never be married, that he's too set in his ways and too afraid of sex."

While that made Carla sad on one level, it helped her to put the relationship in its proper perspective, and to deal with what was possible rather than what wasn't. She and John ended up remaining close friends. They go to an occasional movie together, take drives, have dinner. It isn't what she originally dreamed of, but she is able to appreciate what she and John can give to each other, and to realize that had her dreams, by some wild stroke of the imagination, become reality, the result would most likely have been disastrous for both of them.

There's one more thing about "words." People often use them to try them out, to see how they fit. Or they may be trying to convince themselves of something. So what you're taking as a communication is actually only a dry run, in which they, like you, may be hearing these words for the first time. Needless to say, this crossing of signals makes true communication very difficult, confirming the fact that we cannot afford to rely upon words alone in our attempts to understand another. We must depend upon other sources of information in order to achieve maximum clarity of perception in a situation.

Buddhist wisdom guides us in this direction with the following advice:

1. Listen to the *words* more than to the *person*.
2. Listen to the *content* more than to the *words*.
3. Listen to the *ultimate meaning* more than to the *content*.

4. Listen to your *internal experience* more than to the *intellectual meaning*.

And once we've perceived the situation for what it is, we have to let go of it in order for it to reach its full potential. Chogyam Trungpa has a beautiful reflection upon gaining true spiritual awareness through surrender. He is speaking here of the relationship to one's "spiritual friend," one's guru, but I believe it applies to all love relationships:

Surrendering is not a question of being low and stupid, or of wanting to be elevated and profound. It has nothing to do with levels and evaluations. Instead we surrender because we would like to communicate with the world "as it is." We know where we stand; therefore we make the gesture of surrendering, of opening, which means communication, link, direct communication with the object of our surrendering.

9

Divorce: From Pain to Peace

The very word "divorce" sends a shudder of mega-negativity through most people. After all, divorce is associated with an infinite number of unpleasant experiences, from hostilities that turn otherwise reasonable, loving people into raging beasts coming at each other with fangs bared, to the wrenching pain of dealing with children, the innocent victims. And, of course, the equally wrenching pain of facing what most of us perceive as our own inadequacy, as we try unsuccessfully to salvage a relationship that society still tells us should have lasted forever.

However, after the painful experience of my own divorce, coupled with the countless divorce cases I have mediated and a generous dose of Eastern philosophical wisdom thrown in along the way, I am happy to report that divorce need not be a totally negative experience. In fact, with a healthy outlook and intention, divorce can be one of the most liberating steps we can take toward renewing our relationships with both ourselves and others.

Divorce is usually condemned on religious and cultural grounds as a failure—the failure of a man and woman to live up to the requirements of their social, religious, legal and sexual roles. It doesn't seem to matter that today, unhappy marriages and divorce are the norm and happily-ever-after marriages the exception. We still hunger for the romantic dream of the perfect partnership, and still punish ourselves with a lifetime of guilt if our marriage does not turn out the way it was "supposed" to.

Don't misunderstand me: I am not necessarily in favor of divorce. In fact, whenever I act as a professional mediator to couples in troubled marriages, I generally spend our initial time together trying to see if there is a basis for staying together and/or making sure that a divorce is actually necessary. Because I have a bias in favor of couples remaining together whenever possible, I want at least one of them to be certain that a breakup is best for all concerned.

But neither do I perceive divorce as either a failure or an unrelentingly miserable state of affairs. While admittedly a life-shaking experience, divorce is also a major transformation. Whether it is a negative or a positive one depends entirely on the outlook of the people involved.

All growth is painful, all change disturbing. On the University of Minnesota stress test, which was developed some years ago and has since become a landmark in the evaluation of the effects of stress on one's health and lifespan, many of the situations considered to be stressful merely involve some sort of change. Death of a spouse, divorce and marital separation head the list in terms of stress "points." But a change in financial state, a change to a different job, a change in residence, a change in church activities are also considered stress producers. None of these changes are necessarily for the worse—one can easily change to a better job or a higher income and still experience the effects of stress. In fact, "marital reconciliation" is, according to the experts, on the top-ten list of stressful activities that can adversely affect one's health!

In other words, most human beings do not adapt particularly well to change. So, we have to change our attitudes toward change before the positive aspects of those changes in terms of our self-growth can be realized and utilized.

Therefore, I would like to help you to change your attitude toward divorce.

DIVORCE IS NOT CONFLICT

One of the first ways to begin is to understand precisely what divorce is—and what it *isn't*. When we hear the word "divorce," most of us immediately think of a conflict of some sort. But *divorce is not a conflict*! Divorce is simply a desire on the part of either one or both partners in a marriage to *restructure* the relationship. The present partnership is no longer workable; thus it must be restructured, emotionally, economically, parentally. Now, divorce often is a *result of* conflict or *leads* to conflict. But in and of itself, divorce is not a conflict.

This is a very subtle distinction, but it's a very important one in the conduct of the divorce, for the principals as well as any professionals involved in it. If every couple contemplating divorce fully understood what I have just said, there would be far less need for most representational lawyers to whom divorce was, is and must always remain a conflict, till death do us part. For in this society, divorce is, more often than not, a battle waged not so much by the couple as by the lawyers they have engaged to fight for them. It is interesting, in fact, how the term "fighting for" the client already prejudices the situation at the very beginning of divorce. Divorce is considered synonymous with conflict, not to mention germ warfare, depending on how high the stakes are and how much the lawyer stands to profit from stimulating, escalating and/or coattail-riding of an unnecessary battle.

Although I myself am a lawyer by education and license, the misuse of the art of litigation never ceases to sadden me. Not only do many couples who choose to go the representational lawyer route experience unnecessary financial and emotional anguish as proceedings drag out for months or even years, but they never know the profound joy of self-healing so often experienced through a more direct approach to divorce. Instead, having hired others to "do their fighting" for them, they find themselves cheated out of the opportunity to discover better means of communication with their partner, an awareness of ways in which they need to change in order to have a satisfying relationship in the future and a method of mutual nonantagonism that tremendously speeds the healing of the very real divorce wound.

So, if you are willing to explore the possibility of "restructuring" your present relationship with your husband or wife in a compassionate, noncombative way, remember: A divorce is not a conflict. It is merely a change. How you handle it depends on whether or not it will escalate into a conflict.

It's interesting to note that legally, divorce is considered a "dissolution" of the relationship—a word I find intriguing because of its resemblance to "dissillusion." A dissolution is a dissolving, which is how many people feel in a divorce. Not only is the marriage dissolving, one's entire world can seem to be dissolving, not to mention one's very self. And what is disillusion? Seeing and curing oneself of whatever illusions—unrealities, fantasies, unrealizable hopes and dreams—you may have had and beginning the process of dealing with reality. That process is usually accomplished in a series of stages that parallel our reactions, as human beings, to loss in general.

THE STAGES OF DIVORCE

When one spouse moves toward a divorce, there is always a certain amount of emotional upheaval, even if the decision to pursue divorce is a relief. Many couples have seen separation or divorce on the horizon for years, but have avoided the inevitable as long as possible. When one of them finally acknowledges it, the response of the other can be one of near-gratitude, to have the cards finally out on the table.

On the other hand, the statement of intentions or the act of moving out often seems to come "out of the blue," for instance, after the confession of an affair that the wife or husband knew nothing about, setting the stage for major emotional trauma.

Whatever the circumstances, the pain of impending separation from a marriage, a home, children cannot be minimized. And with this pain usually comes anger, guilt and an onslaught of related feelings guaranteed to block communication until they are accepted and properly dealt with.

The emotional stages of divorce parallel the famous stages of dying first described by Dr. Elisabeth Kübler-Ross in her book, *On Death and Dying*. Divorce, after all, is a death, the end of a crucial phase of one's life. In fact, Kübler-Ross's observation of the response to death and dying probably applies to many critical passage points in life. (It is interesting to note that in ancient methods of divination such as the Runes and Tarot, the card or stone signifying death was not interpreted literally, but rather as change, transformation, the end of one phase and the beginning of another.)

Whether it is only one spouse's idea, or whether it is mutually agreed upon, the divorce will usually engender the same stages of emotional response for each spouse.

1. *Denial.* "This can't be happening to me."

Denial is often the first response to the awareness that your marriage is ending. Denial may take several forms. You may find yourself focusing on all of the good aspects and memories of your marriage and blocking out the difficult times. You may refuse to accept responsibility in any way, shape or form for the breakup, even though your wiser self knows that no marriage is a one-sided affair. Or you may insist that the marriage can be saved, all the while knowing, down deep, that it has ended.

In the case of my friend Ron, whom I mentioned in the previous chapter, denial took the form of refusing to accept reality when his wife, Lena, was having an affair under his nose. Their marriage was already troubled and they had been working on it. They were both enrolled in a marriage and family counseling graduate program when Lena felt an instantaneous antipathy to one of their professors. Immediately after their first stormy meeting, Lena came home ranting and raving about how much she hated him. Out of the blue, Ron told her of an immediate intuition he had—that they would have an affair.

Lena was properly indignant. She told Ron point blank that he was crazy, but that at best she would "try to tolerate the SOB."

To her great surprise, Lena and the professor did become friends. In fact, it was her first real adult friendship with a man, and she regularly reported its ups and downs to Ron. Ron wasn't threatened; he and Lena were still together and everything was moving right along. It wasn't until many months later that he found out that the professor and his wife were indeed involved with each other.

Lena and the professor eventually went off together and got married. All the signs, of course, had been evident from the beginning, blazing as if in neon. Everyone else knew, but Ron was wearing the dark glasses of denial. After his initial intuitive "hit," he simply hadn't wanted to see what was going on—to really accept, once and for all, that their marriage was ending.

2. *Anger.* "Damn him/her! If only he/she hadn't gone out on me, we'd still be together."

When you realize that the dream of your marriage is dying and the fragile thread of intimacy between you has snapped, the sense of despair can be overwhelming. You need someone or something to blame; it may be your spouse, a third party or yourself. Whoever it is, you must realize that like a fever, anger needs to run its course before healing can begin.

During this time, logic and objectivity take a back seat to raging emotion. (In her book, *Mom's House, Dad's House*, Dr. Isolina Ricci calls this the "off the wall" stage.) You need to allow yourself to let go and express any negative feelings in a safe, nonthreatening way. Above all, don't let guilt over having these feelings compound your misery. If you find yourself acting "inappropriately," by "taking it out on" your spouse, your children, your best friend, realize that you are out of control, that you don't mean to hurt anyone else, that you're still a good person. Then get some sort of counseling as soon as possible, to begin putting your anger in perspective.

3. *Bargaining*. "If I change my cleaning habits, will you stay? . . . If you stop that affair, I'll remain with you and the kids . . ."

One or both of you may put great effort into a last-ditch attempt to salvage your marriage. After all, loss and rejection is just about the worst kind of pain we can experience. So it's natural to do anything to make the pain go away.

But putting a Band-Aid on a gut-ripping wound will stop neither the pain nor the bleeding. Bargaining for time does not address the deeper issue of the lack of communication that caused the rupture in the first place. Once a divorce is set in motion, you can't turn the clock back. There's only one direction to travel in, and that's straight ahead. You may learn how to communicate with each other in such a way that you can get back together. Or you may discover that a reunion is impossible. Whatever happens, you will have learned something. But if you simply try to keep the house cleaner, or pretend that your wife never fell in love with someone else, you'll soon realize that you're just prolonging the agony.

4. *Acceptance*. Once you realize that denial is futile, once your anger has begun to dissipate, once you've played your bargaining chips and lost, acceptance of the reality of your situation becomes possible.

Acceptance may be grudging, ambivalent and slow in coming. You may fight it and resent it. But you are beginning to see that you can live with it, and in fact, that it is the only spirit in which you can survive.

Accepting the inevitable is a giant step toward recovery and growth. It is the necessary prelude to forgiveness, of both yourself and your spouse. And no genuine healing can take place without forgiveness. But remember: Really letting go of your marriage may take years. Everyone has his or her own timetable for moving on. And the experience of death is an individual affair, not a shared activity. Even though you may be experiencing the divorce together, your own reactions and needs are unique and must be honored as such.

ARE YOU READY TO LISTEN TO EACH OTHER?

Before any sort of meaningful encounter can take place between the participants in a troubled marriage, each spouse must be willing to listen to the other.

By listening I don't mean waiting patiently until the other person has finished talking, so that you can have *your* say. True listening is not the act of remaining silent while someone else is talking, all the while planning your own response. When I use the term "listening," I mean it in its most profound sense: being present to and for the other person.

"I'm present!" you may argue. "I'm sitting right here in this chair!" But to be present does not refer to physical presence. You can be present for somebody and be thousands of miles away, and you can be lying in someone's arms and feel as if you're thousands of miles away. Being present involves a wholly empathetic response, your willingness to focus all of your attention and energy on what the other person is saying.

Being present requires you to check your own judgments, prejudices and preconceptions at the door, in order to understand as fully as possible where the other person is coming from. Being present means to respond "in the moment," rather than out of past hurt or future fear. Above all, being present means wanting the best *for* the other person. Being present is the only form of listening that invites deep, satisfying communication because it is the highest compliment you can pay to another person.

Admittedly, this is extremely difficult in the early stages of divorce. During this difficult time, emotions can barely be fathomed, let alone controlled. Hurt, rage, fear, relief, love, hate—all may be jumbled up together, making for some highly irrational moments between husband and wife, who no longer even have a clear idea of who they are, as they hang suspended between spouses and strangers.

Take the case of Jean, who called me one day to inquire about the possibility of my mediating a particularly unhappy divorce between herself and her husband, Dale. Jean had just discovered, after thirty years of marriage, that Dale had had a fling with a young woman. Enraged, she hired a detective, who unearthed the painful information that Dale had had many clandestine affairs throughout their marriage. When Jean phoned me, she was on the brink of initiating legal proceedings that would likely bankrupt Dale. The following is an example of the initial phone conversation, which is typical of the type of dialogues I've had with a husband or wife who is still in the intense anger stage of divorce.

JOEL: Hi, this is Joel. How can I help you?

JEAN: Hello, Joel. Actually, I would like to murder my husband. But since I can't, you've been referred to me by my daughter, who would like us to mediate our divorce before we go into a knock-down, dragged-out legal battle.

JOEL: I see. So you're extremely angry, which sounds like it's probably stemming from some recent event.

JEAN: Yes.

JOEL: But you don't want to act on that anger. Or you'd like to act on it, but it seems impractical. Is that right?

JEAN: Well, it doesn't seem impractical to me. But it's mainly for my children that I'm calling you.

JOEL: I see. For your children.

JEAN: Because they're afraid I'll deplete the family fortune.

JOEL: You mean by the murder?

JEAN: No. I want to sue my husband for everything he's worth. I want to ruin him! But the lawyers will cost a fortune.

JOEL: Um hmmm. Why don't I just get a little bit of background on this. First of all, how long have you and your husband been married?

JEAN: Thirty years.

JOEL: Are you still living together?

JEAN: No. He moved out last month.

JOEL: And what was the immediate cause of the separation?

JEAN: I found out that he was having an affair with a young woman! Twenty years old!

JOEL: Was this brand new information? Or had he had other affairs of which you were aware?

JEAN: I wasn't aware until I hired a detective and I found out that he's been having affairs under my nose for twenty years. I can never trust him again. Never!

JOEL: Uh huh. Well, what is it that you want at this point? Am I correct in assuming that you don't want to be married to him anymore? Or you're not sure?

JEAN: Well, my daughter wanted me to talk to you because she thinks I still love him. But I feel like I hate him.

JOEL: Well, sometimes those two emotions aren't very far apart. But that's a tough one. Only *you* know how you feel about him, and nobody can tell you how to feel or what to do.

Now, I don't know if you know anything about the kind of work I do, or what mediation is.

JEAN: Actually I don't.

JOEL: Let me just say a few words about it. Basically this work helps people to resolve their own conflicts as peacefully as possible, without having to resort to either litigation or hit men. In other words, I help people talk to each other and understand each other as to what they both really want. I don't represent one person *against* another; I just provide a service to help the two of you make some decisions together. Now, does this make any sense to you?

JEAN: Well, I'd like to say that my husband Dale is a terrible listener. It's very hard to get him to talk about anything. So I don't know if this is going to work.

JOEL: I don't know either, but let's forget about *him* for a moment and talk about *you*. If he decided that he wanted to do this, is it something that is fitting for you?

JEAN: I don't know. I'm very angry right now.

JOEL: What are you doing with all that anger?

JEAN: I'm getting sick a lot. I've had terrible migraines and I've lost twenty pounds. And I'm planning my revenge.

JOEL: Have you talked to any family members about the reality of the situation, particularly in terms of your desire to make your husband a pauper?

JEAN: Yes.

JOEL: Well, I'm not sure then that I can help you, given your current state of mind. Basically I work with couples whose primary intention is to reach an agreement that they both feel good about. I'm not willing to be the instrument of aiding anyone's desire to hurt another person, either economically, emotionally or physically. However, if after *getting past* these feelings—and by the way, a substantial percentage of the people I deal with started out being as angry as you are—if after putting those feelings in their proper context, you're willing to sit down with Dale and work something out, I'd be willing to help both of you. You can still be angry, but we can deal with that. These feelings *can* be dealt with and processed.

JEAN: I can't believe that I'll ever get over this anger.

JOEL: Well, you will. Either in five minutes, or five months, or five years. Sometime before you die, you'll get past it. The question is, how costly is it going to be for you in terms of money, time, energy and anguish?

JEAN: Do you think we could be reconciled?

JOEL: I don't know.

JEAN: Have you seen couples in the same situation as ours get back together?

JOEL: Absolutely. In fact, if I have any bias at all, it's in favor of people staying together. So I always start out by finding out whether or not that's possible. At any rate, if you do decide that you'd like to explore this process further, I'd suggest that you talk to Dale, or write him a letter letting him know that you're considering what I've just described to you. Ask him to give me a call, so that I can hold a similar conversation with him. And we'll go from there. Okay?

JEAN: Okay.

OFF TO THE RACES

Jean's reaction to Dale's affair falls into the response category I term "Off to the Races." When she discovered Dale's infidelity, Jean was so devastated that she could only react with blind rage. The gun went off and her emotions shot out the gate.

The sad thing about it was that, underneath all the layers of hurt and anger, Jean was still in love with

Dale—at least in the state of feeling that so often passes for love in our culture.

Have you ever noticed how the most vicious displays of emotion often seem to occur between the people who are closest to each other? It seems incredible, to watch love turn so easily into "hate." But that's because what people usually mistake for love isn't the real thing. They may have confused love with expectation, jealousy, envy, ego gratification, sexual desire, the desire for power. The list of subtle substitutes for true love is quite extensive.

True love—true compassion and caring for the other—doesn't turn into hatred. Unfortunately, so much of what I see in very severe divorce wars is the lack of true love. Two people may be utterly convinced that they are in love when they exchange their vows and drift off into their new "altared" state. But the motivation behind their marriage may be the direct antithesis of love.

A lot of people believe that once they're married, the other person will change, only to discover that they'll do nothing of the kind. I've seen plenty of mental shotgun marriages, that were motivated by peer pressure, age or even parents anxious to get rid of their kids. And all too often, people who never received enough attention in their formative years are so overwhelmed by the fact that someone is actually paying attention to them now that they mistake gratitude for love.

So, if you are in the beginning stages of a divorce, you must first determine whether or not you truly love your spouse—and if so, whether or not reconciliation is the best path for both of you to try first.

The Marital Reassessment Survey

When I act as a professional mediator to couples in troubled marriages, we sometimes begin by doing a "marital reassessment." So at this time, if you are not yet totally certain that divorce is inevitable for you, I suggest that you do as some of my clients do and fill out the following chart. As you fill it in, work quickly, without too much pondering. Put down the first response that comes to mind; it is usually the most trustworthy.

While doing this reassessment, you may experience strong emotions. For instance, your hurt and anger may be so intense that, like Jean, you feel incapable of forgiveness. That's okay; you have a *right* to be angry. But you are doing yourself a disservice if you feel wrong or guilty about being angry, or if you allow your anger to negate the positive aspects of your relationship. While doing this reassessment, try to accept your emotions without letting them cloud your objectivity. You have the ability to separate facts from feelings; use it.

The Marital Reassessment Survey

In assessing the following categories, check the appropriate column as to the degree in which they are fulfilled in your marriage.

Aspects of Relationships	Works Well	Barely Working	Doesn't Work at All	Possibility of Change Yes No
Loving feelings				
Communication with spouse				
Mutual respect				
Spiritual connection				

Aspects of Relationships	Works Well	Barely Working	Doesn't Work at All	Possibility of Change Yes No
Parenting your children:				
• Division of tasks				
• Agree on treatment				
• Dealing with problems				
Money:				
• Earning				
• Spending				
• Investing				
Sex:				
• Desire				
• Frequency				
• Enjoyment				
Friends and Relatives:				
• Quality				
• Quantity				
• Frequency of contact				
Lifestyle:				
• Satisfying				
• Condition of home				
• Location				
Leisure time:				
• Amount				
• How used				
Time spent together:				
• Quality				
• Quantity				

When you have completed this evaluation, examine the vertical groupings as to what works and what doesn't in your relationship.

If you are considering ending your marriage, you might want to focus on those areas in which change is *not* possible. There are situations in which a person is a slave to repeated patterns of behavior, and change is highly unlikely unless he or she is willing to make the effort to choose more positive forms of communicating and relating. For instance, in Jean's case she must decide if Dale's "fling" (which was all *he* perceived it as) is a temporary or a permanent, momentary or endemic condition of their marriage. Certainly the fact that Dale had many of these flings indicates that his behavior is more than temporary. If he is unwilling to forego his extramarital affairs, Jean's next question is, "Am I willing to live with that?" Sometimes if the other person has qualities that you truly value and appreciate, you may be willing to put up with his or her frustrating behavior. It all depends on how willing you yourself are to change *your* approach.

Nonetheless, a preponderance of these "no change possible" instances may indicate that divorce could indeed be the best course. However, if the "change *is* possible" column predominates, I would encourage you to consider such options as individual or joint therapy, and/or temporary separation.

After you have assessed your responses, you will need to decide whether or not you want to show your completed chart to your spouse. This may take a lot of time and energy, as both of you will be very vulnerable. You can either share your response in the safe environment of a therapist's or mediator's office, or you can practice the essential communication techniques we've talked about in previous chapters.

One of my more unusual experiences with the marital reassessment survey involved a husband and wife who were determined to go through with a divorce. Although we discussed the possibility of reconciliation, neither of them was open to it. So we proceeded with the divorce and its attendant agreement.

The two moved to separate living spaces. The husband, a successful businessman, sold his business and prepared to retire and move to Utah. The agreement I helped them draw up was mutually accepted, the divorce was about to go through—when I suddenly got a call from the husband.

"Put the brakes on," he said.

"Why?" I inquired, amazed.

"Because we're having doubts."

So, both of them showed up at my office the following afternoon—to finally tackle the marital reassessment survey! And what resulted was definitely one of my most extraordinary cases: a divorce, a reconciliation *and* a "pre–living together" agreement!

After completing the survey, the two of them agreed that although there were many positive aspects to their relationship, divorce was probably the best solution. However, it turned out afterward that the wife still loved her husband and wanted to stay married, and that her husband had decided to divorce her not because he really wanted to, but because the whole process had been so hard on him emotionally that he wasn't able to deal with the possibility of getting back together. He was being a "businessman" with his feelings, escaping into the unemotional approach he was used to and looking at the divorce as a business transaction, and she was going along with him.

After the divorce they reconciled and moved in together. Soon afterward I received a call from them, wanting me to help them draw up a pre–living together agreement, as they had now decided to move in with each other and possibly to renew their vows.

Had they filled out the marital reassessment survey at the outset, perhaps both of them could have been spared untold stress and heartache. Instead, they went through whatever it was they needed to go through. However, my suggestion to you is to confront reality as early as possible. Look at your relationship as objectively as you can; make a checklist of the pros and cons. Once it's on paper, out in the open, it's much easier to decide whether or not a divorce is truly appropriate.

THREE COMMON DIVORCE MISTAKES

I was divorced in 1976, two years before I ever handled a divorce case as a professional mediator and several years before I embarked upon the Eastern philosophy leg of my journey toward inner awareness. Which is to say that I probably made all the mistakes before, during and after my own divorce that I try to help others understand and prevent today.

Most of those mistakes were ones that I made during the marriage as well. Most people, I discovered, generally make the same dumb moves in the process of *divorcing* as they do in the process of the *marriage*. And almost all of these moves can be directly related to a tunnel-vision approach not only to marriage but to life.

Here are the three biggest mistakes I made.

1. *Not doing alternative thinking.* Like many people who are faced with a giant upheaval in their lives, I took a black-and-white approach to the situation. I believed that I had only a very limited number of choices and that I had to proceed a certain way, period. There were no other possibilities. Sitting down and meditating on the crisis, going for a walk on the beach or gathering people around and saying, "Okay. What do you think about this?" were not options that I considered. In other words, I didn't do enough information gathering.

Now, if I'm an expert today in anything—and I don't even believe in experts anymore, which is why I do the work that I do—it's in gathering information. But seventeen years ago I was as much a novice in this field as the next guy, and therefore could not assess my marital situation calmly and positively. For instance, one of the things I did was to allow my house to be sold because I thought I couldn't afford to keep it. This was fear, not reality. If I'd really thought about it and checked out where I could obtain some money on a temporary basis, I could have kept the house, which would have been much better for me and our five-year-old son, Adam, who ended up living with me in a somewhat nomadic fashion for several years after the divorce.

So, today when I counsel clients, I emphasize all the alternatives and how to be aware of them. Sometimes I even go a bit overboard in examining every possibility, but I see this as a positive overreaction to the painful but productive lessons I learned from my own experience.

Never feel stymied by a situation. If you do, realize that you are only bound by the limits of *your* own mind, your own emotions. There is always a way to maintain your sense of power in a situation, even if it involves total surrender—an activity well known to any spiritual warrior. But usually there are alternatives that can satisfy both parties in a divorce. The only reason they haven't been explored is fear or ignorance.

2. *Relying on the wrong people for advice.* Although I had a lawyer "helping" me, he really wasn't independent. He was such a close friend and was dealing with so much of the same madness himself in his own divorce that all he did was to reinforce my own nonsense. I relied on my friend to an overwhelming degree, instead of having an objective person around to give me a second opinion.

The emphasis here is on the word "objective." There will be plenty of people around to give you opinions— friends parents, coworkers, you name it. The trouble is, most of those opinions will be clouded by the giver's own experience or prejudices. When one of my clients, Rachel, was separating from her husband, her best friend, Hazel, was on hand to give her "expert" advice based on her own divorce.

"Go down to the bank, take all the money out and gather up the financial records," Hazel instructed Rachel. "You need to look out for yourself now. My lawyer told me I shouldn't even talk to my husband, except when he picks up and drops off the kids. Maybe you should call my lawyer."

One of the things I insist upon with my clients is that before they sign anything, get it reviewed by somebody who's totally *independent*. I didn't do that, and my mistake haunted me for many years. I've seen far too many couples listen to faulty, one-sided advice from well-meaning friends and family members, only to re-gret it later.

One of the problems is that we are especially vulner-able and in need of emotional support during a divorce. Not only do we rely on those closest to us more that we ordinarily would, but the last thing we want to do is alienate them. In Rachel's case, she had decided upon the course of mediation, despite Hazel's disapproval. I suggested that she respond to Hazel in the following way:

"I appreciate your friendship, Hazel. Your support has been a big help these past few months, and I know I'll need more during my divorce. Thanks for your advice; I know you want the best for me.

"But I have decided to try mediation. I don't intend to try to convince you of the wisdom of this decision, and I won't argue about it. If this doesn't work for me, I can always call your lawyer or another lawyer. I know you don't agree with me; I'm simply asking you to accept my decision and support me in it. Can you do that for me?"

Don't compound the agony of divorce by taking hasty or vindictive actions just because your best friend tells you to. Make sure you visit a therapist, a clergyperson or a sympathetic friend who can listen to you without automatically taking your part. You need to be able to sort out your own feelings through talking, but you don't need to be directed at this stage so much as you need a supportive, nonjudgmental shoulder to lean on. And once you are formulating agreements, make sure an independent third party examines any documents before you sign them. I guarantee it will save you a lot of wasted time, energy and heartache down the line.

3. *Not realizing that nothing is permanent.* In the seventeen-plus years since my divorce, my ex-wife and I have been in every conceivable situation with each other that it's possible for two ex-spouses to be in, all the way from becoming one-time lovers again to going to court over parenting issues. Court—and I'm a mediator!

One of the most important things I learned in the years following my divorce is that no feeling is ever permanent. Life changes. Whatever you're feeling now is going to be different in five minutes, five days, five years or five microseconds. Whether it's anger, or joy, or feeling greedy or wanting to withhold . . . the one thing I can absolutely guarantee is that it's going to be different at another point in time.

The other day I had a couple in my office who were tearing each other's heads off. After they left, I went outside to put money in my parking meter, and I saw the husband on the street. He was still cursing! "I'm so mad at that woman!" he thundered.

Well, I listened to him as calmly, as I never could have seventeen years ago, and then I said, "It's not a permanent condition, you know."

"Oh yeah?" he yelled. "How do you know?"

"Because this too shall pass," I replied.

"When?"

"That I don't know. But don't worry. It'll pass—sometime before you do."

Allow yourself to experience your emotions. But never extend their importance beyond that moment. Never ignore or suppress your emotions, but never take action or make a decision strictly on an emotional basis either. One of the things I always say to my clients is, "If one of your goals is to make decisions and act upon those decisions and you're going to either totally ignore your emotions or be completely ruled by them, then you're out the door. You're a fool, and I'm not willing to deal with you."

And if I'm ever so foolish not to listen to my own advice, then I should divorce myself!

THE FOUR DIVORCES*

And finally—how do I divorce thee? Let me count the ways.

Contrary to popular belief, a divorce is not a single event. Two people do not simply part ways in one fell swoop. How could they? Through the years their lives have become intertwined in many different areas, all of which are affected by a divorce. It's like a tree that's wrecking the foundation of your house. You can't simply chop it down because the roots are the problem and they're still there. And just as it's murder to get at all of those roots, so it's extremely difficult to sever the various kinds of connections you've had with your spouse, his or her family and friends, the finances, the children—not to mention your connection to yourself.

There are four different kinds of divorces that we experience: One is the legal divorce, which involves the formal documents and paperwork. Another is the economic divorce, in which property and debts are divided and spousal and child support are decided. Then there's the social divorce, involving mutual friends and relatives. And finally we have the emotional divorce,

* Thanks to Hugh McIsaac, former director of the Conciliation Court of the Los Angeles County Family Court, for this concept.

which is not complete until each person has truly let go of the other so that someone new can come in.

To complete these steps can take years. That's why it's extremely foolish to get involved with anyone who hasn't had all four divorces happen. In my own case, I can honestly say that none of the women with whom I became involved within three or four years after my divorce took into sufficient account my continued attachment to my ex-wife—and neither did I. I was still being affected by my divorce—or divorces—far more than I could be by anyone new. If I had met these women a few years later, I probably would have been able to marry at least two of them, because the quality of the relationships was excellent. But the seeds of those new relationships could not withstand the winds of my divorce, which were blowing too strongly for them to take root.

One piece of advice I give to anybody who is considering becoming involved with someone who is separating, separated, contemplating divorce or recently divorced is: Have a mental checklist ready. Make your own assessment; don't even ask the other person for answers he or she probably isn't capable of giving. Decide for yourself whether the four divorces have taken place, and if they haven't, either enter into an involvement with your eyes wide open or keep your distance. What we're dealing with in this book is avoiding conflict as well as resolving it, and a realistic assessment of the situation early on is the wisest move for all concerned.

By the same token, if you yourself are divorced, be honest with yourself as to how distanced you actually are from your divorce and its effects on you. And then be honest with whoever you want to become involved with. I'm not saying that everyone has to take a vow of celibacy until all four divorces are complete. But it is absolutely necessary to be as upfront as possible with yourself and others about the fact that it's going to take some time to fully release past hurts, fears, guilts and attachments.

10

Nine-to-Five Disputes: Handling Conflict in the Workplace

Vic is the stereotype of the tyrannical supervisor. He's arrogant and pompous and is always on the lookout for acts of employee "subversion." He's also incompetent, and constantly blames others for his own mistakes. When he doesn't meet a deadline for *his* boss, Vic will come down on his employees, accusing them of poor performance, even though he expects them to work overtime to cover his ineptitude.

The politics in Vic's office rival the goings on in Washington for sheer intrigue and ingenuity. Here's how one of my clients, a former employee of Vic's, describes the inner workings. There's the office "rat," Bill, the most recent employee, who has slavishly ingratiated himself with Vic and acts as his confidant, chauffeur and informant. Bill is a double-agent; he's befriended his coworkers, who mistakenly consider him one of them, and Vic can count on Bill to bring him juicy reports of any dissension in the ranks.

Then there's Gail, the office "social climber." Gail is the receptionist, but because she considers this job painfully beneath her, she has aspirations of quickly moving up the ladder. In her first week on the job, Gail was already circulating memos to the other employees, Vic and the president of the company, giving her opinions on how things in the office could be improved. She made herself extra available to Vic—at the expense sometimes of doing her own "menial" duties like filing and relaying messages to the other employees—and is now in line for a big promotion as Vic's "personal assistant."

And of course, we can't forget Gary, the office "gossip." Gary wields tremendous power; a human wire service, he can be replied upon for up-to-the-minute, behind-the-scenes info on everything and everyone. He artfully cultivates confusion and backbiting among his coworkers and is probably the most popular member of the staff because people rely on him to make them feel better by putting others down.

Needless to say, Vic's office isn't a particularly safe or happy place in which to work. People fear for their jobs every minute, and it's the rare employee who doesn't succumb to the "dog-eat-dog" mentality that Vic has so successfully fostered. We'd like to think that Vic's office is atypical, or even fictional in the annals of workplace horror tales, but unfortunately it happens to be a true story, and one that's probably distressingly familiar to many of us.

WHY WORKPLACE CONFLICTS ARE UNIQUE

Some of the most annoying, confusing and stressful conflict situations we're likely to encounter in our lives occur in the workplace, that crucial activity center where most of us spend at least a third of our lives, and where our performance often directly impacts how we spend the other two-thirds. The rules of most workplaces do not naturally foster a sense of peace and relaxation. The nature of the "job" being what it is, most of us are under constant pressure to achieve an optimum level of productivity while at the same time keeping our emotions under control and putting our best face forward.

If you've ever worked for anybody, however, or if you've ever been in a management position, you know that the above expectations present a built-in dilemma. On the one hand, in order for things to run as smoothly and efficiently as possible, conflicts on the job need to be kept at a minimum. On the other, precisely *because* expectations and demands are so high, stress levels mount and the workplace becomes, more often than not, a breeding ground for disagreements, resentments, power plays and all sorts of other dubious dynamics in which human beings, being human, tend to engage.

The elements of workplace conflict prevention and response are the same as in other types of conflict, with one important exception. Conflict on the job has a unique aspect to it, in that you are obligated to be at that job eight hours a day, five days a week. Although you may be able to get a "divorce" by changing jobs, workplace conflicts have a great effect on income, self-concept and issues of status and power, all of which directly affect our relationships with spouses, lovers, family and peers.

In other words, job conflict impacts our sense of self-esteem and emotional and physical security in a way many other types of conflict do not. We become attached to our jobs because they provide us with an identity and the financial means by which to survive. Thus, when conflicts or potential conflicts arise in the workplace, they may be more difficult to deal with because of the strong element of fear present on the part of *both* employees and management, each of whom may feel that their sense of self-worth and/or job security is being threatened.

But as we have seen in so many conflict and potential conflict situations, our fears have often very little to do with reality. When it comes to handling problems and disagreements on the job, we generally have far more power, and many more options, than may at first seem evident. The key steps involved in the process of preventing and responding to conflict—stepping back and viewing a situation objectively, gathering information, exploring alternatives, understanding and respecting the other person's position, and having the intention and willingness to come to an amicable and mutually beneficial solution to the problem—help us to realize that conflict situations can actually be opportunities for improving our work environments, our relationships with our coworkers, employees or employers and our sense of personal power and self-esteem.

THE MOST COMMON CAUSES OF ON-THE-JOB CONFLICTS

In my many years as an employee, supervisor, co-owner of a small business, chief executive of a community public service organization, lawyer, mediator and conflict consultant to businesses, it's been my experience that most job-related disputes do *not* concern poor performance on the part of an employee. Rather, they usually have at their core at least one of the following incendiary aspects of human behavior:

1. Misunderstanding or miscommunication
2. Disrespect or disregard for other people
3. Conflicting egos
4. Impatience
5. Fear and insecurity over perceived "loss of control."

By its very nature, the workplace is a potential hotbed of conflict. A sense of competitiveness is often fostered; one person vies with another for a higher position, or, if layoffs are imminent, employees fight to retain their existing jobs. Misunderstanding the concept of authority, management often puts a higher emphasis on "maintaining control" than on being open and flexible.

Thus, being honest and vulnerable and giving priority to other people's needs and feelings has not been a traditional component of workplace dynamics in our society. But if conflicts on the job are to be prevented, or responded to appropriately, at least one of the parties involved must be willing to:

1. Communicate clearly and calmly with the other person;
2. Respect the other person and their position;
3. Detach one's ego from the situation, and have the intention to settle differences amicably and in a mutually beneficial manner;
4. Take as much time as is necessary to explore the problem, understand and empathize with the other person, and decide upon the best course of action;
5. Be honest and vulnerable, knowing that true control and security lies in one's ability to feel secure in oneself, not one's job or position.

CONFLICTS OVER PROMOTIONS AND RAISES

Jack has been working at his company for two years. While he's received good evaluations, he's gotten neither a raise nor a promotion. Jack is angry and hurt, but feels backed into a corner when it comes to confronting Pete, his supervisor. What can he do, after all, if his request or demand for fair compensation is denied? He doesn't want to quit because he likes and needs his job. He doesn't want to antagonize Pete or go above his head because he may be accused of being a "troublemaker." So Jack keeps quiet. But inside he feels helpless, like a victim of the workplace fates.

What are some of the likely results of Jack's unwillingness to ask for what he feels he deserves? Well, he may slack off in his work, doing less of it or not doing it as well. He may take more sick leave—and he may need it, because of stress-related illness stemming from the unexpressed anger he feels at being taken advantage of.

He may become resentful and negative on the job, complaining about the job and Pete to others. Or, he may go to the other extreme and become a "whistle-blower," trying to prove his value to Pete by monitoring the activities of others and trying to "run things better."

None of these actions or inactions, of course, are very productive. They are *indirect* responses to an uncomfortable situation that has not yet become a conflict, but that, because of Jack's negative behaviors, has a good chance of escalating into one, with either his supervisor or his coworkers.

What can Jack do to resolve the problem? First of all, he needs to step back from the situation, go to a quiet place, take a few deep breaths and figure out where he's at and where he wants to be.

DOING A LITTLE INFO-GATHERING

What are the elements of the situation? Is Jack the only one who has not received a raise and/or a promotion? Has *anyone* at the company received one? If so, why does he think he's been passed up? Is there something he could be doing better? Is it merely an oversight on Pete's part that won't be corrected until Jack makes him aware of it? Has his communication with Pete been good? not so good? Why? What does he really want to communicate to Pete? What does he really want for himself? How can he get his needs met by not putting himself in an either-or situation—"Either I get a raise or I quit!"—or by putting Pete in a defensive position?

In other words, Jack has to do some information gathering. He needs to gain clarity as to what his own needs are. How does he feel about his performance at his job? Does he genuinely know that he's been doing his best? Or is there part of him that has to admit he could be doing better? How much of a raise does he feel entitled to? Would he like a promotion? If so, to what position?

How does he feel about Pete? Have they gotten along? Or is there some resentment on his part, some "unexpressed conflict" with his superior, as we explored in chapter 2, that he's not voicing—and possibly vice versa?

What's the company policy regarding raises and promotions? Does Jack know for a fact that others who've worked there as long as he has have received an increase in pay and/or status? Or is there a freeze in those departments?

The issue of getting a raise or a promotion can be very much a "structural" type of dispute. (See chapter 1.) There may be a number of circumstances that have nothing to do with the individual. The organization might be tightening its belt; in one case I know of, a woman who hadn't received a raise on schedule, but who never questioned why, harbored a great deal of anger against her boss and his boss and the entire company, until she found out that all wages had been frozen due to the company's financial difficulties. Or, a boss might be the type of person who as a matter of principle only gives raises for superior performance, not simply good work. And even if an employee is told that his or her work is not up to snuff, this still isn't a personal issue. It's a professional problem. The employer might like the employee very much, but simply may not be happy with his or her performance.

In Jack's case, he may be assuming that (a) a dispute exists between him and Pete, and (b) that dispute is a personal one. Pete has overlooked him for a raise or a promotion; Jack takes it personally. Period. But in reality, the perceived problem between Jack and Pete may be of a structural nature—or it may be a mixture of structural and personal. And until Jack becomes a spy and does his research, he won't know what sort of dispute he's actually dealing with, or whether there's even a dispute to begin with.

Above all, how does Jack's attitude toward the problem contribute to its "conflict level?" If he's angry and resentful, he may already be engaged in a silent dispute, for just as it takes two to make war and one to make peace, it can take one to make a dispute out of a merely unharmonious situation. If, however, he's merely puzzled and curious, a dispute does not yet exist.

If Jack can manage to act as if he's just curious and is getting information—even if he's feeling angry and frustrated—he'll be much more likely to get the information he wants and move things forward. He can gather the basic data he needs regarding company policy and practice before making any sort of a preliminary judgment. And if, when he meets with Pete, he's of a calm and inquiring disposition, he won't put his supervisor on the defensive, nor is he likely to respond defensively to Pete. As a result, the problem has a good chance of being resolved amicably, with negative feelings at a minimum.

And what about Pete's response? If he says, "I've recommended you for a raise but I don't make the final decision," there's no dispute, at least not with Pete. If he says, "Well, your work's been good but there are areas in which you need to improve," Jack can either disagree or reply, "Okay. I'll try to do better. When can

I be reevaluated?" In both of these cases, however, the problem is a structural, not a personal one.

If, however, Pete says, "I don't like the way you dress," or "I disapprove of your going out with Mary Ann the receptionist," or "If you lose fifty pounds I might consider it," Jack will find himself dealing with a personal dispute, one that may or may not be capable of being resolved.

THE MYTH OF EMPLOYEE DEPENDENCY

The most important thing for Jack to realize is that he's not a victim. He's not in a position of dependence upon Pete unless he chooses to believe that he is. For the simple truth is that in the workplace, relationships between employees and employers are always *interdependent*. Even though it may sometimes seem otherwise— the boss has control, the employee doesn't—in reality there are two truths that most employees forget:

1. Bosses need employees every bit as much as their employees need them, and
2. Unless it's a very small organization, every boss has a boss.

In other words, unless Jack is doing a very poor job, which doesn't seem to be the case as he's always gotten good evaluations, his supervisor—and his company— needs him. And his supervisor has a supervisor to whom he must answer.

Although it may not seem that way at times, the goals of management and employees are not necessarily opposed. Both want to achieve good performance and high productivity. And when the goals of both parties in a problem situation are similar or parallel, there is not a conflict—only a disagreement over how those goals can best be reached.

Time and again, when I'm helping couples who are going through a divorce, or who are already divorced to come to a financial agreement, I'll remind them that "What's good for one of you is good for the other."

At first this may not be obvious to the parties; hostilities may be hard to overcome, and each may be looking for a way to make the other "pay up." But regardless of how they may feel about each other, both spouses or ex-spouses are still joined together in one economic unit. If there's any money passing hands between the two of them—child support, alimony or money to be paid in property settlements—the economic happiness of one is directly dependent upon the economic happiness of the other.

In other words, the zero sum game—whatever I get he doesn't get and vice versa—is a myth, in divorce, business and life in general. When exs get together to argue about money, or when management locks horns with labor, the tendency is to jump into the hot scramble for bucks on the table. But the reality is that a business or a marriage—severed or not—is an ongoing dynamic process in which money is being earned and paid out all the time. Thus, what's good for one is almost always good for the other. And what's bad for one is generally bad for the other.

The traditional "boss as ogre" image, in which the boss gets the most out of his employees by being a dictator and cracking the whip, may still exist in the movies, on TV or in certain specific instances. But my observation is that the "Big Stick" philosophy of how to run a business or company or corporation is much less prevalent than it used to be.

Because of the style of management being taught in today's MBA schools, much of which draws upon the example the Japanese have set in terms of a cooperative, team-spirited, participatory approach to business, there is much more of a tendency within organizations today to realize the *interdependent* nature of employer-employee relations, as well as a willingness to protect the rights of both employer and employee in the form of recognized procedures incorporated into the organization's standard operating policy.

Let's go back for a moment to Jack and Pete. Jack realizes (a) that he has power in his job; (b) that he and Pete ultimately share many of the same desires and concerns; (c) that Pete is answerable to someone else for his actions; and (d) that there are legal procedures he can make use of to assure, at the very least, a "fair hearing" of his grievances. Jack can then decide how to approach Pete. He may want to discuss the matter face to face with Pete, over lunch or at a specified appointment time. He may feel more comfortable sending Pete a memo, clearly and calmly stating his feelings and why he feels he's entitled to a raise or promotion and suggesting that the two of them meet to discuss the matter. Whichever avenue Jack chooses, the important thing is that he is dealing with the issue in a manner that's both direct and nonadversarial.

If, after he meets with Pete, Jack is still not satisfied, he can then inform Pete that he's going to appeal the issue to the appropriate higher-ups. Here it's very important for Jack to make sure that he documents everything, starting with his initial memo to or conversation with Pete. And again, he should be calm, direct and as non-accusatory as possible.

Chances are that his initial conversation with Pete will solve much of Jack's dilemma. Pete will be made aware of Jack's feelings, will have to offer an explanation and will probably try to either correct the situation or inform Jack of what he needs to be doing in order to get a raise or promotion. Going above Pete's head is a more serious action, and one that generally doesn't need to be resorted to if communication lines have been kept open, Jack has been as honest as possible and has exhibited the intention to understand Pete's point of view and to come to an agreement that will benefit both of them.

THE MANAGEMENT END: RESPONSE TO AND PREVENTION OF CONFLICT

An article in the November 1990 issue of *Spirit* magazine, the in-flight publication of Southwest Airlines, took an intriguing look at the question, "How Well Do You Manage Conflict?" While the article was geared toward managers and employee conflicts, the basic principles it dealt with apply to conflict in general. Here are a few of the "test" questions readers were supposed to answer.

1. When trying to resolve a conflict, you should first state what's important to you and then ask the other person what is important to him. True or False.

2. If you communicate to an employee that you are afraid he or she will act irresponsibly, the employee will

try harder to prove to you that he or she is responsible. True or False.

3. When the flow toward a conflict resolution does not occur naturally, you should first suggest alternatives and then invite the other person to do the same. True or False.

4. As a manager, you should always give honest consideration to alternative solutions. True or False.

5. Complete the statement: "Well, Lisa, there doesn't seem to be any other alternative for getting this done correctly."

A. "I'm sorry, but my decision stands. We're depending on you to help us out on this one."
B. "You have a right to feel differently, but my decision stands. We need your experience to meet this deadline."

The answers to these questions were:

1. True. It's essential to state simply and clearly what is important to you and why, and then confirm your understanding of the other person's needs. This can sometimes lead to an immediate solution.

2. False. People respond not only to your actions, but also to your expectations. "Self-fulfilling prophecy," or the process of confirming the expectations others have of you, is a natural result based on the human response to peer evaluation and acceptance.

3. False. People are likely to be more committed to carrying out a solution they've developed. Let the other person suggest alternatives first.

4. False. Unless you genuinely want to consider alternatives, and are not restricted by any organizational policies, exploring and generating alternatives will be frustrating all around.

5. B. In this statement, the manager acknowledges the other person's right to disagree, states the decision and explains why it has to be that way.

Well, how did you do? If you've grasped what you've read in this book so far, you probably got an A. On the other hand, you may have found that some of the answers were not as clear cut as they might have seemed. For instance, while the answer to (1) is true, the answer to (3) is false. On the surface, the situations seem almost the same. But in reality, there is a distinct difference between first stating your needs in a conflict situation and initially suggesting alternative approaches to a solution before inviting the other person to do so.

Or, while the answer to question (4) might have seemed to be true, effective management often requires one to be able to narrow down alternatives in order to increase efficiency, and to stick by one's decision regarding the most productive course of action to follow.

As we can see, in the complex area of response to and prevention of disputes, a fine line often separates a well-meaning manager from one who clearly understands the dynamics of conflict prevention and resolution. Ideally, as a manager, your goal is to have respect for your employee, listen to his/her position, be open to suggestion and still know when to make a decision and stick by it. This is perhaps the best definition I can think of for the correct use of "authority." And it applies equally to parents and to managers in any field. The ability to understand and keep the balance between flexibility and control, reasonableness and firmness, understanding and commanding, is a creative talent that some people may be born with, but that most of us have to acquire, usually through raw—and usually bad—experience.

TERMINATION: FIRING WITH LOVE

One of the most difficult experiences any manager will encounter involves firing an employee. I myself have had to deal with this highly uncomfortable situation, and I learned a number of things from the experience.

Some years ago, when I was the director of a community service organization in L.A., I hired a young woman—let's call her Sandy—to work in the office. While she was still in her probationary period, she began to question the way in which I was running the center and to make her views known to the other employees in a loud and definite manner.

I took Sandy aside and confided my concerns about her behavior to her in as pleasant a way as possible. She replied that she thought I was too lackadaisical in my approach as a director. I thanked her for her opinion and reminded her that I was running the operation, not her.

When Sandy continued to try to assert her own authority, I called her into my office and told her that I didn't like what she was doing and that I found it highly inappropriate. She responded by showing up at the

next Board of Directors' meeting and airing her grievances in public, causing the Chairman of the Board to
question just "who's in charge here?"

Although I tended to be a very laid-back authority
figure, I realized I'd let things get out of hand. I'd
given Sandy several warnings, but never an ultimatum.
And perhaps she was right—perhaps I didn't assert as
much authority in my position as I should have. I
resolved to correct the error immediately, by calling her
into my office again, presenting her with a written list
of what I found to be her unacceptable behaviors and
firing her.

This was not an easy thing for me to do. In fact, it
made me very uncomfortable. But I knew that if I
continued to allow Sandy to run roughshod over me,
the entire organization would suffer. I needed to take
back my own power as the director, and at the same
time to give a loud and clear message to the other
employees that although I might be a Mr. Nice Guy, I
was still in authority, and those who questioned that
authority inappropriately would be terminated. Period.

NO SUBSTITUTE FOR PREPARATION

Yet *how* does one person fire another? What's the best
approach to terminating someone? What are actions to
take, and actions to avoid?

1. *Give early warnings.* When an employee is engaging in conduct of which you cannot approve, start
giving him or her warnings. If your first warning isn't
heeded, make the second warning more severe, with
very specific consequences. If the undesirable conduct

happens again, document the occurrence. You may then give the employee a dismissal.

2. *Document everything.* As a manager or supervisor, protect yourself with a paper trail. From the first warning to the final dismissal, make sure that every incident is documented in writing. If you gave the employee a warning face-to-face, make a note of it. A file should be kept with memos and dates, times and summaries of conversations held with the difficult employee or any other employees or supervisors.

3. *Respect the employee's dignity.* When you're ready to terminate someone, call them in at a time when others are not around. Ask to see them after work or tell them to come in early, before others have arrived.

4. *Be factual, not personal.* When you are sitting with the employee, go over the relevant history of the problem. Show them the file; explain that since the problem has been a repeated one, you've decided to terminate them. Stay as calm and empathetic as possible, and be willing to answer any questions if they have any.

5. *Do your own self-talk.* Not many of us relish the thought of firing someone. We generally have very mixed emotions. Part of us doesn't want to cause them an economic hardship, especially if they're supporting a family. Part of us hates to deal such a severe blow to their self-esteem. And yet another part of us is angry and resentful and would like to do far more than simply fire them.

If we deny one of these parts in favor of another, we

risk coming off as either an "ogre" boss or a "bleeding heart." We'll either totally get into our anger, or we'll repress it because we don't want to look like a bad person, to ourselves or anyone else.

So, we need to do some self-talk. We need to acknowledge both parts of ourselves. We need to make eye contact with the person we're terminating, because that lets them know we're sincere and serious, and that we're owning our power, but in a human, feeling way. We want to communicate to the person that we aren't afraid of them, but that we respect them as a fellow human being. If we feel guilty or badly, we may want to admit this to them. "This doesn't feel very good to me. I have nothing against you as a person. But I believe that this is in the best interest of the organization."

6. *If it's appropriate, maintain helpful contact after the dismissal.* Paula is a telecommunications supervisor in a prestigious bank. A "super-manager," she's known for the high productivity and motivation of her department. Her employees love her, and with good reason. Paula works with them to help them achieve their best performance. She pitches in, stays late and is always available "just to talk." If an employee has a problem, Paula's attitude is, "How can we solve this together," rather than "You'd better shape up or else."

Even when she has to fire an employee, Paula's relationship with that person doesn't necessarily end. That's because she knows the secret of firing with love.

"I don't often have to fire someone," she says. "And I hate it when I do. But my employees love me even if I fire them. I talk with them, explain my reasons. I'm sympathetic, and I listen to them. And if it's a situation where they were just wrong for my particular department, I even try to help them get another job, either within the bank or at another bank."

Paula has managed to separate the *act* of firing someone from the person themselves. She doesn't throw the baby out with the bathwater she doesn't throw the employee out with their termination. She respects her staff as individuals and human beings, and they return that respect with a loyalty that's as devoted as it is rare.

CONFLICTS BETWEEN COWORKERS

Most of us have probably come up against a problem with a coworker at some point in our lives. Whether it's a business partner who just doesn't see things your way, a secretary who's jealous of her territory or a fellow employee who's loud and opinionated, life on the job can be frought with emotional peril when you and the person you're forced to work with don't get along.

Coworker conflicts are especially bothersome because (a) there are many more employees than there are bosses, meaning that there's more opportunity for conflicts between employees to arise; (b) given the nature of office politics and structure, they are rarely private; and (c) because of the generally close and constant proximity between the antagonists, they are difficult to escape from.

But as in all the other dispute situations we've discussed, the problem is not the conflict so much as the failure to *deal* with the conflict. And this failure often stems from the fact that you have to work with this person every day. You can't fire them; they're part of the working family. So, if there's a difficulty with a coworker, most people tend to avoid the issue, preferring "not to make waves" or possibly create what they fear will be an intolerable working environment.

MAKING AN INTOLERABLE SITUATION TOLERABLE: THE PAYOFF OF OPEN COMMUNICATION

Larry and Hank, for instance, were engineers at an aircraft company. Larry is one of those mild-mannered nice guys who tries his hardest to get along with everybody. Hank, on the other hand, is loud, opinionated, abrasive and manages to royally annoy virtually everybody with whom he comes in contact.

When he wasn't at work, Larry complained a lot about Hank. "That guy is such a jerk!" he fumed. "He drives me crazy! He's always telling me what to do, and giving me advice I didn't ask for. On top of that, he hangs around me all the time!"

But Larry never revealed his frustration to Hank. Instead, he was as affable to Hank as he was to everybody else. And Hank, who, needless to say, wasn't exactly Mr. Popularity, mistook Larry's nice-guy mask for friendliness and adopted him as his bosom buddy.

Larry's irritation with Hank grew, to the point where he dreaded going into work. Eventually, he was faced with several options. One was to tell Hank to leave him alone forever. Another was to quit. A third was to try talking to Hank. And the last was to allow things to remain as they were, and to try to make the best of an obnoxious situation.

Larry decided to try discussing his feelings and frustrations with Hank. At first, Hank was very defensive— and also very hurt. But Larry's honesty allowed him to feel friendlier toward Hank. And eventually, Hank was able to appreciate Larry's openness and respect his needs.

The upshot of all this is that Larry and Hank have now worked together for nearly two decades. Through the years, they and the rest of their coworkers have become, basically, like bickering members of a family. They have known each other for so long that protocol and politeness have long since ceased to be a priority. Instead, they argue and fight and, at the same time, provide each other with support and nurturing.

The Workforce as an Extended Family

There is a definite correlation between the workplace and the home environments in which its members grew up. Unconsciously and intuitively, many of us make our coworkers into projections of individuals who have been in our lives from an early age. The result is that a family dynamic often develops on the job, with coworkers unconsciously assuming family roles for each other.

One person may become the mother, another the father. Ted may remind Jack of his older brother with whom he was very competitive; Thelma may remind Ted of his favorite aunt. (In Larry's case, Hank, who was much older, treated him paternally and paternalistically, like the son he never had. And Larry, whose father abandoned him at an early age, made Hank the recipient of a lot of unconscious anger he was holding against his own father.)

Kathy, a woman in her forties, had a pattern of getting into disagreements with women supervisors. She rebelled violently against any kind of female authority, and would become so irrational that she either quit or was fired from a number of positions. It was only when Kathy came to grips with *who* these authority figures represented—her mother, who had been abusive to Kathy in childhood—that she had a chance of ending this destructive pattern and creating a satisfying and productive work environment for herself and others.

If you are involved in conflict situations with a co-worker or coworkers, examine these situations closely. Do they remind you in any way of the conflicts you had—or have—in your own home? Are the people with whom you're in conflict reminiscent of anyone else in your life—mother, father, brother, sister, grandfather, ex-lover or spouse? Just as many of us marry people who remind us of our parents or other influential childhood figures, so we often carry past relationships over into the workplace.

Of course, the longest journey begins with a single step—in this case, the step of awareness. As I've said throughout this book, awareness is the first and most important step toward changing ourselves, our relationships, our lives. Once we are aware of why *we* are behaving in a certain way with certain people, we can then try to become aware of why they may be behaving in a certain way with us. Are they simply reacting to our behavior? Or do they have their own unconscious agendas that they're not aware of? Awareness is the prelude to understanding, and understanding is the prelude to change.

There may, however, be instances in which you just can't get along with someone else on the job. No matter what you try, nothing seems to work. If that's the case, go back to the Conflict Continuum in chapter 1. How would you rate this particular relationship? Is it a case of an "unclarified feeling of hostility"? Is it an all-out personality clash? Or are your difficulties with this individual "situational," that is, related specifically to on-the-job issues?

Once you've defined, as closely as possible, the nature of your relationship, you can then decide what to do about it. If you or the other person is experiencing an unclarified feeling of hostility, do you want to clarify it? If you're having a personality clash that makes it difficult for the two of you to be within a five-mile radius of each other, do you want to ask for a transfer to another department? Another state? Do you want to just plain quit the job altogether?

Bear in mind that, all things being equal, I always maintain that it's a lot better to remain in any situation and try to work it out. Whether you're talking about a marriage, your relationship with your parents or a relationship on the job, hang in there and work it out if you can. If you can't, you can't. If the job or a person you work with is making you physically and emotionally ill, and it's a situation you can neither control nor change, it isn't necessarily running away, or "doing a geographic" to quit and look for another job or work environment that's less stressful. But if you remain in the ring and do your best to *intend* and *attempt* to improve the situation, chances are high that you'll succeed—whereas if you don't, there's a high probability that you'll manifest in another work situation or personal relationship the conflict that you didn't resolve this time around.

And remember: There's nothing "wrong" with conflict, on the job or anywhere else. It happens to be very human. In fact, there's everything "right" with it, in

the sense that (a) once you realize the kind of unconscious relationship you're having with a boss, supervisor or coworker, you've just catapulted yourself into
an area of choice and consciousness, and (b) you're
uncovering yet another aspect of your own truth,
which is the most exciting and worthwhile journey we
can make in this life.

11

Creating Business Partnerships That Work

Jerry and Frank are business partners. They co-own and operate a small handmade furniture shop. They have a dozen employees and a round-the-clock operation that is quite successful. But they also have a partnership problem that has practically destroyed their friendship, and threatens to destroy the business as well.

Jerry and Frank are very different personalities. Jerry is quiet, modest and extremely affable. He's also plodding, overly conscientious, a perfectionist who prefers to see that the job gets done absolutely right, no matter how many hours he has to put in. In addition, he's extremely frugal, and often holds back his own wages until the bills and his employees' salaries are paid.

Frank, on the other hand, is more social. He likes to "shoot the breeze" and is highly popular with many of the customers, whom he treats almost like family. While this is helpful to the business on one hand, Frank sometimes talks more than he works, which annoys Jerry no end. And because his sense of money is not as keen as Jerry's, Frank sometimes loses track of the cash-flow situation, drawing himself a salary when Jerry feels they both should wait.

Frank is also a substance abuser. While it wasn't a problem in the early years of their partnership, as time went on and Frank grew more addicted to drugs and drinking, Jerry found that he couldn't count on Frank to show up on time, or even at all, from one day to the next.

But when Frank was arrested for driving under the influence one too many times, Jerry was in a real bind. Frank not only lost his license permanently, but went to jail for ninety days, at the time of year, of course, when the shop was at its busiest. Jerry ended up working eighty- to ninety-hour weeks because there was no one he could hire or train who even approached Frank's level of knowledge and expertise in woodworking. He pushed himself past the point of exhaustion, but ratio-nalized that because Frank was very remorseful and had promised to "finally get his act together," things would be better when he got out of jail.

When that happy day arrived, however, Frank went to California to "recuperate." Furious, Jerry decided at last that he just wanted to be rid of Frank. But that was no easy task. As a co-owner of the business, Frank would demand his share if he left, and Jerry didn't have the money. The business was at a critical transition stage, with more orders coming in than they could fill without expanding, and Jerry simply could afford nei-ther to lose his partner's expertise nor buy him out.

"I just wish I had the time and money to hire and train someone else," Jerry says wistfully. But given the kind of slow-but-steady profit business they're in, the time and money might not come for another ten years. Jerry feels stuck, helpless, resigned. What can he do to get himself out of this Partnership from Hell? Better yet, what could he have done to prevent these partnership blues in the first place?

GOING INTO PARTNERSHIP: SOME BASIC CAUTIONS

As business partnerships go, the example of Jerry and Frank is not an unusual one. In the rocky terrain of these relationships, it's the rare seed that falls on hospitable soil. The statistics of the Small Business Administration are bleak: *Most business partnerships fail.* In fact, the "divorce" rate among business partnerships is much higher than the divorce rate among married couples.

What gets people into bad business partnerships? The biggest mistake is having expectations that were based not upon the reality of the situation but upon what the partners wanted the situation to be, or thought it could be. The second biggest mistake is thinking that you can change the situation—or the other person. And the third is making rosy forecasts about the future in the midst of undercapitalization—not just in dollars and cents, but in terms of the creative ideas necessary to keep a business flourishing.

In reviewing their fifteen-year friendship and ten-year business partnership, Jerry realized that he and Frank had committed all three of these partnership "sins of omission." They had both talked vaguely of owning their own cottage industry, and when they heard that a shop in the area was up for sale, they made the quick decision to buy it without having done enough advance mental preparation. Instead of sitting down and mapping out a preliminary strategy *before* committing to buying the operation, Jerry and Frank bought first and thought later.

Both of them also knew each other's strengths and weaknesses. But they made the fatal assumption that, in business, personal flaws and idiosyncrasies didn't matter. And besides, they might improve in a new milieu with dynamics and demands that were distinctly different from those of a friendship.

And for the first six years of business, undercapitalization was a major issue. Because Jerry and Frank had a severe cash-flow problem and could basically afford to pay only themselves, they lacked the creative and physical resources that could have come through hiring others or bringing in a third partner. In addition, undercapitalization not only threatened the life of the business; it created a highly stressful environment that put an added strain on their relationship.

How could Jerry and Frank have tried to prevent some of these difficulties? Well, before entering into any business partnership, here are some guidelines that can minimize the danger of problems further on down the line.

1. *Know thy partner—before they're your partner.* Perhaps the most important bit of advice I ever received in law school came from the professor of the property course I took at NYU Law School.

This gentleman's name was, believe it or not, Elmer Million, and what he said to us at the end of the last class of a three-semester course was worth a million: "Most of the statutes and cases that we've studied for the past year in this class have involved handling a breach of contract," Professor Million observed, as he bid us adieu. "But if you follow one, and only one, rule in business, you can throw out everything you learned in here. That rule is simply this: 'Deal with an honest man.' "

There is no substitute for making sure, *in advance of a contract or agreement*, that the people we do business with keep their word, are trustworthy and have integrity. In other words, if you want to avoid the possibility of conflicts, you should know who you're doing business with.

By "know," I don't simply mean as an acquaintance, a good friend or even a lover. People involved in these types of relationships often go into business partnerships, just as often with disastrous results. "Knowing" your potential business partner means doing your homework: doing some outside research, gathering some business history, talking to others who may have worked with or known the person and using your own intuition and best judgment.

A business partnership is not only *like* a marriage; it *is* a marriage. While you might not be in love with your partner, you will have a financial, emotional and perhaps social bond with him or her. You may have to live with that person for a good part of your waking hours, and in this close and constant proximity you will probably have to learn the invaluable marital arts of communication, compassion and compromise if you want your relationship to strengthen and grow rather than weaken and rupture.

Remember what we said in our chapter on love relationships about listening to early warning signs that might indicate that after the initial fires of passion have died down, all may not be bliss? The same advice applies to business partnerships.

Jerry and Frank, for instance, had been friends ever since college. When they went into business, they already knew a lot about each other. Jerry was aware, for instance, that Frank liked to drink beer and smoke marijuana. This didn't bother Jerry, however, because as a buddy, Frank was a great guy to kill a few beers with. And pot was just pot, wasn't it? All of them had smoked it at one time or another.

Jerry also knew that Frank was the sort of fellow who "embellished" the facts and spent a lot of time in the future rather than the present. But Jerry chose to see Frank not as a liar or a loafer, but as a fun conversationalist and visionary, who would be a support to him in the realization of their mutual business dream.

And Frank's tendency to let money slip through his fingers wasn't exactly a well-kept secret. More than once Jerry had loaned him a few bucks for beer, or a few more to fix his old car that was just this side of auto heaven. But Jerry reasoned that for his part, Frank was generous with whatever he had, and besides, when the business really got going, his friend's money worries would be over.

As for Frank, he knew that whenever Jerry got an idea in his head, he could be "pigheaded" about it. They had clashed more than once about the way to do this or that. And Jerry's slow thoroughness was often frustrating to Frank, who liked to do something quickly and move on to the next project. But wearing the rose-colored glasses of the budding business partner, Frank preferred to see Jerry's stubbornness as persistence, and his perfectionism as cautiousness, which was certainly necessary in any business venture.

In short, both Jerry and Frank had enough information about each other before they went into business together to be able to predict trouble down the pike. In the spirit of friendship and the excitement of a new venture, however, they chose to disregard the unmistakable warning signs of incompatibility.

2. *Start off small.* When deciding to go into business together, it's a very good idea to "test" the prospect before jumping into a full-blown partnership. It would have been much better for Jerry and Frank to try a few small projects together before forming their partnership. They might have collaborated on a test design-and-marketing venture for one of their prospective products, working together on a trial basis for several months to see just how they got along. Or, they might have tried setting down—in writing—their respective business strategies, working methods and goals, comparing the two to see just where they might or might not coincide.

Just as many people decide to live together before getting married, so it can be equally illuminating to work together before tying the business partnership knot. And give yourselves a reasonable period of time to get to truly know the other's work habits and lifestyle and ride out the "honeymoon" period where you and your prospective partner will be on your best behavior and at your most enthusiastic.

Kim and Eileen are good examples of two friends who decided to go into a consulting business together, but who started small. They each made a minimal financial investment in business cards and advertising. And they took only a few projects on at first, to see how well they worked together and what the degree of commitment was to the business on both their parts.

Their caution paid off. It turned out that Kim worked much slower than Eileen, who became frustrated because she felt they could be getting more work if Kim speeded up her process. And after six months, it became evident to Kim that while she was totally committed to the business, Eileen had a lot of other irons in the fire that she wasn't willing to give up. Their trial partnership ended amicably; Eileen went on to another job and Kim eventually found another partner whose working style and personal goals coincided more closely with her own.

3. *Examine the alternatives.* Before entering into any significant business relationship, look at the alternatives to this particular relationship. If it doesn't work out, who else is available to do the job?

This portion of your homework is absolutely crucial to any long-term investment you might have in your business venture. If we go back to Jerry and Frank, we can see that Jerry's most critical problem, at the moment, is his lack of an alternative to Frank. He has no one to replace him in a crunch period, no one with his expertise and experience. As a result, Jerry's in a real double bind. His choices are dismal: Assuming that buying out Frank is not, at the present time, an option, Jerry can either work Frank's hours as well as his own, continue to ride on Frank's emotional rollercoaster or quit the business.

Chances are, however, that even after they'd decided to go into partnership, this crisis state could have been avoided. Long before Frank was arrested—years before, in fact—it was obvious to Jerry that they were having problems. As soon as he was aware of them, Jerry should have begun looking for someone to hire on a part-time basis, whom he could have trained at his leisure as a possible replacement for his errant partner.

It's the rare employer who hires an employee without maintaining a file of runners-up for the position. By the same token, no matter how close you think your friendship with your partner is, it's never too close to take precautions. Always give yourself options in terms of other people who can be on hand to take over in case this partnership just doesn't work out.

4. *The partnership checklist.* Most prospective partners think that a legal agreement is all the protection they'll ever need. And, because partners often start out as friends and want to trust each other, even this document may be minimal.

Prospective partners will probably hire a lawyer, who may pull out a standard partnership agreement form, or may dig up the same basic agreement he used for his last ten clients.

Because these "generic" agreements usually take into account *past* case law, it's a little like providing well-constructed weapons to fight the last war. They are hardly personal, hardly preventive. And they consist primarily of "boiler plate," written in incomprehensible legalese and guaranteeing the future translation services of a lawyer should anything go wrong.

This written agreement itself rarely causes problems. What is *missing*—what was avoided or not sufficiently considered—are the typical sources of partnership problems later on. Therefore, it may be much more useful to discuss a checklist of issues with your partner-to-be and to fashion your own agreement before you ask a lawyer to draft one for you.

Here's a list of fourteen key elements that should be discussed in any partnership agreement you might make. As you go through the checklist, take notes on each decision. When you're finished, draft an informal memorandum of agreement that you can both approve before taking it to a lawyer.

1. *Capital requirements.* How much capital is needed, and by what date? What will be the sources for this capital? How much will come from investors, and how much from loans or personal money?

2. *Form of ownership.* What is to be the form of ownership? Partnership? DBA? Closely-held corporation? Subchapter S corporation? What percent of ownership will each of you have?

3. *Time commitments.* What is the expected time commitment from each partner? Is there to be "sweat equity"? What about outside business activities? What's the nature and amount of time that is allowable for each partner to devote to other projects or ventures?

4. *Distribution of profits.* How much for each partner?

5. *Salaries or draw.* What is the starting salary for each partner? How will raises be decided in the future? Will salaries have to be held back? If so, in what instances?

6. *Decision making.* Which decisions require concurrence among all partners? which can be made by any partner?

7. *Division of responsibility.* What will be the duties of each partner? How much authority does each have, and in what area?

8. *Hiring other employees.* Who has authority to hire other key employees? What about hiring family members or friends?

9. *Disbursement of funds.* Who signs checks and who decides which banks to deal with?

10. *Partnership meetings.* How often will you meet? What is to be discussed at these meetings? what isn't?

11. *Financial reports.* How often will you schedule financial reports? Which of you is to be responsible for preparing them?

12. *Changing the partnership agreement.* How can the agreement be altered? How can it be expanded or ended? Are there to be mutual buy-out provisions? What about an ending date for the agreement—a "sunset" provision in which the agreement would expire unless all of you agreed to continue it?

13. *Partnership benefits.* What will each partner receive in the way of health care, expense accounts, vacations, etc.?

14. *Contingencies.* What could go wrong? Make a list of the most likely contingencies and decide how to deal with each of these worst-case possibilities.

Even if you have a watertight partnership agreement, remember: Statistics show that *most business partnerships do not succeed*. In my opinion, the majority of these failures are due to *unrealistic expectations*—of each other, yourself, market conditions or capital requirements, to name the most obvious.

How does one guard against unrealistic expectations? By injecting oneself with megadoses of reality. Regardless of how compatible you and your partner or partners believe you might be, regardless of how bright your projected economic future looks, make present reality your first priority by doing plenty of information gathering, discussing and communicating your wants, needs and expectations and planning in advance for all that could go wrong as well as all that can go right.

Well, you might say, hindsight is great. But what do you do if you're Jerry and Frank and you want to try to save a sinking business ship?

When things have reached the crisis stage in a business partnership, emotions are running high. Frustration and anger tend to cloud reason and clear-headed judgment. Therefore, the first thing to do in this sort of a situation is to *step back* from it.

Try to get away from the business for a couple of days. Go somewhere where you can relax, breathe deeply, deep sea dive, fish, meditate—whatever it takes to clear your mind and reduce your blood pressure.

Do some of the internal research exercises we've discussed throughout the book. Ask yourself what you really want. Do you really want to remain in the business because you love it or because you don't want your partner to get it if you leave? Do you really want to try to work things out with your partner and do you think it's possible? Or does your intuition tell you that it's a dead end and you'd be much better off, and happier, working with someone else—or even giving up the business?

If you think there's still a chance to salvage the partnership, what is it going to take? How much effort are you willing to put into it?

If the effort isn't worth it, what are the possibilities for buying your partner out? What legal recourse do you have if he or she has not lived up to his obligations as a partner and has endangered the business by his/her actions or lack of them?

Once you become clear on what it is that you want, from both the business and your partner, you can take the following actions.

1. *Arrange a meeting with your partner.* Tell him or her that you'd like to sit down and discuss both of your options at this point. Don't lay any blame or pass any judgment. Simply say, "I know we've been having some difficulties and I'm sure you'd be as happy to see them resolved as I would. Why don't we meet and talk about what it is that we both want, and how we might be able to work things out to our mutual advantage?"

2. *Put down your objectives, and a possible strategy for meeting them, in writing.* When you meet with your partner, you'll want to be as calm and objective as possible. In order to reach this state of mind, you need to have a written plan that you can present to him or her. If you plan on "winging it," there's a good chance you and your partner will end up with an emotional free-for-all rather than a successful business meeting.

Never underestimate the advantages of advance preparation. Write down everything—what you want, what you've been happy and unhappy with in your partner, ways in which you think the two of you can work things out. Make a copy of this document and give it to your partner at the outset of the meeting. Better yet, tell him/her that this is what you're planning to do, and invite him/her to do the same. If both of you have a written strategy, it's that much easier to see where you converge in your feelings and intentions, which in turn makes it that much easier to come to a peaceful resolution of the conflict.

3. *Set a deadline.* Agree upon a time limit for testing whatever strategy the two of you decide to implement. In Jerry and Frank's case, Jerry should give Frank a time frame in which to "get his act together" and to prove that he cares enough about the business and the partnership to make some changes in his personal life. But *how* he does this is crucial. It's important not to state things in terms of an ultimatum—"Clean up your act or else!" Jerry has a much better chance of getting what he wants from Frank if he says, "I know you've been trying, Frank. But when you fall off the wagon, the business suffers and I suffer. I care about you as a friend. But I can't afford to take chances with the business. So, here's my suggestion. I'd like you to go for counseling and make a real attempt to get off the drugs and the booze. And I'd like you to show me that you care about the business enough to put your share of time and effort into it.

"How does a three-month deadline sound to you? Do you think that gives you enough time to get it together? Or, would you rather discuss dissolving the partnership? You don't have to decide this minute. But let me know, say, by Wednesday, what your decision is."

4. *Draw up an agreement or revised contract for the future.* Let's say Frank is willing to try to save the partnership and abide by Jerry's three-month deadline. The next step is for them to draw up an agreement or revised contract that will protect Jerry and the business in the event that Frank is again "incapacitated," and that will also protect Frank in the event that something happens to Jerry.

Such an agreement can be checked by a lawyer after it's drawn up.

5. *Agree on regular meetings to review progress and agreements.* Holding regular meetings to get a status report on the relationship is excellent preventive medicine. The partners agree to get together at regular intervals to discuss how they're doing emotionally and financially, if everyone is doing his or her job, what needs to be done that isn't being done. Mutual intentions can be reclarified; the question, "Why are we in this partnership?" can always benefit from being reiterated and reexamined.

Imagine your business partnership as a car, and these meetings as tune-ups that will catch small problems before they become major ones, exposing hidden agendas and realigning intentions with actions.

6. *Mediation.* If bad feelings have gotten so out of hand that your partner isn't willing to meet with you, it's a good time to suggest mediation. Here an objective third party will meet with you and your partner to listen to both sides and help you to resolve your differences as amicably as possible. If your partner refuses to meet with you and refuses to try mediation, it's a pretty

clear sign that "working things out" is not an option, and that you'd better begin to think in terms of dissolving the partnership.

7. *When all else fails . . . see a lawyer.* When a business partnership goes awry, many people make the mistake of assuming that consulting a lawyer should be their first step. "I want to know my rights!" they say. "I'm not letting that SOB take advantage of me!"

Nine times out of ten, you will pay a lawyer to do a job you could have done yourself, for a fraction of the time, money and stress. In most cases, either by yourselves or with the help of a mediator, you and your partner can make up your own agreements. It's only when communication has totally broken down and you need to extricate yourself from a bad situation that you should seek legal consultation. To arm yourself with a lawyer first is to broadcast your intention of going to war.

Before you sound the legal cannons, try every other avenue you can to work things out with your partner. Going to court is not an option; it's a last resort.

BUSINESS AND MARRIAGE: THEY DON'T ALWAYS GO TOGETHER LIKE A HORSE AND CARRIAGE

Many marriages involve husband-and-wife-owned businesses. This is a particularly delicate balancing act, and one that demands careful forethought, a commodity all too scarce among couples in love.

Take Tom and Nancy. They met in the MBA program of a midwestern college, fell in love and married. After several years, they decided to open a toy store in their old college town. Nancy was in charge of inventory and teaching toymaking classes. Tom ran the financial end of the operation. They opened small, and within a year business was so good they were able to expand their shop, build a large, rambling house in the woods and have a second child.

But while the business blossomed, the marriage was withering. Nancy had gained nearly one hundred pounds since their wedding day. She devoted most of her energy to the business and their two daughters, with little left over for her husband. And she had become a leading "expert" in handcrafted dolls and the author of numerous best-selling books in the field. Suddenly she was bringing tens of thousands of extra dollars into the family/business coffers. She became bossy and irritable. And she filled every corner of the house with handmade dolls.

Tom was horrified. Because truth to tell, he hated dolls. To him, making them was a lucrative business venture, not an interior decorator's dream. To Nancy, however, it was her livelihood, as well as her chosen form of creative expression. Deaf to Tom's pleas, Nancy slowly but surely transformed their home into a giant dollhouse. The only room that was off limits to her was Tom's office, on the top floor of the house—a room distinguished by its sparseness, orderliness and the absence of dolls.

Tom was miserable in his marriage. But when he finally brought up the subject of divorce to Nancy, she went through the roof, assuring him that he'd lose everything, from the house and the kids to his share of the business.

So, Tom stayed in his unhappy marriage. He'd learned the hard way that mixing business and marriage is like going to Las Vegas, winning on one number and taking all your chips and putting them on another. You're not hedging your bets; you're either going to come out a big winner or you're going to lose everything.

Was there any way Tom's unfortunate situation could have been avoided? Only if, at the outset of his business venture with his wife, the two of them had agreed to admit that they were in an "altered state," and to make a business agreement accordingly.

An "altered state" is one where one's perceptions are clouded by one's emotions. When we're enraged, we're in an altered state. When we're ecstatic we're in an altered state. And of all the altered states I know, there is none so exquisite or so dangerous as being "in love."

If two people who are married decide to go into business together, my advice to them would be to be aware that they're in an altered state and that while that condition could cause them to have the impulse and the desire to form a business partnership, they must make an agreement with themselves that they will finalize that partnership only when they're in a nonaltered state. They must, in effect, *make a contract with themselves* that the venture will not be viable until their altered and unaltered states agree.

Does this sound patently ridiculous? Well, better ridiculous than devastating. Combining business and marriage successfully takes an almost superhuman degree of foresight and fortitude. Can you be with your spouse twenty-four hours a day? Can you both withstand the double-whammy stresses of making a marriage and a business work? How much quality time will you have for each other? For your children? What are your short-term goals? long-term goals? And what will you do if the marriage doesn't work out?

Such vital questions can only be answered in a state of utter practicality and clarity. And that state can only be attained when you are able to trust not simply the other person, but yourself. The contract you have with *yourself*, to only act when reason has overtaken emotion, is, in fact, far more important than any contract you might have with anyone else.

Trusting yourself involves relying on your intuition, your assessment of the facts and your judgment to tell you whether or not something or someone is right for you. Most of us use the word "trust" in the context of the other person: "I trust him," or "I don't trust her." But when it comes to trust, the other person isn't that important. Because if you trust yourself, you can always make necessary adjustments and changes in relation to new circumstances.

If you and your lover or spouse are contemplating going into business together, do some inner work. What are your gut feelings about the venture? What are your hopes? your fears? How might being in business together affect your marriage? What's your contingency plan if things don't work out? What are some alternatives to actually forming a business partnership?

Never assume that just because you're in love and committed to each other that a joint business venture is a built-in sure thing. It's as important to go through a partnership checklist with your spouse as it is with anyone else—even more important, perhaps, as the contingencies you need to foresee must take into account your marital as well as your business relationship.

DIVORCE AND BUSINESS: CAN EXS REMAIN PARTNERS?

Fred and Angie were husband-and-wife partners in their own literary agency. After eight tempestuous years of marriage, they asked me to mediate their divorce. And some months after that, they came back to me with an unusual request. They wanted to know if I could help them remain business partners.

Talk about sticky situations! Because of their complicated financial arrangement—which involved Fred keeping the house, Angie moving to an apartment and the business paying for both—as well as the fact that they each had put their entire lives into the business and didn't want the other to enjoy all the profits, they had been unable to sever their work relationship.

But you didn't have to have a crystal ball to predict that their heroic attempt at business togetherness would end in fireworks.

When they came to see me, Angie was on the verge of murdering Fred. "He's absolutely impossible!" she screamed, during one of our more energetic sessions. "He's an obsessive-compulsive neat freak! And he's invasive to the point of abuse! Why, the other day he got so angry at me for something he thought I wasn't doing that he picked up my desk and dumped the papers all over me!"

Angie admitted to feeling "physically violated" by Fred, who, although he had never been physically abusive, had a violent temper that only seemed to erupt in her direction. "You're probably the kindest, gentlest person I know," she observed. "And everybody would say that about you. But nobody else can cause fear in me except you."

As Angie talked, it became evident to both of them that Fred was the only one who could push her buttons, and vice versa. Because they knew each other so intimately, each knew intuitively just what to say, how to look or what to do or not do in order to get the other's goat. "He's a badgerer," Angie reflected. "And I'm a digger. I'm really good at sticking the knife in and turning it." This wasn't conscious behavior, however, until it showed up in the merciless mirror of mediation.

My job, as I saw it, was to help them do whatever it was that they wanted to do. If they chose to stay together as business partners, I could help them give it a try. If, on the other hand, they decided during the session that there was no way they could really make a go of it, I was equally willing to help them separate.

I gave them the up and down sides of both possibilities. "If you decide to stay together," I said, "you'll learn a lot more about yourselves and each other because you won't have a choice. If, however, you split up, life will definitely be easier. You'll be more relaxed; you'll have more fun. This mess won't be the focus of all your energies. That's not to say, however, that it won't happen with the next person. But for the moment you both will breathe easier."

Both of them still wanted to try to remain partners. "Okay," I said. "What would you both like to change in yourselves that would make a partnership possible?"

They had to do some thinking about that. Finally Angie said, "You know, with everybody else in the world I tend to act humble and downgrade myself. But with Fred I feel the need to get overblown and puff myself up. I wish I didn't do that."

"What do you think makes you do that with Fred?" I asked.

"I don't know. I think that down deep I don't believe I'm as good as he is."

When Fred, who had been understandably on the defensive throughout the session, saw Angie become more vulnerable and honest, he immediately grew gentler.

"I guess I'm really anal and picky and obsessive-compulsive," he confessed. "I know that must bother people. I infiltrate other people's spaces and I'd like to change that about myself."

From this point on, they opened up to each other. "You know," Fred remarked, "this is the first time we've been able to talk straight with each other since we were here last."

"Yeah," Angie agreed. "I was feeling so angry. But I'm not angry anymore."

"So—you still want to stay in business together?" I asked.

"Well . . . Can you be business partners and not like each other?" Fred inquired.

"And Joel, you said something earlier, about learning a lot if we stay together," Angie cut in. "What's the fine line between masochism and learning?"

"Those are both wonderful questions," I replied. "And they dovetail beautifully. The answer to Fred's question is, 'Yes.' But it depends upon whether the not liking each other is a research question or a conclusion."

"Go on." Both Fred and Angie were intrigued.

"If you just don't like each other and you conclude that there's no way for either of you to change, then you really won't be able to remain together. You've already come to the foregone conclusion that no matter what, you're going to continue disliking each other.

"If, on the other hand, you turn it into a question—'We don't like each other, but is there any way we can change that and succeed in creating a viable working relationship?'—you're in a different frame of mind. Now you can explore the disliking, see what it's about. As long as the incentive is there—if it's a money incentive or whatever—and you're willing to discover what it is about both of you that contributes to the disliking, you can remain partners. And that, Angie, is the fine line between masochism and learning."

Both Fred and Angie stated that they were willing to examine the source of their feelings about each other. They decided to hire me as a "business consultant," and to meet with me for a two-hour session twice a month. So far they're still in business together, due to the fact that they are now *aware* of their actions and are able to observe them and reflect upon them.

So, when Fred gets picky, instead of going into the old knee-jerk reaction of rage and fear, Angie calmly and nonjudgmentally points out what he's doing and he recognizes his behavior accordingly. Similarly, when Angie feels the urge to "stick the knife in," Fred will ask her why she feels the need to go digging. This isn't to say that they still don't get angry at each other. But because they now know what they're doing and are willing to take responsibility for their actions rather than blaming one another, they have a much higher chance of maintaining a tolerable work relationship.

WHEN IT'S TIME TO CALL IT QUITS

George is forty-seven and Clark is forty. The two Atlanta real estate developers were partners for twelve years. Even before their partnership began, they were good friends; their twelve years together increased their closeness. George was considered the "senior partner," serving as a mentor to Clark, teaching him the business and helping him become successful at it. He was, in effect, like an older brother, and for Clark, who had no wife or children of his own, George's family was *his* family.

So, when George decided to make a career change and open a practice as a marriage and family therapist, Clark's world suddenly fell apart.

Although George had given Clark warning for approximately four years that he was thinking of eventually making such a move, when he actually announced that he wished to dissolve their partnership, Clark was stunned. He felt abandoned and betrayed; not only was his closest friend "deserting" him, but he was forcing him to change his own life as well.

Money was not the issue. Their net property holdings totaled more than $10 million. Each drew an annual salary of approximately $250 thousand. Thanks to hard work, sound investments and a booming real estate market, both men had done extremely well. But the hour of reckoning for the partnership was at hand, and Clark couldn't face it.

To George's bewilderment, Clark went into a depression. He couldn't work, couldn't function. He saw a therapist for the first time in his life. And finally, when he was ready at last to face the inevitable and begin talking about the dissolution, he demanded his "revenge" in the form of what George considered to be exorbitant financial compensation.

George and Clark came to see me hoping to resolve their conflict without having to resort to the courts. At first their ability to communicate calmly and constructively was at a low ebb.

GEORGE: When I said, "Let's talk about dissolving the partnership," what happened was not what I had in mind. In twelve years we've always been able to work things out. This is probably the toughest issue we've ever faced.

CLARK: Right now I'm drained. I don't want to fight, but I'm not going to let you take advantage of me anymore.

GEORGE: Dammit, I'm not trying to take advantage of you! Let's stop this; it's getting us nowhere.

As the session progressed, however, they began to discuss rational alternatives.

GEORGE: I'll tell you what. Let's give ourselves another weekend to think things over. We'll be back together in the office on Monday; let's both give ourselves some questions to think about until then.

George wrote down the following questions and made a copy for Clark.

1. Do you want to continue alone or with a partner? Or do you also want out of the business?
2. Even assuming that you put in more hours than I did these past few years, what about the first few years? What about all the time I spent teaching you the business?

3. If you want to continue the business, what can I do to help assure its success without being available as a partner?
4. If you want to buy me out, what method do you want to use to pay me off?
5. How do we decide what the whole partnership is worth for purposes of selling it or dividing it? What if pieces are sold to pay me off? What are the other options?

"What about you, Clark?" George asked, as he handed Clark the questionnaire. "Do you have some questions or issues for me to think about prior to our next meeting?"

"Yes," Clark replied. "I'd like to know what Charlie, our lawyer, and Linda, our accountant, have to suggest about the situation. I'm concerned about the tax consequences if we start selling properties or buying each other out. Maybe we should wait until we have had a chance to talk to them.

"Next I want to know your time schedule. How soon do you want out and how much time can you devote to the business during the next few months? How much longer can I count on you?"

When they next met, their "dollars-and-cents" discussion, which had served to mask the real issues underlying the conflict, gave way to honest interaction on a "feeling" level.

GEORGE: I want you to know how much our partnership has meant to me. It's not as easy as it may sound for me to give it up. It's taken several years for me to come to this decision, which has nothing to do with any dissatisfaction with you or any complaints. But I'm changing careers. I have an-other calling now.

I know I must be causing you pain, anxiety, anger, insecurity and who knows what else. But it's not my intention to hurt you. I know it's difficult right now for you to look on the bright side. What's of primary importance to me is that you try to understand *why* I'm changing careers—that it's not something I'm doing *to* you. Am I making sense? And do you believe me?

CLARK: I guess so. You've always been strong-minded; you've always basically done what you wanted. Why should this be any different? I saw it coming years ago and I didn't want to face it. But I can't help taking it personally. I'm the one who's being left in the lurch. I haven't been preparing for five years to do something else. What the hell am I going to do while you're having a great time shrinking all those needy clients?

GEORGE: Well, what are you *intending* to do? Have you been able to think about it? Are you going to continue in the business, sell out and take some time off or jump into something else?

CLARK: My first instinct is to keep up what has worked well for me. But I'm open to chang-ing, just as long as I don't work for someone else.

GEORGE: That sounds like a good start to me. I know you think I'm running out on you and that you've been carrying me for years. If I were in your place, I'd probably see my conduct the same way.

CLARK: I'm glad you finally see it my way.

Although their ability to empathize with each other had increased markedly, there was still the thorny issue of how to divide their joint assets. After several weeks of fruitless wrangling over a number of possibilities, Clark and George were at a standstill—until Clark came up with the following solution.

CLARK: Tell me this, George. You *say* you want to be completely out and I believe you. I've even grudgingly begun to accept the partnership break up. But does it make economic sense for you to jump ship now?

We got into this partnership to build up equity, which we certainly have done. So let me ask you this. What if we could find a way to keep your equity building up, to keep income coming to you and for you to have no responsibility?

GEORGE: You're losing me. It sounds impossible.

CLARK: Stay with my train of thought, please. It's so simple I don't know why either of us didn't think of it sooner. Here's the idea: You and I continue to jointly and equally own the property, almost like limited partners. I do all the managing, buying, selling and other decision making on our behalf. I'll get a fee for that service and you won't have to do much more than get a check each month. You've trained me well and I've learned a lot. I think I can do it. What do you think?

GEORGE: I don't know. It's interesting. I'd be putting a great deal of trust in you and I'd have very little control. But it would certainly keep me from having to decide how to manage my investments. I must say, you've turned the tables on me. Here I

was readying myself to withdraw from the partnership, and now you're thinking of using our assets
and experience for our mutual benefit!

CLARK: That's right. Maybe you don't need to
"take the money and run."

GEORGE: Well. This is a real show-stopper. Give
me a few days to think about it and we'll talk
again.

The happy ending is that George and Clark agreed
to continue joint ownership of properties, with Clark
managing and controlling the enterprise. Through
mediation, and the willingness to take each other's
needs and wants into account, George and Clark were
able to save their friendship *and* their partnership,
turning a conflict into a new phase in their business
relationship.

When one person wants to end a business partnership and the other doesn't, it's as painful as a divorce involving one willing and one unwilling spouse.
Fortunately, however, in the case of a business partnership there are always options. You just need to
give yourself enough time and space to think of them.
In the case of George and Clark, their frequent meetings and conversations were actually brainstorming
sessions in disguise, with the right solution finally
coming up unexpectedly as a result of their discussions.

But it wasn't just talking that resolved their conflict.
It was the *intention* and *willingness* on the part of
both George and Clark to work things out amicably,
to see the other person first as a human being and
a friend and secondly as a business partner, and to

respect his perspective, as much as possible, in all of their interactions.

George and Clark were fortunate. They were each doing business with an honest man. And honesty, trust and mutual satisfaction were the results.

12

Creating and Conducting Successful Meetings

One of the best places to begin using the techniques in this book to improve your working relationships with friends, family, coworkers and superiors and *their* relationships with each other is at a typical gathering that, sooner or later, all of us are subjected to: a meeting.

MEETINGS: COMING TOGETHER EFFECTIVELY

At various times in our daily lives, we are all participants, either willing or unwilling, in *meetings*. Family meetings, school meetings, partner meetings, church or synagogue meetings, department meetings, board meetings . . . We are all familiar with the experience of interacting within a group environment, in the hopes of setting and accomplishing a larger goal for the common good.

It's interesting that the origin of the word "meeting" comes from the Anglo-Saxon *metan*, which means "to come together." The original intent of meeting with others, then, was a positive and harmonious one: to unite people in a mutually beneficial activity.

All too often, however, meetings are drudgery. In many cases they are a necessary evil, a requirement of the job or organization in which we're involved. They're something to endure—to sleep through, daydream through, fidget through, until at last we hear the magic words, usually uttered by the "leader" of the event: "Well, I guess that about wraps things up," at which point we can bolt from our seats like kids barreling out of school at the eagerly awaited sound of the bell.

Some people, particularly those who work for organizations of any size and who have so-called white collar or creative jobs spend a substantial amount of their time in meetings. For example, a high county official I know spends at least half of his time in meetings, some of which he "runs," and some of which he simply participates in as a staff person. He would be the first to admit that a large percentage of these meetings are either a partial or complete waste of time and that they are not run in ways that are either effective, efficient or pleasant.

Ask yourself how many of the meetings that you've attended were necessary. How many were well run? How many were enjoyable? How many accomplished anything useful proportional to the amount of time they took up? If you answered, "very few," your experience is the norm. The sobering truth is that *most meetings are not necessary, and that therefore most of us whose work involves regular meetings spend a substantial part of our lives in ways that are ineffective, inefficient and unpleasant.*

Meetings often disintegrate into empty rituals. They're a little like reciting poetry in the third grade: You may be great at memorizing it, but it probably won't have much meaning to you. People who attend a lot of meetings may find themselves in a rut, parroting words or approaches that have become meaningless and empty through overuse. Instead of a live, *living* interaction, many meetings have a mortuary cast to them. Getting any enthusiasm or energy out of the participants is a feat akin to raising the dead.

This reminds me of a billboard I often pass on one of the L.A. freeways for a rock station whose claim to fame is its selection of current hits. Their slogan reads, "Less Music by Dead Guys." The goal of the "perfect" meeting, as I see it, is to provide "more music by live guys." But how can we turn meetings from cemetery visits into positive, productive, invigorating experiences?

Think about how you might be able to *energize*, *enervate* and *change* the next meeting you're going to attend. The nature of the meeting is immaterial. It could be a meeting at work, or with the PTA or a club or organization you belong to—even a meeting with family members. We're interested here in the *vehicle* of the meeting process, as an opportunity to facilitate meaningful and effective communication.

Similarly, your "official" role at the meeting is of secondary importance. Whether you're the chairman of the board, president of a company, officer of a club, department supervisor or staff employee, your goal is, ideally, the same: to help energize and facilitate personal interaction so that all the participants feel as though they're an important part of the process and the meeting becomes a true *coming together* of ideas and goals.

MAXIMIZING YOUR MEETING STRATEGY

How can you make the most of and get the best out of the meetings in your life?

1. *Write down your own needs and goals.* Become focused; do some internal research. What do you feel is the purpose of the meeting? What would you personally like to get out of it? What do you hope it accomplishes in terms of short- or long-range goals?

2. *Do some advance preparation.* Meetings can be divided into three quite separable phases. The first is *set up and creation*. The second is the *meeting itself*. And the third is *following through on the meeting*.

Let's talk about *set up*. Most of us come to meetings unprepared. We are often unclear as to our role in the process; we will often try to "wing it" unless we have to make an actual presentation. Remember the case of Steven, the aerospace employee who was having problems with his supervisor, Sylvia? (chapter 5). Although he did not have a "meeting" with her in the way meetings are categorized here—as a group rather than one-on-one activity—Steven prepared thoroughly in advance before he went in to discuss his concerns with Sylvia. He did his research, finding out about her background, some of the reasons for her behavior, the best time and the best way to approach her and other crucial information that maximized his chances for successful communication with her. Had he "winged it" without clarifying his own feelings, needs and goals and getting vital information about Sylvia beforehand, Steven would not have been nearly so focused, calm and ultimately successful.

So, in order to maximize any meeting, you want to get people to do much of the work of the meeting in advance. You want to get them thinking about it, preparing for it, so that by the time the meeting takes place, they can already be on board as to what the intention of the meeting is. Hopefully they're in agreement as to that intention; hopefully they're already sparked and ready to go.

Discuss the intention with the participants beforehand, or write to them. State your own; invite them to state theirs. What is the meeting intended to accomplish? What do they think are some of the best methods of realizing this? Have them write out their needs, goals, concerns and ideas beforehand. Remember: You don't have to be the designated "leader" or facilitator of the meeting to do this. Your input as an attendee probably is just as valuable as anyone else's. This is a crucial concept to communicate to the other participants: That their concerns are important, and that once they take responsibility for their own needs, they are far more likely to have them met.

This is particularly important for passive participants—those people who, if they are not responsible for the meeting, will automatically take a back seat, acting as if they're little more than auditors, sitting in on a course for noncredit. Your goal is to "activate" these passive participants, help them to feel personally connected to and an important part of the process. For this reason, you'll want to set up the meeting in the most consensual way possible, so that instead of feeling summoned to be there, the participants *want* to be there.

3. *Label the meeting as to type and function*. Every meeting should, at the outset, be clearly defined. Is it a *brainstorming* meeting, for the purpose of generating ideas? Is it a *decisional* meeting? If so, who is going to make the decision—one person or a majority? Is it an *electoral* meeting? Is it a meeting of *department heads*? A routine *staff* meeting? Whatever the type of meeting, it should be clearly defined in advance, and a decision made as to who exactly needs to be there.

Much of the inefficiency and frustration in meetings is due to the fact that people who don't need to attend them are required to put in an appearance. A boss, for instance, might like to round up an entire department simply for his or her convenience, so that he or she can "get the whole picture," when in reality that picture can be effectively and efficiently provided by a few people and 90 percent of the meeting will be a total bore to many of the employees forced to sit through it.

4. *Running the meeting*. After the preparatory phase, second phase of the meeting is the actual conduct of it. I don't like the term "running," because it implies that someone in some sort of authority position is taking control of the proceedings.

Unless the primary purpose of gathering people together is to bring the word of God to them, a *real meeting should never be "run" by the authority figure in the room*. This statement may sound surprising, because it runs so completely counter to the way most of us have been conditioned. It is nearly always expected that the person "in charge" of the organization, section or group—the CEO, the department head, the club president—should be the automatic engineer of the proceedings.

Now, some meetings have the aura of passing out the stone tablets about them. The president of a company might hold a meeting simply to inform his or her employees that a merger is about to take place. An army general might call a meeting to pass along orders to his subordinate officers. In these instances, the speaker is the person in charge and they're going to run the meeting the way he or she sees it.

But most meetings are *not* for the purpose of simply passing orders along. And if they are, they should be clearly labeled as such. The majority of meetings will *not* benefit from having the highest authority figure in the organization at the helm, because (1) subordinates may feel inhibited from taking an active and honest participatory role. If we're afraid that our opinions might conflict with those of the authority figure, we aren't likely to express them; (2) It gives the authority figure too much power—not only the power of the final decision but the power of the gavel. When the *substantive power* and the *process power* come together in one person, you have your basic dictatorship. That's one of the great beauties of the U.S. Constitution— that it provides for a separation of powers, so that one branch of the government can't become too strong. Well, the same principle applies here: *If you want to have a good meeting, you must have a separation of powers.* You must separate the legislative, executive and judicial functions, delegating them to more than one individual.

Moreover, effective and productive conduction of meetings is a skill and a working experience that very few of us—especially chief executives—possess. I mentioned the real importance, in mediation, of *facilitating* the communication process rather than simply "knowing what to do" when the door closes and the mediation begins. Well, it's the same with meetings. Most of them are set up and run according to what I call the "amateur mediator's mistake": focusing most of one's attention on what to do when the door closes, and not enough on the preliminaries and preparations, as well as the surrounding circumstances and the most effective way in which to run the meeting itself.

The *process* is the issue here. It doesn't matter what the topic of the meeting is—whether it's a meeting as to what type of offer to make to settle a court case, how to increase sales, how to refine an existing product or what the agenda is going to be for the *next* meeting. *How* that meeting is going to be run is the most important decision that needs to be made, for that will determine its context and feeling, and therefore how productive or unproductive it will be.

One can use the analogy here of a marital relationship. I believe that just as most of a meeting is determined by *how* it is run, so most of a relationship is concerned with *how* the people communicate. How they talk to each other, how they fight with each other and what they think they're fighting about. Because what they are really fighting about is concerned far more with *how* they are dealing with each other than the actual subject itself.

In order to maximize the chances for a meeting's success, have it conducted by someone who is *successfully experienced in facilitation*, who can help all the participants to become aware of *how* they are talking to each other as much as *what* they are talking about. The goal is to make everyone feel part of the process, from both a personal and professional standpoint, and to feel that their contribution is just as important as anyone else's in the room, regardless of position—all of this in the service of having *more productive* and *shorter* meetings.

The facilitator's chief objective is to get the best out of the people who are there. So, he or she needs to have an intention to stimulate and motivate. He or she needs to be skilled in "mining," unearthing ideas, opinions, feelings and other matters relevant to the situation. At times the facilitator must take the role of provocateur, at other times the role of ally. The best facilitators I know are people who are more focused on *listening* than on talking themselves, who are genuinely interested in the opinions and feelings of others and who don't need to be constantly expressing their own.

But facilitating isn't easy; it's a skillful practice that involves being able to maintain the delicate balance of power in a group environment. A good facilitator must be on his or her toes at all times, cognizant of everyone in the room, involving people without making them feel intruded upon, hearing what they're really saying and responding accordingly, making sure that no one is left out of the process and that no one person is allowed to take too much of the stage. In other words, the facilitator's own ability to maintain his or her balance will greatly affect the balance in the room.

And in the process, the "boss" can truly sit back and "take it all in" without having to perform. Doing an effective job of conducting a meeting is, in itself, a task requiring a person's full attention. If the authority figure in the room is also conducting the meeting, he or she is really attempting to do two jobs. Something is bound to suffer; others may not be able to get the feedback they need from their superior, and the true purpose of the meeting may be lost. But when the authority figure is more relaxed, he/she and everyone else has more access to all of his/her faculties, the most important of which may be his/her experience. *Not* having to conduct the meeting can allow more of these qualities to shine through.

5. *Following up on the meeting.* Whether or not a meeting was productive can be judged by what occurred at the meeting itself. But whether or not a meeting was *effective* can only be determined by following up on it.

Follow-up, the third phase of the meeting process, is just as important as setting up and conducting the meeting. In some ways it is even more important, because it will greatly influence the long-range effectiveness of the meeting—whether or not agreed-upon tasks are being carried out and various issues and concerns are kept in focus.

Ron and Maria Reifler, who make up the Los Angeles consulting team of Reifler Associates, Inc., are experienced educators and consultants to management. They help both corporations and school systems learn skills in team building and self-esteem, and their clients range from General Motors, Chrysler Corporation and Walt Disney Studios to some fifty-five school districts throughout California and the Southwest.

The Reiflers are noted for their ability to motivate groups, to energize and activate participants who, because they are usually required to attend a seminar scheduled by their company or school, are often not initially excited about being there.

"We spend a lot of time helping people to feel comfortable in the seminars, with themselves and each other," notes Ron Reifler. "We encourage them to express their feelings, to get to know each other, to really participate in the event. At the end of the day, or the weekend, most of the people we work with are really excited and revved up about new techniques and attitudes we've shown them, and are eager to try them out in their work environments.

"But we've found that unless the company or organization schedules follow-up sessions with us, there's a higher probability of their employees losing their motivation and forgetting much of what they learned. Correspondingly, when follow-up seminars and workshops are scheduled, employees are likely to be far more successful in utilizing what we've taught them and making the initial seminar 'pay off.' By discussing their progress, their successes and problems, people can keep their original intentions and goals in focus. At the same time they are better understanding and refining the new skills they've learned, and better incorporating them into their lives."

After a meeting, then, either follow-up meetings should be scheduled or someone should be designated to check in on people's progress. The lines of communication must be kept open, so that difficulties that crop up along the way are dealt with, triumphs congratulated and enthusiasm maintained. In this way, the experience of effective, honest communication—and conflict prevention—will not be merely a "one-shot deal," but can rather become part of the normal routine.

MEETINGS AS DISPUTE-PREVENTION DEVICES

It's a statistical fact that groups and organizations that hold regular meetings have better long-run efficiency and productivity than those that don't. The reason is simple: Affording people a chance to express their ideas, feelings or grievances on a regular basis clears the air and helps to insure that disagreements or dissatisfactions will not be allowed to escalate into full-blown conflicts.

Families who have weekly or monthly meetings to discuss their issues will tend to be happier ones because communication has been made a top priority. Business or staff meetings that are not perfunctory, that discuss genuine concerns of the employees rather than delivering glowing reports about how wonderfully everything is going, will help to foster a work environment in which people feel better about themselves and consequently do a better job.

On the other hand, environments in which silence reigns, in which denial plays a major role and the opinions, feelings and needs of the members are not valued will tend to foster confusion, fear, anger and resentment. In such an environment, people are not likely to be operating at an optimum level of productivity and efficiency because too much energy will be spent cultivating negative rather than positive attitudes and emotions.

Take the following example. Mr. Adams was the president and publisher of an entertainment magazine. Because he only felt powerful when he was controlling his environment and everyone in it, Mr. Adams took a dictatorial approach to running his publication. He was careful not to praise his employees and made sure to go heavy on the criticism. He was habitually indecisive about everything, so that people never knew what he'd like or dislike or where they stood. He underpaid everyone and never gave raises. Once, when the magazine was running late to the printer, he even expected part of his staff to come in on Christmas Day without giving them overtime. In short, he was a genuine Ebenezer Scrooge.

The constant state of tension and confusion he created among his staff weakened their sense of self-esteem, made them fear for their jobs and gave Mr. Adams a feeling of absolute authority.

So, it almost goes without saying that Mr. Adams hated meetings. He didn't want to hear his staff's opinions, didn't want his own challenged and certainly didn't want to let anyone else feel as though they were important or valuable. Once that happens, he reasoned, it's all over. They'll get uppity. They'll start asking for raises, trying to run things . . . Maybe they'll even try to edge me out!

Because of Mr. Adams's paranoia and his insistence on wielding complete authority, his magazine was neither a happy nor a particularly productive place in which to work. As a result, he was constantly losing top writers and editors. In a single week, three of his key employees quit. And those who remained resented him so much that they did the minimum amount of work, taking long breaks whenever he was out of the office and not giving their "all" to the publication.

Finally Mr. Adams realized that if he wanted to keep his publication going, he would have to begin recognizing and valuing his staff members. Reluctantly he held a staff meeting, where many grievances were aired and issues were discussed and clarified. People immediately felt calmer and more cheerful. Productivity increased, and soon Mr. Adams began to hold regular staff meetings.

To his surprise, Mr. Adams discovered that instead of posing threats to his authority, staff meetings actually enhanced it. His employees respect him more and became far more loyal than they had been in the past. The meeting process served not only to clarify issues and increase motivation and productivity within the office—it became a highly effective dispute-prevention device.

MEETINGS AS A FINAL STAGE OF DEVELOPMENT

We usually view an initial meeting as a beginning stage of getting something accomplished. But sometimes a first meeting can actually be the *final* stage in a process, particularly when that meeting involves conflict resolution.

In 1985, I did a major mediation inside Wilson Learning Systems, a relatively small corporation (owned by a large publisher) that provided training curricula in management, sales and supervision for industry and that in 1985 boasted two hundred of the Fortune 500 companies as clients.

The chairman of the corporation, Larry Wilson, who also happens to be the coauthor, with Ken Blanchard, of the book *The One-Minute Salesperson*, brought me in to deal with a serious dispute. Let him describe it:

"I had envisioned a new, more efficient and effective way to deliver learning through a self-instructional 'interactive video' process. In order to make this new 'IT' [Interactive Technology] group succeed and to keep it from being destroyed by the mainstream of the parent organization in Minneapolis, we decided to move to Santa Fe. The separation concept is similar to what IBM did in moving the PC development group to Boca Raton, Florida. [And, later, what General Motors did in setting up the Saturn division in Tennessee.]

"Within eight months from start-up we had a conflict brewing. It looked like a territorial conflict between the people who ran the Minneapolis studio and the people in the Santa Fe art shop who were creating their idea of how the new interactive video process should look.

"The dispute became very serious. It developed into a corporate crisis situation, escalating way beyond normal boundaries and bouncing up to the top of the company. Now, it would not be uncommon to have the CEO listen to all sides, render a judgment, send it down and say, 'Now let's get back to work.' That sometimes is appropriate. However, most of my experience shows that rendering a judgment from above never really solves the real problems. It's treating the *symptoms*, not the underlying cause. And it was clearly our goal to provide a sense of mutuality and partnering, not to create a further rift between the two groups.

"At that point, it occurred to me that we needed to bring in an unbiased person—a new player. I was looking for someone who understood underlying human principles, someone who understood the nature of negotiation from the point of view of arriving at a win-win type of growth experience for the players."

So, Larry contacted me. My first action was to talk individually with everyone involved before I called a meeting between them. Because I thought of this corporation as a family, and of the disputing factions as family members, I made my approach a personal one. I spoke with people either in person or on the phone and got them to express their feelings and concerns. At the same time, I made sure they were informed as to exactly what was going on. I explained to them who I was, that the chairman had decided to call me in to mediate the dispute and that there would be a meeting for that purpose.

Both Larry and the executive vice-president of the corporation were careful to keep the lines of communication open as well, so that everyone had an opportunity to not only be briefed, but to have their say in advance, and to feel that their position was being valued and taken seriously. As a result, when we finally held the meeting, the dispute resolved itself because, essentially, there was nothing left of it. People had talked themselves out with me beforehand! Not that I did anything other than to listen to each of them. But I discovered, to my surprise, that while the meeting was necessary as a device to physically bring everyone together, it had become, by the end of the preliminary discussions, a ritual to acknowledge the fact that there was nothing more to fight about.

So, by *thoroughly preparing the participants for the meeting, allowing them to vent and clarify their positions in advance and making sure that they felt valued and unthreatened*, the meeting became not the beginning but the concluding stage of a dispute resolution, a successful coming together of participants who were no longer adversaries, but individuals sincerely desiring a peaceful end to their difficulties.

13

When Service Becomes Disservice: Handling Conflict in the Marketplace

Your mechanic fixed your car for $300, and you discover that all you needed was a new battery. The guy you hired to paint your house promised three coats, but only gave you two, and insists that was all you'd contracted for. The IRS is sending you pointed letters reminding you that if you don't file your income tax return from 1965, they're going to take everything you own, from your house to your underwear.

These are examples of some of the kinds of problems we run into in the marketplace—that vast region somewhere between heaven and hell in which we must deal with the goods and services that keep our lives, and society's, running on a daily basis.

It seems to be a law of the universe that before we die, we're destined to encounter at least one nasty teller, rude cashier, unscrupulous builder, incompetent physician, blind-deaf-and-brain-dead loan officer, or intractable bureaucrat. How do we respond in these situations?

Because most of us (a) want to believe that others are good, sincere and trustworthy, and (b) hate the idea of conflict, we tend to experience temporary paralysis when confronted with unethical or obstinate marketplace personnel. After the shock of having our illusions shattered, we may experience feelings of rage or helplessness. The result is that we are likely to act either out of anger, or not at all. But if we are able to respond to conflict or potential conflict situations in the marketplace skillfully and in the spirit of making as few unnecessary waves as possible, we can maximize our chances of success and maintain our sense of personal power without having to resort to avoiding, attacking, accommodating or holding out on the object of our dissatisfaction.

WHAT MAKES MARKETPLACE CONFLICTS UNIQUE

Marketplace conflicts differ from the previous types of conflicts we've been discussing in that we're usually dealing with strangers—people whose histories and lives we don't share. There is thus an element of "impersonality" in marketplace interactions, although in reality there is no such thing as truly impersonal contact, a fact which I'll discuss shortly.

In the marketplace, then, we are generally communicating with people we don't know, who have goods or services that we need. Most conflicts stemming from marketplace relationships will tend to involve either unsatisfactory merchandise or unsatisfactory service on the part of the company or business, or unsatisfactory remuneration on the part of the customer.

Like the rest of this book, this chapter is as concerned with preventing and responding to conflict as it is with resolving it. So, the first question to ask is, how can the chances of marketplace conflicts (a) occurring and (b) escalating be minimized or avoided altogether?

RULE NUMBER 1: BE YOUR OWN TROUBLESHOOTER (INSTEAD OF YOUR OWN TROUBLEMAKER)

If you're familiar with the basic principles of this book, you know by now that information gathering is a crucial skill in conflict prevention. And nowhere is it more necessary to cultivate this skill than in marketplace interactions.

During my half-century of experience, personal and otherwise, upon this planet, I have formulated a number of life rules-of-thumb, based on observations I've made about human behavior. In the area of marketplace conflict, here is one of these observations: *Most workers are neither completely competent nor completely ethical.*

Did you know that according to their peers, only about 5 percent of people in all professions are both ethical *and* competent in their business dealings?

As the former chairperson of the state board in charge of licensing marriage and family counselors, social workers and educational psychologists, I had a first-hand chance to observe the people who were applying for the chance to be in charge of the social and mental well-being of their fellow men and women.

Believe me, it was scary. In fact, there were very few of these individuals to whom I personally would entrust the psychological safety of anyone I knew and loved.

The more experience I had with the state licensing process, the more uneasy I became. So, I began to present the following scenario to every licensed professional I came across. "Okay. Let's say you're a marriage and family counselor, and you have a close friend or relative who is in need of the kind of service that you provide. However, because they're so close to you, it wouldn't be right for them to approach you. But you want to refer them to somebody in your profession. Based on your experience of all the people you know who are licensed in your field, what percentage of those people would you feel comfortable referring your friend or relative to?"

What do you think the answer was—50 percent? 20 percent? 10 percent? If you guessed the last figure, you're closest to being right, although I never heard an answer of greater than 10 percent. Usually, in fact, it was less than 5 percent. And this was not just a reflection of the sorry state of affairs in the counseling field; later, when, I began asking the same questions of medical doctors, lawyers and other licensed professionals, the answers were basically the same.

This response reveals a sobering statistic indeed: Most professionals don't trust 95 percent of the people *in their field who are licensed*! What does this say in terms of satisfaction in the marketplace? Basically, that you'd better be your own troubleshooter and do your homework ahead of time if you want to minimize the possibility of future dissatisfaction, disillusionment and conflict.

Remember that wonderful sequence in *The Wizard of Oz*, when the Wizard—himself a master at concealing impotence behind a mask of omnipotence—presents the Scarecrow with a Th.D., or Doctor of Thinkology? "Where I come from," the Wizard pontificates, "we have universities, seats of great learning, where men go to become great thinkers, and when they come out they think deep thoughts—and with no more brains than you have. But they have one thing you haven't got! A diploma!"

The Scarecrow receives his diploma, and immediately begins to spout mathematical theorems, a feat which leads to his becoming the new ruler of Oz. The idea that a diploma, or license or any sort of external certification could suddenly invest one with the intelligence and competence to take charge of society is ludicrous, of course—but when it comes right down to it, most of us take that piece of paper very seriously.

When they're looking for a professional in any area, most people will be impressed with a license. "A license?" they'll say. "Well, then, he/she must be competent." But I have news for you: A license is in no way an indication of an individual's competence.

Let's take the medical profession as an example. One of the reasons there's a malpractice crisis in our country is that it's becoming clear that medical doctors can and do make mistakes—terrible ones. A recent report in the *New England Journal of Medicine* summarized the findings of a Harvard study done by the School of Public Health. According to this study, *fewer than 2 percent of the physicians who are guilty of negligence are ever sued by their patients*! By the judgment of those in the know, the actual occurrence of malpractice in this country is so staggering that if 100 percent of the victims sued, the system would come crashing down!

But this study is not just applicable to the medical profession. Unfortunately, it's an indication of what's happening across the board, in virtually every profession. In California, for instance, bar dues have tripled in the last three years. Why? Because people are finally coming to grips with the fact that a significant percentage of lawyers are either incompetent, unethical or both.

When you understand the "5 percent rule," you realize that you cannot go into any situation with the assumption that the person you're dealing with either knows what he or she is doing or is going to do it ethically. This is not cynicism on my part; it's simply a fact of the world we live in. The 5 percent rule covers pretty much every profession and activity that I've ever had dealings with, from car mechanics to brain surgeons. And let's not rule out librarians: Someone I know recently had an eye-opening experience at the main library of a local college, where the only available reference librarian was Chinese, spoke almost no English and had substantial difficulty spelling titles and subjects correctly, let alone understanding what her patrons wanted!

Thus, when you're looking for a service, you have to take responsibility for your own well-being. You don't have to be high-handed or aggressive and you don't have to take a negative approach. Rather, you simply need to use your research skills, in order to find the best person for the job.

Finding a Good Professional Service

In looking for a professional service, there are many avenues you can explore. I'll list some of them, from the least effective to the most effective.

1. *The Yellow Pages.* Anybody can advertise in the Yellow Pages. The phone company isn't going to check to see if somebody's really what he or she claims to be; competence is not a prerequisite for admission into this particular book. A less-than-qualified lawyer or chiropractor or podiatrist can take out a full-page ad in the Yellow Pages, shining smile and all, and nobody—*nobody*—is going to stop them. So, if you're starting out cold, avoid the phone book. It's more likely to add to rather than alleviate your ignorance.

2. *Official referral services.* The next worst way to find a competent service is to use an official "referral service." For instance, as long as you've been a member of the bar for a reasonable period of time and you've paid your dues and haven't committed a crime, you can get on most Bar Association referral services. Such services almost never check into the names they list, and so, if you use one of them, you're basically following the "licensing principle" of competence, which, as we've already shown, doesn't hold water.

3. *Referral to an organization.* In general it's wise to never let yourself be referred simply to an organization, such as a law firm, medical center or any other group service. You're looking for a competent *individual*, not a whole company, corporation or team of associates. Organizations are comprised of people with different

talents, styles and ways of handling things, and since you're looking for the person who will be most likely to meet *your* needs, you want a referral to a specific individual.

4. *Referrals from others in the field.* This means of locating a reputable service is slightly better than the above methods, because at least you have a chance that the person you're asking will know somebody who's a member of the elite 5 percent of their profession. On the other hand, they might give you the name of their sister, uncle, best friend or colleague they "owe one" to. I get calls all the time from people who, when they find out that my services aren't exactly what they need, say, "Okay, if you don't do that, who can you send me to?" They don't know me; they don't know why I'd recommend somebody. Will I get a fee? Did I go to school with him? Did I have an affair with her? Do I owe them money? Of course, if you know the person you're asking, you're in better shape. But again, your source may be going on something as insubstantial as reputation in the community rather than the fact that they've used the service themselves. Which brings us to the best way to find a service.

5. *Referral from someone who's used the service.* It seems obvious enough, but you'd be surprised how many people neglect this tried-and-true method of selection. The opinion of a satisfied customer is the most reliable way to maximize your chances of finding a reputable service. An example would be Lucy, who needed a dentist who specialized in dental phobics like herself.

One of Lucy's friends who had a similar problem was

quite pleased with her dentist. So Lucy called that dentist and was treated with immediate understanding and courtesy during her initial contact. Lucy was happy with her new dentist, whose specialty was "children and the fearful," and was thankful to her friend. Remember, satisfied customers and clients, especially friends, usually base their referrals on their actual *experience*, not on hearsay, reputation or advertising.

And once you've got a referral, your information gathering continues. Don't assume that just because you've found what you feel is a reputable person, you're automatically going to engage him or her. Spend some time doing your own checking-out. Call the person up and listen carefully to how they sound. Are they being helpful, courteous, sympathetic? Will they talk to you at all? If a person, no matter how highly he or she is recommended, says, "Talk to my secretary," or "I don't do free phone consultations," take my advice and be the first to hang up.

I'm reminded of Dick, who had cancer and was referred to the best surgeon in the area. The surgeon was abrupt with Dick, dismissing his questions with "That's nothing to worry about," or "We'll cross that bridge when we come to it," and showing an evident desire to get on to his next patient. Although Dick did not like the way he was being treated, he felt that he couldn't question the surgeon's reputation and competence. He had his operation and during his painful recovery period, the surgeon was often unavailable for consultation. When he did choose to pay Dick a brief visit, he was pompous and all-knowing. Eighteen months after Dick's operation, his surgeon pronounced him "cured." Three months later Dick's cancer returned, and he lived only six weeks more—the victim of both disease and neglect on the part of the doctor to whom he'd entrusted his life.

I've found time and again that how you are handled at the first phone call is probably the *best* treatment you're likely to receive. If you're treated in a cavalier way, you'll probably be in for similar treatment—or worse—later on. So look at every instance of contact carefully, as an example of future behavior.

And although I've said it before, it bears saying again—and again: *Use your intuition.* Listen to your gut reactions, about how the person looks, sounds, smells, dresses. Are you happy with their appearance and how they respond to you? or do you feel nervous, frustrated, dissatisfied? Most of us have been conditioned to repress our intuitive responses, especially when dealing with authority or professional figures. "Oh, he's a member of the blankety-blank-blank and he has eighty-five honorary degrees so he must be good," we tell ourselves, even when we don't like what we are seeing, hearing, feeling.

Remember: Your emotional needs are as important as your physical ones. You're entitled to courtesy and respect at all times. You don't have to settle for less. If someone comes recommended to you as the best in their field and your intuition tells you that they're going to ignore you, overcharge you or generally treat you with arrogance or disdain, listen to your inner voice and find someone else who has both the competence and integrity you deserve.

And While We're at It . . . How Competent and Ethical Is Your Work?

In keeping with our observance of the process of internal as well as external research, you might want to rate yourself in terms of your own performance in your field. If we assume that 5 percent of the population is both very ethical and very competent, there are perhaps 5 percent below that who are reasonably competent and reasonably ethical. Then there's a fairly large group below that—say 50 percent—who are reasonably competent or reasonably ethical, but not both. From there it's like a bell curve, with 5 percent of people who are super incompetent and super unethical at the bottom, and a middle range that includes everything in between.

Where do you fit on the curve? Where do your friends fit in, and the service people with whom you've dealt in the past? If you do a brief rating of yourself and those you know and know of, it will give you a valuable picture of what, exactly, you're dealing with when you go in search of quality, expertise and integrity in any area of life.

GETTING SATISFACTION: CHECKING ON YOUR OWN ATTITUDE

How do you handle disagreements about unsatisfactory products and services? What attitude do you take when confronted with credit card difficulties, misunderstandings with a merchant or a customer, computer glitches, bureaucratic red tape?

If you're like most people, your initial reaction is one of either anger or fear or both. If a service hasn't given you what was promised, or a client hasn't paid his bills for six months, you feel enraged that you've been "taken." If the guy from the collection agency is hounding you, you're scared that your credit rating will be ruined, your car repossessed or your children abducted. If a computer error has caused your favorite department store to close your account for nonpayment, you feel helpless and paralyzed at the very thought of taking on the entire technocracy.

When faced with a potential conflict in the marketplace, put the tools that I've given you throughout this book to use. First, stop. Take a deep breath, calm down and take a look at yourself.

What are your assumptions? If you're enraged, are you automatically assuming that the other person is "out to get" you or doesn't give a damn? Are you fearful because of beliefs like, "I'm just one little person. I can't fight the system," or "The bureaucracy's the bureaucracy. They won't listen" or "I don't even know who I'm dealing with. It's all so impersonal."

Analyze your beliefs. How realistic are they? Are they grounded in the now, or floating in the yet-to-come? What steps can you take to minimize your anger and fear, and maximize the possibility for constructive, sympathetic dialogue?

First of all, beware of slipping into the four unconscious reaction patterns of *avoidance, attacking-defending, accommodating* and *stalemating*.

If you're the type of person whose immediate reaction is, "It's just too much; I'll never win," when facing a conflict with a merchant, company or bureaucracy, examine your tendency to *avoid* confrontations. Recall those times in the past when you avoided dealing directly with a misunderstanding or a full-blown conflict.

How did you feel about how you handled the situation? Did you get what you needed? did the other person? If not, how would you change your modus operandi? What things would you do differently? How will you go about doing them differently now, in the current situation?

Since the fear of rejection, failure and the wrath of others is a primary motivating force in avoidance behavior, your goal is to work at believing that there is a nonadversarial way to approach your dilemma, that honesty and openness will greatly reduce the possibility of rejection and anger on the part of the other person, and that no situation is irremediable, no decision irrevocable. Instead of deciding in advance that your creditors will be hostile, your landlord intractable or that the plumber who charged you $100 not to fix your toilet is going to argue his defense all the way to the Supreme Court, visualize the other party as being understanding and willing to listen to your side of the story. And visualize yourself—and the other person—as being worthy of proper consideration and respect. Then practice getting your facts together and relating them in a calm, self-assured manner. You can do this in front of a mirror, or with a friend; the latter might be a better arrangement, as your particular goal is to improve your ability to communicate directly with the other party. Above all, you need to affirm your power to make a reasonable case on your own behalf, and assume until proven otherwise the other person's willingness to come to a mutually beneficial solution to the disagreement.

If you tend to be an apologizer when involved in disagreements with merchants, service providers, customers or bureaucracies, your job is to direct your attention to what *you* want, need and deserve. Getting in touch with your own issues and articulating them in a firm, nonthreatening manner is your goal. Unlike avoiders, *accommodators* will generally be less concerned with communicating smoothly (as that is one of the high points of their behavior). Rather, if you tend toward accommodation, you need to get more in touch with your own issues and putting them out to the other person, preferably at the outset of any meeting or conversation. A good way to do this is to write down what you want and refer to it as often as you need to during the contact.

If you're an accommodator, you'll tend to bend over backwards to make the other person happy and preclude his/her anger. In this way, you're like an avoider. So, you need to affirm your right to be satisfied. If, during contact, the other party becomes argumentative or defensive, prepare for this in advance by visualizing yourself going over your story and sticking to the facts, no matter what the response on the opposite end might be. This doesn't mean that you shouldn't be open to what the other person is saying—simply that as an accommodator, you particularly need to reinforce your belief in your own self-worth and your right to life, liberty and the pursuit of personal satisfaction.

If you react to a marketplace disagreement by grabbing the phone and making a nasty call, or firing off an angry letter, you'll need to call a halt to your *attacking* pattern. You want to engage the other person in mutually beneficial dialogue, not back him/her into a defensive position. Because attackers have an unparalleled talent for complaining, they are often successful at getting what they want through sheer intimidation. Your goal is to maintain your complaining skills while toning down your bark, so that the other person does not feel attacked or threatened.

If you're a stalemater, your first reaction is to maintain the "rightness" of your position, to prove that someone else, not you, did something wrong. Your strength is that you know your story well; your weakness is that you know it too well, and the other person's not well enough. Because stalematers are traditionally not great listeners, you need to improve your intention and ability to hear what the other person is saying, and to respond in a nonjudgmental manner. A helpful hint: Put yourself in the place of the other person and give him or her your same reactive style. This is a little like a lawyer training to speak for both sides of an argument. If you can make this switch, your view of the situation will change accordingly.

And if you've come to the conclusion that many lawyers are holdouts, you're correct. Their talent for memorizing and relating facts, figures, dates, times and other details is admittedly very useful in any marketplace dispute or disagreement. But they'll be more likely to get real satisfaction if they use their admirable minds to gather *full* information rather than to just build up a case for their clients.

PREPARING FOR CONTACT

In preparing to talk with the other party in a marketplace conflict situation, don't make the preliminary and deadly error of assuming that the service provider, customer or client is intending to pull a fast one on you, or does not care about your feelings.

We all know that how we *think* precedes how we *act*, and that what we believe has a powerful tendency to materialize. When we assume that the other person is an adversary, when we second-guess their intentions, we're likely to create the scenario for a negative self-fulfilling prophecy. If, on the other hand, we decide to assume that the other person actually wants to know what took place, why we feel the way we do and how they can satisfy us, it's more likely that they will respond in exactly that fashion to our conciliatory approach.

Before speaking with the other party, *clarify your intention*. What exactly do you want? To get your money back? to get a fee or bill paid? to get something fixed? to get someone fired? Once you're clear on what you want, *explore your acceptable alternatives*. If you can't get your money back, for instance, would you be satisfied with the service provider redoing the job or giving you credit or a comparable item? If your client or customer can't pay their bill, will you accept other goods or services from them? Are you willing to take payment in monthly installments? Don't insist on one and only one alternative; be flexible.

Ruth's new optometrist told her that she would need two pairs of glasses—one for regular use and one for working at her computer. But when she got the glasses, she discovered that her regular prescription was all she needed.

Ruth felt like she had just donated $160 to her wastebasket. A classic avoider who would do almost anything to avoid an uncomfortable situation, she immediately became certain that her optometrist would refuse to take the computer glasses back. "I'm probably stuck with them," she sighed.

When she complained to me one day over lunch about the situation, I challenged her beliefs. "Why do

THE TAO OF NEGOTIATION

you assume that your doctor won't be willing to satisfy you?" I asked.

"Well, the last optometrist I had was a real jerk," she replied. "He gave me the wrong prescription and insisted that I wasn't giving myself enough time to get used to the glasses. Well, I never got used to them and he wouldn't give me my money back."

"You're confusing apples and oranges," I replied. "One situation has nothing to do with the other. This is a different optometrist. But you've put him in the category of jerk already, without giving him the least credit for possibly being an intelligent, sympathetic human being."

Ruth was surprised when she began to see that in practicing avoidance behavior, she might actually be being unfair to the other person. I worked with her on distinguishing fact from fear, and on being clear as to what she wanted.

"I want my money back," she said.

"Okay," I replied. "Is there any other alternative you'd be satisfied with?"

"Well," she thought for a moment. "I've always needed prescription sunglasses. I guess I'd be willing to take the price of the computer glasses and put it toward a pair of sunglasses instead. In fact," she brightened, "that's exactly what I want to do!"

When Ruth went back to her optometrist, she not only found him apologetic about his mistake—to her delight he was more than willing to rectify his error in any way she felt was fair. They agreed upon the sunglasses. As Ruth later reflected, "My fears were really ungrounded. I could have gotten my money back if I'd wanted it. But talking with you helped me to define my real needs, and to articulate them without assuming that my optometrist was going to be a bastard about it."

Use self-observation. Are you using this disagreement to express other unrelated feelings? Are you upset over other things, like the loss of your job, a divorce, your kid's mounting college expenses? To what extent might you have contributed to the situation? Did you run your new car's engine too hard? Did you wait too long before returning damaged merchandise? Did you eat your entire dinner and then tell the waiter he brought you the wrong meal?

If you're not sure as to what's the right thing to do, *get an independent opinion.* Talk to a friend, relative, coworker. They can help you to get a clearer perspective and explore alternatives.

As always, *do your fact gathering.* Have all receipts and records of names, dates, conversations, agreements or contracts ready before you make your first phone call. This way you'll feel more secure, and your side of the story will have much more credibility.

DECIDING ON THE FORM OF CONTACT

When making your initial contact, should you write, phone or appear in person?

Although in previous chapters I've counseled taking the approach that's most comfortable for you, marketplace conflicts are slightly different. The rule of thumb in the marketplace is, *the smaller the organization, the more personal contact you'll want to make.* If, on the other hand, you're dealing with a large corporation or government agency, a communication by letter or fax, sent to the pertinent person with a copy to the company president, is most appropriate and effective.

When making a phone call, here are a few tips.

1. *Be personable.* If you talk to a secretary or receptionist, ask her how she's doing. And it helps to give her a little insight into your dilemma. "I'm wondering if you can help me. I received a bill for services that seems to me to be too high. Who do you think is the best person to talk to about it?" Not only will your middleman or woman be inclined to be sympathetic; he or she will be likely to turn you over to someone higher up who will be equally willing to help you.

2. *Try to make contact early in the day.* You want to give yourself a head start, after all. Not only will the other party's energy tend to be higher earlier in the day, but it will give him or her a chance to look into the matter and get back to you in a few hours, rather than postponing it until the following day.

3. *Tell your story to the right person.* You don't want to start in on a monologue until you (a) have contacted the person with the proper authority to help you, and (b) have that person's undivided attention. Be sure to ask, "Am I speaking with the right person? Can you help me?" And then, "I need a few moments of your time. Is that possible now, or is there a better time for me to call you back?"

Once you have the go-ahead, identify yourself by name and write down the other person's name and position. As briefly as possible, explain the problem and state what you want up front.

4. *Separate facts from feelings.* Try to be as calm as possible. Stick to the facts as closely as you can. If you

know you're getting emotional, recount the facts and say something like, "By the way, as you can probably tell, I'm really upset about this." Then tell your story in chronological order, checking in with the other person to make sure that he/she is listening and following you.

If you're dealing with a large organization, be prepared to recount your summary a number of times. You may not get the right person at first, so you need to make your summary as brief as possible. And don't get frustrated at having to repeat it; expect that you'll have to.

5. *Remember: Everybody has a supervisor.* If you feel you aren't getting satisfaction from the person you're talking with, ask to speak to their superior. If a clerk or manager is insolent or doesn't know what they're doing, don't keep bumping your head against the wall of their incompetence. Simply give up on that person and ask to talk to the person above them. If they tell you that their supervisor isn't in, ask to speak to their supervisor's supervisor. Most bureaucracies and organizations expect people to go up the line; in law there's a principle that states that people in higher positions are not going to listen to you until you've exhausted the possibilities below.

Be aware that this process, however time-consuming, tends to work to your advantage. You're most likely to get results with somebody higher up, because the people who are more consumer-oriented are generally the ones that are promoted. They're smarter and they tend to have a lighter, broader view of things. And they're able to give you what you want.

Of course, there are times when it's most efficient and effective to go directly to the top. Some years ago, when the constant delays at a certain airline ruined my girl-friend's and my weekends together, I wrote directly to the president of the airline detailing the inconveniences we endured and expressing my indignation at the shoddy performance of his outfit. Within two weeks I received a letter of apology from the president—and a check for $100.

Here's an example of how important it is to contact the right person at an organization with whom you're experiencing difficulties. Jill, a freelance artist, was owed money by a magazine. She made numerous phone calls to the art editor, who kept promising Jill to "look into it." But weeks went by and Jill still didn't have her check.

Jill next tried talking to the managing editor, who promised her he'd "get right on it." A week went by; frustrated, Jill called the Graphic Artists Union to find out about taking the magazine to small claims. They sent her forms to fill out, but the process was a long one and Jill needed the money yesterday.

Two weeks and no check later, Jill tried a last resort tactic. She called Michael, the employee in charge of sending in the contracts for payment.

Now, Michael was a notoriously ill-humored fellow, which was why most people avoided him like the plague. But Jill was desperate. She told Michael her dilemma: that payment was two months overdue, she couldn't pay her rent and Christmas was around the corner.

"Michael," she said, "can you help me?"

To her surprise, Michael was not only sympathetic—he was angry at the managing editor, who, it turned out, had just turned Jill's contract in the day before. Michael promised to send it to the accounting office in

New York by courier, with an "urgent" request for payment. Four days later, Jill received her check.

THE MYTH OF IMPERSONAL CONTACT

When we're dealing with a large organization, we tend to balk at the seeming impersonality of things. With computers taking the place of humans, it is admittedly frustrating to find yourself talking to recorded voices or trying to rectify a mistake that's already entrenched in the system. But in reality, *there is no such thing as an impersonal contact.*

Leslie would disagree. When her car payment was fifteen days overdue, she began receiving phone calls from a recorded voice that said, "Please stay on the line. We have an important message for you." Furious, she kept hanging up, until one day she decided to wait and vent her rage on the human being she expected to speak to.

But surprise! Instead of a person, Leslie got a computer. "Your account is past due," it said. "It has been past due before. This pattern must stop. Do you agree?"

"Uhh . . ." Leslie stammered, too flustered to respond.

"Your answer is being played back to you now," the voice said. Sure enough, Leslie heard her "Uhh . . .," loud and clear.

"Do you intend to make a payment today or tomorrow?" the computer continued to nag her. By this time Leslie had regained her fighting spirit.

"I'll make a payment when I'm damn well ready, and I refuse to talk to any f———ing computer about it!" she bellowed.

"Your answer is being played back to you now," the computer droned, at which point Leslie hung up in a rage. She considered calling the finance company or writing them a letter, but as she put it, "I'd probably receive a reply from a computer."

But Leslie's wrong. The decision to harass people via computer was made by a human being in the collections department, who said, "Let's program the system to do this." Then, some computer programmer had to do his or her part. So the whole process is actually very personal. Machinery and electronics might intervene, but the communication between Leslie and director of the collections department is 100 percent personal, a fact she discovered when she decided to call the finance company herself. She was put in contact with a supervisor who expressed understanding for Leslie's indignation, and asked her if there was any way she could help in clearing up the matter of Leslie's delinquent account. They agreed upon a date for receipt of her late payment, and Leslie promised to make a real effort to be on time in the future. "I was willing to keep my part of the bargain with a real person," she said. "But I'm damned if I'm going to jump for any computer!"

Carol had a much different experience with a collections office. When her MasterCard payment was overdue, she came home to find a message on her answering machine, which happened to have an outgoing message that played Dame Kiri Te Kanawa singing a Mozart aria. Like the initial call to Leslie, the call to Carol from her bank also began with a recorded message saying, "Please stay on the line. We have an important message for you." But the recording was followed by the distinctly human voice of a genial gentleman who identified himself as a Mr. Boyd, and went on to say how much he'd enjoyed Carol's outgoing message. "I happen to be an opera fan myself," he said. "Would you mind calling me back to discuss your account?"

Carol called Mr. Boyd back as soon as she got his message. "I'm glad you liked my message," she laughed.

"Oh, it was something," Mr. Boyd chuckled. "You know, I make a lot of calls like this but your message was something special. Now, about that account . . ."

Carol sent in a payment immediately. "He was so nice," she said later. "In fact, I was tempted to ask him if he was married. I've been looking for a nice man to share opera with!"

Niceness counts. A lot. Mr. Boyd was not only nice; he was smart. He knew the value of the old "catching more bees with honey" maxim. People are far more likely to respond positively to a human being, and a pleasant human being, than they are to a computer voice or a threatening communication. A loan officer I know even goes so far as to send people personal thank-you letters for making their payments on time. Needless to say, his clients are rarely in arrears.

And niceness goes both ways. After Jill received her check from the magazine, she phoned Michael.

"What's the problem?" he snapped.

"No problem," said Jill. "I just wanted to thank you for your help, Michael. The check arrived today and you don't know how much it means to me. I know it was a hassle for you, and I'm really grateful."

Michael almost fainted. "Well, I, uh . . . gee!" he muttered. "This is a real surprise. I'm used to people yelling at me, not thanking me."

Need I add that from that moment on, Jill always received her checks from that particular magazine on time?

THE IRS: DEALING WITH THE BEHEMOTH

"That's all well and good advice for 'normal' marketplace conflicts," you might say. "But how about the IRS? How the hell do you deal with them?"

To which I would reply, "The same way you deal with anyone else."

True, when it comes to inspiring a feeling of awed terror in the breast of humankind, the IRS is unsurpassed. It's an entity unto itself; a feudal kingdom within a democracy, an institution that does not seem to be bound by the laws and principles to which the rest of society, at least on paper, is beholden. Having acknowledged this, I still maintain that every one of the principles we've seen in this book applies to any and all conflict or potential conflict situations, even those that involve the IRS.

If you're receiving threatening letters from the IRS, or you're in danger of being audited, your first step is ... what? That's right. Stop. Breathe deeply. And take as objective a look as possible at the situation.

What does the IRS want from you? What can you do to satisfy them and keep yourself out of trouble? Or, if you're already in trouble, how can you minimize the chances of the conflict escalating to all-out war?

In his excellent book, *How to Get Out of Debt, Stay Out of Debt and Live Prosperously*, author Jerrold Mundis discusses how to approach bureaucracies. Interestingly enough, his observations bear a striking resemblance to the ones in this book. "There are no monsters," he insists. "Only problems, which can be dealt with and resolved." And that includes problems with the IRS.

"The Internal Revenue Service is not irrational or without understanding," says Mundis. "Approach them as you would any other creditor—honestly, and with complete documentation of your situation. They are stern and determined, but in most cases a liveable payment schedule can be negotiated."

What are the underlying principles at the basis of Mundis's assertion? You should recognize them by now. (1) Take a positive attitude—assume that the other party is willing to listen and negotiate; (2) clarify what you want, and what you think the other party wants; (3) do your research, both internal and external; (4) be honest and upfront in your approach; (5) document your case as completely as possible; (6) have the intention of resolving your difficulties in as mutually satisfactory a manner as possible.

The IRS is really no different from anyone else. They want money that's owed to them. They don't want you, or your house or your wife—they want payment. Period.

If that's the case, how can you best satisfy them? The first step is to understand how and why the IRS operates the way it does, and to gear your approach accordingly.

Most governments still retain a belief, an assumption that's a holdover from the age of monarchies. In those times, the theory as well as the practice was: Anything the monarchy or the kingdom does in the name of the kingdom is okay. They're all-powerful; they don't have to explain their actions because it's not a two-way relationship. You owe something to them; they owe nothing to you.

Now, unless they have absolutely no competition, most private businesses can't afford this kind of arrogance. But unfortunately, there's only one government and one Internal Revenue Service. So it isn't as if you can say, "I'm not going to deal with you anymore—I'm giving my business to the DRS!" You must understand, at the outset, that the IRS won't take no for an answer, that if you owe them money and penalties and anything else, you will have to pay them. But you must also understand that if you are as diligent as possible in following their requirements and exhibiting an intention to satisfy them, they are unlikely to scorch the earth that's yours.

"But how do you deal with the impersonality of the IRS?" you ask. "Have you ever gotten a slew of their computer letters? Or tried to contact them by phone?"

Dave has. He received a computer letter from the IRS demanding that he file back taxes. It took him awhile to gather all of his information and to meet with his tax man, during which time he received two more letters, with an increasingly urgent tone to them. "Please contact us at the above number," they read.

Anxious to show the IRS that he was in the process of complying with their request, Dave called the number. For two days he received a constant busy signal. Finally he reached a real live woman.

"I've been receiving letters regarding back taxes," he began.

"Just file as soon as possible," the woman replied.

"But aren't you going to take down my name, and

note the fact that I called you as you requested?" asked Dave.

"No," the woman replied. "We don't do that. Just file as soon as possible."

Dave was thoroughly perplexed. If the IRS wasn't even going to acknowledge the fact that he'd called them, why did they ask him to do so in the first place?

This is actually an interesting question that says a lot about both government entities and the communication process. The IRS and other government agencies actually have a great deal of intelligence about human behavior and the communication process. They know the same thing that a lot of people who deal with people who owe money know: There is almost nothing more important than getting those who owe you money to believe that they should be in communication with you.

The IRS knows that if you *think* you should call them and you *do* call them, there's a much higher probability that you're actually going to file a return and pay your taxes. They're not interested in *talking* to you per se, and they're not going to do anything with your call. What they're doing is to provide you with the *desire* to contact them, which in turn leads to the desire to file your return and pay them what you owe.

So, the IRS knows that *communication precedes action*. They may not have created a mechanism to record the information you want to give them or to hold two-way communication, because that requires a level of internal sophistication which simply doesn't pay off, especially in what they consider to be nickel and dime cases. But they do know that if you make an attempt to communicate with them, you're far more likely to give them what they want than if you close your eyes and pretend that they'll go away.

This, of course, is using the term "communication" in a different sense from the one with which most of us are familiar. This isn't two-way communication because, as I said before, your relationship with the IRS is not a two-way relationship, anymore than a serf's would have been with his lord, or a subject's with his king. Rather, it's communication in the sense of *contact*. The IRS wants to stimulate *contact* and *action* on your part, not communication. Once you understand this most basic reality, you're in a much better position to deal with them efficiently.

And remember the myth of impersonal contact? Well, at a parent-teacher gathering at my son's school, I once had the good fortune to meet a genial woman who, when I asked her what she did, replied, "I'm an IRS agent."

Having never met a real genuine IRS agent, I was intrigued. "That's some job you have," I said.

"Oh, yeah," she laughed. "It has its perks. Wherever I go, all I have to do is tell somebody I work for the IRS and they want to give me all sorts of deals. Cars, stereos, you name it. Of course, they also want me to give them advice and tips on all their tax problems!"

"Is the IRS as unapproachable as many people believe?" I asked.

"Oh, no," she smiled. "In fact, we really do try to give people as many breaks as we can. When we send letters out, people don't realize how many we send and how far we'll go before we actually take action. For instance, it's my job to contact people if they haven't contacted us. I'll call them on the phone and get them to talk. Through the years, in fact, I get the same cases and it's really funny. You get to know all about them and their families. And every year I'll give them a call and ask how their kids are, and they ask how mine are, and pretty soon the kids are having their own kids and these people still can't pay their taxes on time! But I do develop a personal relationship with a lot of people."

Remember: *There's no such thing as impersonal contact.* At the other end of every computer is a person, and every agency, however gigantic, is comprised of human beings. Look at the other party—even if it's the IRS—as somebody like you who has a need to be met, and you've made the most important step in resolving a conflict or preventing potential conflict courteously, efficiently and relatively painlessly.

Conclusion: Waging Peace

The Tea-Master and the Assassin*

Taiko, a warrior who lived in Japan before the Tokugawa era, studied Cha-no-yu, tea etiquette, with Sen no Rikyu, a teacher of that aesthetical expression of calmness and contentment.

Taiko's attendant warrior Kato interpreted his superior's enthusiasm for tea etiquette as negligence of state affairs, so he decided to kill Sen no Rikyu. He pretended to make a social call upon the tea-master and was invited to drink tea.

The master, who was well skilled in his art, saw at a glance the warrior's intention, so he invited Kato to leave his sword outside before entering the room for the ceremony, explaining that Cha-no-yu represents peacefulness itself.

Kato would not listen to this. "I am a warrior," he said. "I always have my sword with me. Cha-no-yu or no Cha-no-yu, I have my sword."

* Paul Reps, *Zen Flesh, Zen Bones*. New York: Anchor Books, 1989, p. 50.

"Very well. Bring your sword in and have some tea," consented Sen no Rikyu.

The kettle was boiling on the charcoal fire. Suddenly Sen no Rikyu tipped it over. Hissing steam arose, filling the room with smoke and ashes. The startled warrior ran outside.

The tea-master apologized. "It was my mistake. Come back in and have some tea. I have your sword here covered with ashes and will clean it and give it to you."

In this predicament the warrior realized he could not very well kill the tea-master, so he gave up the idea.

The above Zen tale makes, in the true Zen fashion of paradox, a fitting ending and beginning to the journey you have begun with *The Tao of Negotiation*. For while this final chapter is the ending of this book, it is really the beginning of the next phase of "peace consciousness" in your life, as you begin to put its principles and techniques into use.

The story of the warrior and the tea-master is a perfect illustration of the premise of *The Tao of Negotiation*: That it only takes one person to defuse a conflict situation and help turn anger into reason, fear into calmness, the "black magic" intention of inflicting pain into the "white magic" intention of seeing things from the other person's perspective as well as one's own.

In this story, the one person is primed for war. The warrior's mind is made up; he is going to kill the tea-master and there is theoretically no room for discussion. Because he has a sword, the warrior mistakenly assumes that he controls the situation and the outcome—that he is the powerful one. But it's the tea-master who has the real power. His choices determine whether the outcome will be war or peace. If he becomes either an attacker-defender or a stalemater—if he meets might with might, stubbornness with more stubbornness, war is the inevitable result. If he becomes an avoider or an accommodator, denying that there is a problem or acquiescing to the warrior's plans, he dies.

But if the tea-master anticipates his adversary, approaches the situation in an objective, nonthreatening manner, protects himself accordingly and has the intention of coming to a mutual understanding, there is the possibility for peace.

Sen no Rikyu chose the path of peace by cleverly "disarming" his adversary. Anticipating Kato's actions, he was able to catch him off guard and capture his sword. But this, in and of itself, was not a victory to the tea-master. His true triumph came not in physically disarming his adversary, but in *psychologically* disarming him—in creating the kind of environment in which the warrior, faced with the unbeatable forces of respect and reason, was able to relinguish his anger and meet the "enemy" in peace.

There were actually two warriors in this story: One was a warrior for war; the other was a warrior for peace. The term "warrior for peace" may seem incongruous, but as the XIV Dalai Lama has so insightfully observed, peace is *not simply the absence of war*. Peace is an *active* state, not a passive one; conditions of both war and peace require the same amount of energy to sustain themselves.

The Tao of Negotiation was written to help you become a warrior for peace by changing your attitude—and therefore your response—to conflict. In growing more familiar with your own makeup—your needs, wants, motivations, intentions, hidden agendas, how *you* respond to conflict or potential conflict situations—

you have become aware of how you consciously or unconsciously contribute to the conflict situations in your life. At the same time, you've seen how just one person—you—can make the difference in preventing or resolving many of the conflicts and potential conflicts that have been and always will be an inevitable element of human interaction.

COMING TOGETHER

This final chapter can be thought of, on a variety of levels, as a *coming together*.

Coming together here refers to a unity or synthesis of both principles and people.

First of all, it's a chance for the *different techniques and concepts you've encountered in the book to come together* in your mind, as you decide how you'd like to begin incorporating them into your life.

Second, as these ideas and strategies become more a part of your life, you will begin to achieve a balance between the different, and sometimes conflicting, parts of your own nature. In becoming aware of our own motivations, needs and responses, our *various selves can come together* in a more integrated relationship with each other. We can move from "disowning" certain parts of ourselves to accepting and understanding them.

And third, you'll be *coming together with others*, recognizing them as individuals worthy of care and attention who have basically the same needs and desires as you, wanting the best for them as well as yourself.

The principles of *The Tao of Negotiation*, then, begin with the self and radiate from the central core of our own being into the larger universe. It's a little like a

Jungian approach to Jules Verne's *Journey to the Center of the Earth*. We have learned how to go inward, to journey into our own psyches. Armed with a new self-awareness, we become more aware of others—how their minds work, how they communicate or miscommunicate, how we can facilitate *their* self-awareness in order to amicably prevent or resolve conflict. And in so doing, we have changed the earth itself, for the better.

It becomes evident, then, how much we, as single individuals, can and do impact the world. Because we serve as constant influences to those around us, we must never underestimate our own power to *wage peace*, to know that if we ourselves have the intention to create harmony rather than exacerbate or escalate disharmony in our relationships, we cannot help but alter our environments and correspondingly change the attitudes of those with whom we interact.

BECOMING YOUR OWN SELF-MEDIATOR

As I hope I've made clear, my goal throughout this book has been not simply to help you prevent or resolve conflict, but to help you to *enhance the quality of your life and relationships*. You may have picked up this book because you are currently involved in a conflict situation, but once you begin to use its principles, you will discover, if you haven't already, that the very texture of your life, is undergoing a transformation. You're learning how to become even more honest—with yourself as well as others. Your focus, on your relationships, career, personal growth is becoming clearer, and you are learning how to better communicate with, and understand, others in order to get your needs—and theirs—met. You're discovering how to listen better, how to do more thorough research into yourself and other people, how to create a safer, less threatening environment in which to discuss and resolve disagreements as peacefully as possible.

In the process, you have become a *self-mediator* in your daily life.

As a professional mediator, the most important, or at least the most useful, skill I've acquired is knowing how to *facilitate* the process of bringing people together and keeping them positively focused on the doughnut, not the hole. Success comes, I've found, not so much in knowing what to do *for* people who are involved in a conflict situation as knowing how to help people find the *intention and willingness* to peacefully resolve their difficulties.

My job, then, is not to control or direct people or outcomes. Rather, I help *energize* those parts of the participants in a dispute that have the intention of coming together and resolving the problem. And I help *de-energize* those parts that, out of anger or defensiveness, resist direct dealing with each other.

I'd say that 90 percent of being a mediator is precisely this ability to open—and keep open—the lines of honest and healthy communication. Knowing what to do when my office door closes and the proceedings begin is only 10 percent of the job. Yet most people who are "trained" in mediation focus on what to do when the door closes. (Whenever I hear the word "training" in the context of mediation, I think more of dog obedience than a human skill.)

Life is a constant creative dynamic, not a static state of preordained conclusions. Living "in the moment" is not just a highly refined spiritual attitude intended for supreme enlightenment; it is a practical skill essential for anyone who wants to truly understand and communicate with others in a productive and meaningful way.

. A truly successful third-party mediator learns to prepare his clients in advance by helping them become aware of their real feelings, needs and goals prior to the actual mediation. He or she learns to listen, to adapt his or her techniques to the specific situation, to be spontaneous, to hear what people really want and need at any given moment and to help them address those needs.

These are skills that you have encountered throughout this book. You've learned how to free yourself of preconceptions and judgments; how to view conflict situations as objectively and nonemotionally as possible; how to create a safe environment for coming together; how to truly listen to the other person; how to divest yourself of attachment to or expectation of a given *result*, concentrating instead on the *process* of the interaction.

In short, you can now incorporate the basic skills of mediation into your own life. In so doing, you can move beyond simply preventing or resolving conflict, to creating situations with others that maximize communication, self-awareness, growth and personal satisfaction for everyone concerned.

WHERE DO YOU GO FROM HERE?

Take a moment now to stop and think about your life. Where were you when you began this book? Where are you now? Where would you like to be?

The following worksheet is designed to help you focus on how you'd like to incorporate, or continue incorporating, what you've learned in these pages into your daily life. It's my own version of a "follow-up" to our initial meeting; while I can't be there in person to monitor your progress, this exercise can serve as a check-in device, to remind you of your goals and the ways in which you can achieve them.

The principles and concepts you've encountered in this book can be thought of as *antiinflammatories*. When applied, they can serve to calm the passions that inflame most conflicts and enhance the powers of reasoning. And, as you become more aware of how to respond to and prevent conflict, you will correspondingly become more adept at creating an open, honest, joyful environment for yourself and others.

Armed with the honest awareness of your own needs in the midst of disagreement and the "white magic" intention of creating harmony rather than exacerbating or escalating disharmony in the process of getting those needs met, you are ready to *wage peace*.

Conflict, after all, is just another form of human energy. When we talk about conflict, we're really talking about *life*. And learning how to respond to conflict in the interests of peace rather than war teaches us to respond to life itself in the same way.

I hope that this book is the beginning of a journey toward harmony and fulfillment in all of your relationships—a coming together of the many selves and forces of which we are all made, and which, when acknowledged, expressed and balanced with true understanding, can free us to realize our full potential in work, love and life.

Where Do You Go from Here?

Think about the relationships you have with key people in your life—spouse or lover, children, parents, friends, boss, coworkers, others. Has reading this book changed your attitude toward these relationships, and/or the relationships themselves? If so, how? Write your reflections here.

What about your relationship to yourself? What have you learned about yourself through reading this book? In what ways are you becoming more self-aware? Has this awareness helped your relationships and your life in general? If so, how?

Which of the chapters, principles and/or techniques in this book did you find most useful and applicable to your own life? In what ways?

In chapter 1, we asked you to rate the relationships in your life according to the Conflict Continuum. Go back to that page now and take a look at what you wrote. Has the level of conflict in your life changed since reading this book? If so, how?

What aspects of your life and your relationships would you like to improve? Based on what you've read in this book, what steps can you begin to take at this moment to begin changing them?

Index

347

About the Author

JOEL EDELMAN holds a J.D. from New York University, an M.A. in Marriage, Family, and Child Counseling from Azusa Pacific University and an M.S. in Industrial Engineering from Columbia University. Joel has traveled widely and studied intensively with many spiritual teachers and transformational healers. He is a pioneer mediator who, in 1977, was the founding Executive Director of the Neighborhood Justice Center, the predecessor of Dispute Resolution Services of Los Angeles, now the largest local community mediation program in the country. In 1981 he started the first private mediation law practice in Southern California. His clients have included corporations, divorced Hollywood notables, family businesses, warring L.A. street gangs and the LAPD, and he has conducted international dialogues in China and Russia. He was a research analyst at the RAND corporation during the 1960s (spending nearly one year in Vietnam studying U.S. policy) and was a prosecutor and a civil liberties lawyer during the 1970s. He created mediation law courses as an Adjunct Professor at the USC and Loyola law schools and is certified in Holotropic Breathwork™. He is remarried, has a twenty-two-year-old son and lives in Malibu, California.

To contact Joel Edelman regarding lectures, workshops, consultations, or being on his mailing list, please write to him at 169 Pier Avenue, Santa Monica, CA 90405-5311, Fax (310) 392-6331 or call (310) 392-4830.